Swift
for Masterminds

How to take advantage of Swift and AI Agents to program professional apps for iPhones, iPads, and Macs

J.D Gauchat
www.jdgauchat.com

Swift for Masterminds

The source code for this book is available at **www.formasterminds.com**

ISBN: 978-1-0699942-3-3

1st Edition 2026 John D Gauchat
2nd Edition 2026 John D Gauchat

Table of Contents

Chapter 4
Structures

Chapter 5
Enumerations

Chapter 6
Objects

Chapter 7
Protocols

About this Book

This book covers the essential concepts and advanced techniques you need to master the Swift programming language. To help you navigate the content and focus on the topics that best match your goals, each section is identified with one of the following labels:

BASIC

The topics presented in the BASIC sections provide the fundamental knowledge required to develop applications for Apple devices and understand the code generated by AI agents. Study these sections first if your goal is to learn how applications are built, understand how Swift works, and collaborate effectively with an AI agent to finish your first projects.

PRO

The topics presented in the PRO sections introduce advanced concepts and techniques that become important as your skills grow. These sections are intended for readers who want to become proficient in app development or fully understand every piece of code generated by an AI agent.

Every topic introduced in this book is explained through fully functional examples that you can try on your own. We recommend opening Xcode and experimenting with the code as you learn, but you can also download the examples from our website to work through the material at your own pace (**www.formasterminds.com**).

The examples in this book were created for instructional purposes and may not always follow established best practices. There are many programming patterns and techniques you can apply, and the right approach depends on the needs of your application and your development goals. We recommend you to explore the options presented in this book, but also experiment and develop your own.

IMPORTANT

The source code for this book, along with additional information, is available on our website at **www.formasterminds.com**. Apple's official documentation is available at **developer.apple.com**. Additional tutorials, articles, and guides can be found on the Swift official website at **www.swift.org**.

Chapter 1
App Development

BASIC

1.1 - Swift

Swift is the programming language offered by Apple for developing applications across its platforms, including iPhones, iPads, and Macs. Introduced in 2014 as an alternative to Objective-C, Swift was created to reduce complexity and verbosity, making development for Apple devices more accessible. Swift combines a clean, approachable syntax with the low-level power needed to access the full capabilities of modern hardware, which quickly established it as the preferred language for new developers and the one officially recommended by Apple for building applications across its ecosystem.

BASIC

1.2 - Xcode

Creating an application requires access to resources, tools to write and test code, and the ability to work with frameworks, packages, and other components. To simplify this process, developers rely on Integrated Development Environments, or IDEs. An IDE is a program that brings together all the tools needed to design, build, and test an application. The IDE used to develop applications for Apple devices is called *Xcode*.

Xcode is available for free in the Mac App Store. The latest version, and the one we use for the examples in this book, is 27. To install Xcode, open the App Store from the Applications folder in Finder and search for "Xcode" (Figure 1-1, number 1). The window displays the Xcode icon along with a Get button to install it (Figure 1-1, number 2).

Figure 1-1: *Xcode in the App Store*

IMPORTANT

At the time of writing, Xcode 27 is available in Beta mode. To download this version of Xcode, go to Apple's developer website at **developer.apple.com**, sign in with your Apple account, click on Downloads/Applications, and select the latest beta version available.

After downloading Xcode, we can run the application from the Applications folder in Finder. The following is Xcode's welcome screen.

Figure 1-2: *Xcode's welcome screen*

The welcome screen provides buttons to open an existing project, clone a project from a repository, or create a new project. Clicking the button to create a new project opens a popup menu with options, as shown below.

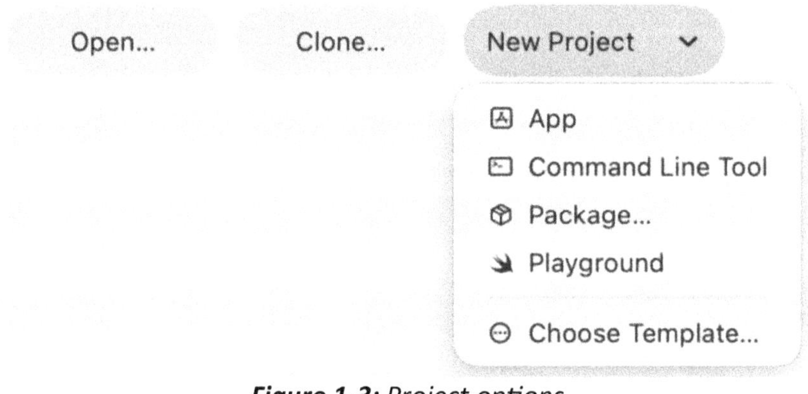

Figure 1-3: *Project options*

The **App** option is used to create a new application, the **Command Line Tool** option is used to create an application without a user interface, the **Package** option is used to create a package with code we can share with other developers, and the **Playground** option is used to create a single Swift file for testing. Of all the available options, the **App** option is the one we are going to use the most because it creates a project that allows us to test our code, learn how to program, and create fully functional applications.

Project

When we select the **App** option, Xcode creates a new project. An Xcode project includes all the information and resources we need to create an application. After the project is created, Xcode opens an interface with all the tools necessary to manage it, as shown below.

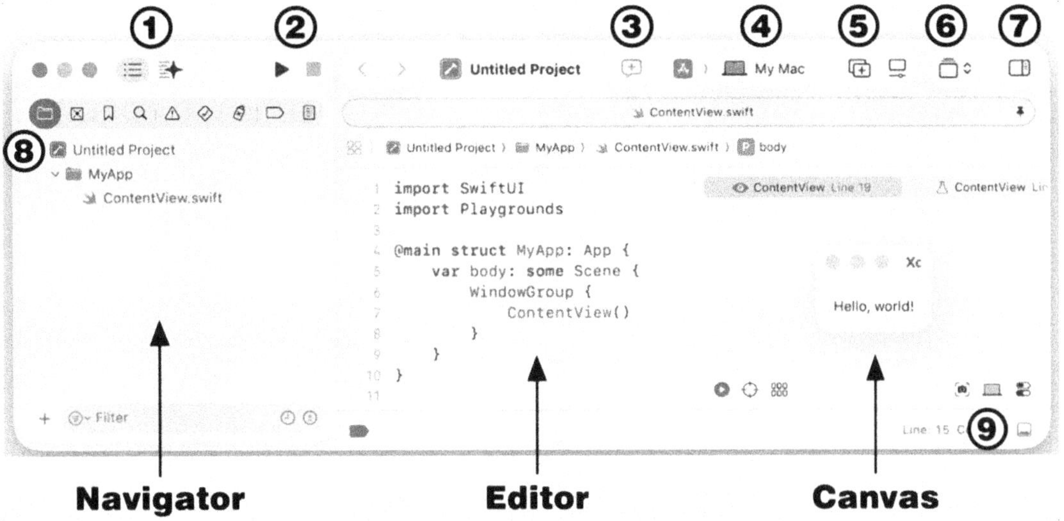

***Figure 1-4:** Xcode's interface*

The Xcode interface is divided into removable panels. The panel on the left, called **Navigator**, shows all the files in the project, including an item at the top to represent the project itself (**number 8**). The panel at the center is called **Editor** and is where we write our code, and the panel on the right is the **Canvas**, where we can see a preview of our app and the results of our code when using Playground (We will learn how to use Playground to test Swift code later).

The interface includes a toolbar at the top with buttons to configure the interface and the project. On the left, we have two buttons, one to hide or display the **Navigator** and another to open a **Coding Assistant** panel to work with an AI agent (**number 1**). Next, we have buttons to run and stop the application (**number 2**), a button to start a new conversation with an AI agent (**number 3**), buttons to select the device or simulator where we want to run the application (**number 4**), buttons to configure the editor (**number 5**), and buttons to change the editor mode (**number 6**).

The interface also includes additional panels that can be useful for configuration and testing. There is a button at the top right corner to open the inspector panel with information about files, targets, and more (**number 7**), and a button at the bottom right corner to open a console where we can see errors and print our own messages when debugging our code (**number 9**).

Do It Yourself

Install Xcode 27 on your Mac as explained in Figure 1-1, or download the latest beta version from **developer.apple.com**. Once installed, open Xcode, click the **New Project** button, and select the **App** option to create a new project (Figure 1-3). You should see an interface similar to Figure 1-4. Click the buttons in the toolbar to get familiar with the interface. Buttons usually perform the opposite action, so if you change something and do not know how to go back, try pressing the same button or simply close the project and create a new one from the File menu at the top of the screen (**File -> New -> Project**).

IMPORTANT

When you create a new project, Xcode generates a template and all the files required for the application to run, but does not save the project to disk. To save it, press **Command + S** or select **Save** from the **File** menu, type a name, select a folder, and click the Save button. Once the project is saved, any further changes are saved automatically.

BASIC

Canvas

There are three ways to test our code and run our applications: a device, a simulator, or the Canvas. Testing on a device or simulator is required when developing full applications, but for learning Swift and testing code, we can use the Canvas. The Canvas is a live preview panel built into Xcode that renders our app's views in real time, without the need to deploy to a device or simulator. It can show the result of a single line of code, simulate a device, or present the interface in a flexible view to test different screen configurations.

When we create a new project, Xcode shows the code generated by the template on the left and the Canvas on the right, as shown in Figure 1-4. By default, Xcode sets My Mac as the destination, so the app runs on the computer, but we can change it to any device or simulator from the toolbar. The toolbar includes buttons to open and close the Canvas and to select the destination we want the Canvas to use, as shown below.

Figure 1-5: *Selecting the device to represent on the Canvas*

When we press the **Show Canvas** button on the toolbar (Figure 1-5, number 2), the panel is opened on the right or at the bottom of the Editor, and the view created by the code is rendered simulating the device selected as the destination (Figure 1-5, number 1). For example, below is what we see when we select an iPhone simulator and open the template generated by Xcode for an **App** project.

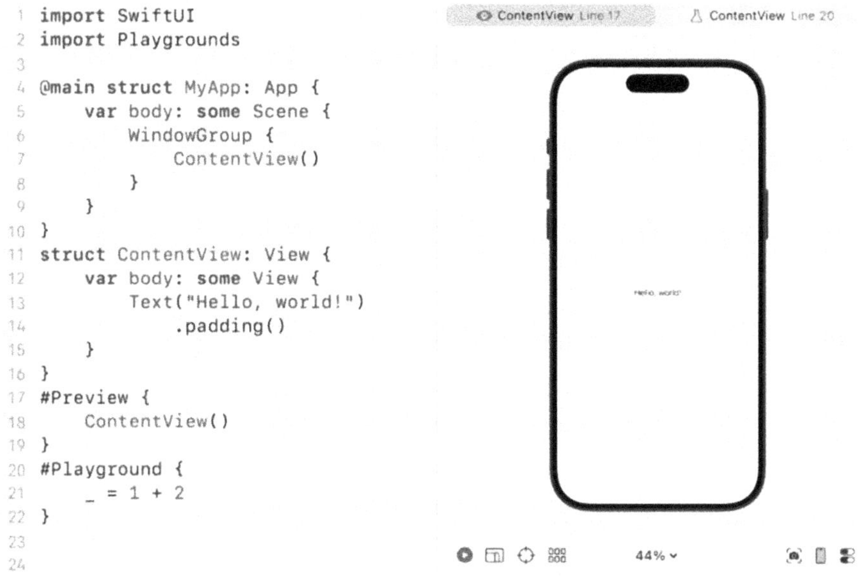

Figure 1-6: *Canvas rendering the initial screen in an iPhone simulator*

> **IMPORTANT**
>
> Although we can use the Canvas to develop an entire application, its most valuable feature for learning Swift is the ability to execute code from a Playground and immediately display the results. We will learn how to create a Playground next.

BASIC

Playground

When we start a new project, Xcode creates a file with the basic code required to run an application. The file is called **ContentView.swift**, and we can find it in the Navigator, as shown below.

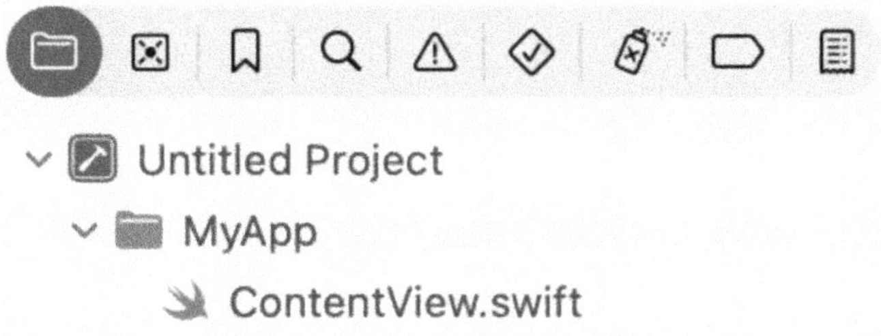

Figure 1-7: *Initial files in the Navigator*

If we click on this file, we can see its content in the Editor. Listing 1-1 below shows the code currently generated by Xcode for an **App** project.

Listing 1-1: Xcode template

```
import SwiftUI
import Playgrounds

@main struct MyApp: App {
    var body: some Scene {
        WindowGroup {
            ContentView()
        }
    }
}
struct ContentView: View {
    var body: some View {
        Text("Hello, world!")
            .padding()
    }
}
#Preview {
    ContentView()
}
#Playground {
    _ = 1 + 2
}
```

This code may look daunting at first, but it is actually quite simple. The first two lines use the **`import`** instruction to include pre-programmed code that adds functionality to our application. After these instructions, the template includes two Swift structures (**`struct`**). In this case, the first structure is called **MyApp** and it is preceded by the **`@main`** keyword to indicate to Xcode that this is the code the system should execute first. The second structure, called **ContentView**, defines the content of the app's initial screen. In this case, the structure just shows the text "Hello, world!" on the screen. Finally, we have two macros. As we will see later, macros generate code and inject it into our source code to simplify our work. The template includes two: the **`#Preview`** macro to generate a preview of the application on the Canvas, and the **`#Playground`** macro to allow us to test Swift code.

The main function of the **`#Preview`** and **`#Playground`** macros is to include the code necessary to preview results on the Canvas. If we open the Canvas panel, we will see two buttons at the top: one on the left to see the result produced by the **`#Preview`** macro (Figure 1-8, number 1) and another on the right to see the result produced by the **`#Playground`** macro (Figure 1-8, number 2).

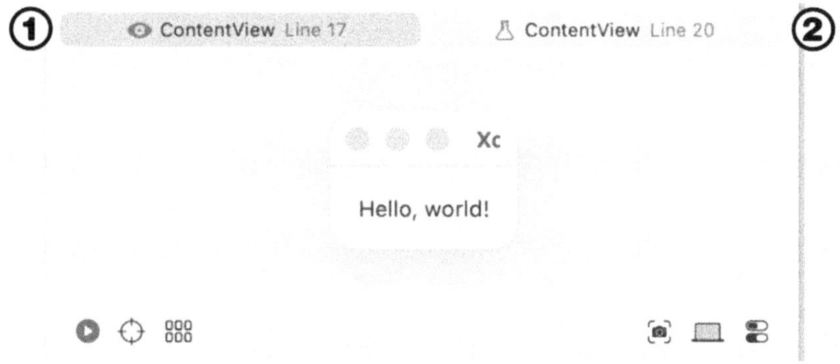

Figure 1-8: *Canvas previews*

The **#Preview** macro processes the **ContentView** structure and shows the result on the Canvas. In this case, this is a small window displaying the text "Hello, world!". On the other hand, the **#Playground** macro executes the code between braces and displays that result, as shown below.

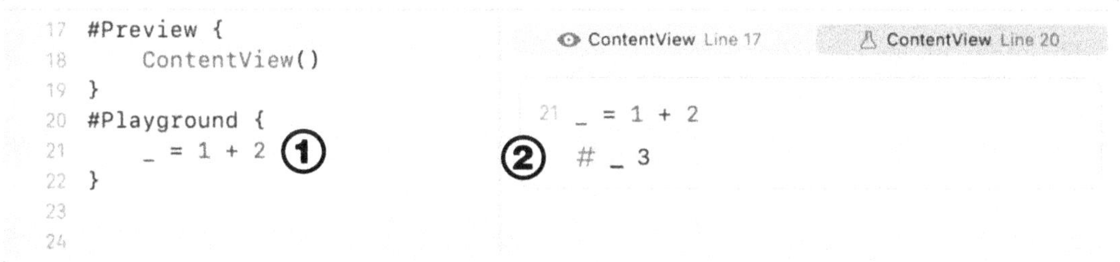

Figure 1-9: *Playground results*

The code included for the **#Playground** macro by the template is just one instruction that adds 1 plus 2 (Figure 1-9, number 1), so the Canvas shows the result 3 (Figure 1-9, number 2).

Do It Yourself

Click the **ContentView.swift** file in the Navigator panel to open it in the Editor. You should see code similar to the one in Listing 1-1. By default, the project is set to work on the Mac and show a preview of the application on the Canvas, so you should see a small Mac window displaying the text "Hello, world!", as shown in Figure 1-8. If the Canvas panel is closed, click the Canvas button in the toolbar to open it (Figure 1-4, number 6). To see the result of the code in the **#Playground** macro instead, open the Canvas and click the button on the right (Figure 1-8, number 2). You should see the statement executed by the **#Playground** macro and the result below, as shown in Figure 1-9, number 2.

As the name suggests, the **#Playground** macro defines a space where we can play around with the code. The code between braces is executed separately from the application's code, and the results are shown on the Canvas, so we can use it for testing purposes or to learn how Swift works, as we will do for the examples in this book.

Files

Because the template generated by Xcode includes not only the code for the Playground but also all the code necessary to run the application, it is recommended to create a dedicated file to test our code and learn Swift. Xcode allows us to add as many files as we need to our project from the File menu at the top of the screen. We must open the Navigator and click the folder where we want to place the file (in this case, **MyApp**) and then select the option from the **File -> New** menu (Figure 1-10, number 1).

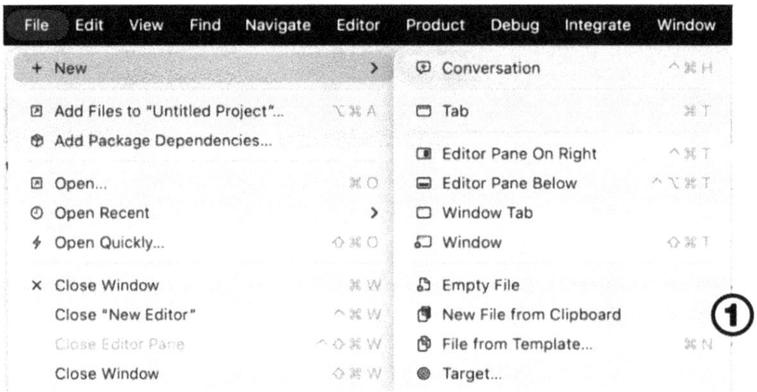

Figure 1-10: *New file options*

There are three options available: we can create an empty file (**Empty File**), create a file with the contents of the clipboard (**New File from Clipboard**), or create a file from an Xcode template (**Create from Template**). If all we want to do is create a file to run a Playground, we just need to import **Playground** and define the **`#Playground`** macro, so an empty file is sufficient. To create the file, we specify a name with the **.swift** extension and then declare the **`#Playground`** macro, as shown below.

Listing 1-2: Playground file

```
import Playgrounds

#Playground {
    let mynumber = 10 * 5
}
```

In this example, we import **Playground** and define the **`#Playground`** macro as before, but we change the instruction between braces. The instruction now includes the **`let`** keyword, the name **`mynumber`**, and a mathematical operation that multiplies 10 times 5. We will learn what all this means later, but for now all we need to know is that the **`let`** keyword creates a constant called **`mynumber`** that stores the result of the multiplication, so the Canvas shows the result of the operation, as before.

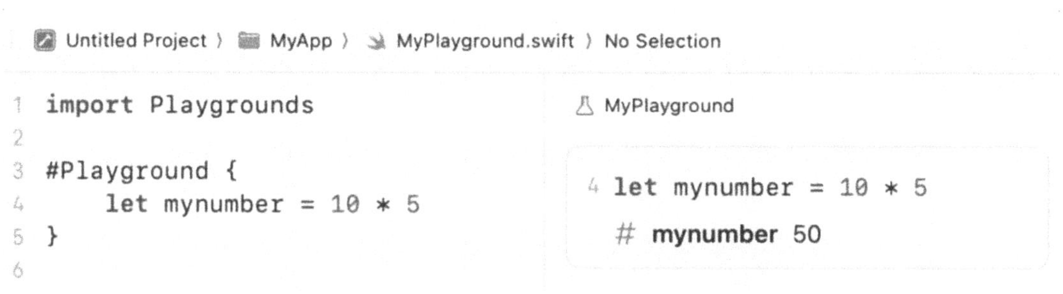

Figure 1-11: *Running new Playground code*

Do It Yourself

Click the **MyApp** folder in the Navigator to select it (Figure 1-7). Open the **File** menu, go to the **New** option, and select **Empty File** (Figure 1-10, number 1). Xcode creates a new file inside the **MyApp** folder and asks you for a name. Type the name **MyPlayground.swift**. Select the new file and update the content in the Editor with the code in Listing 1-2. Open the Canvas. You should see your code in the Editor and the result of the execution of that code on the Canvas, as shown in Figure 1-11.

IMPORTANT

The code defined by a `#Playground` macro works independently of the application, allowing us to explore how the Swift programming language works without first creating a complete app. Because of this, we will use `#Playground` throughout most of this book to test and experiment with the examples. If you want to go further and learn how to build full applications, read our book *SwiftUI for Masterminds* (**www.formasterminds.com**).

BASIC

1.3 - AI Agents

Artificial intelligence has transformed app development, but contrary to early concerns, AI models and agents have not replaced programmers. Instead, they have become powerful tools that help developers work more efficiently. Today, building an application requires a solid understanding of how code works, along with the ability to use AI agents to learn new concepts, improve code quality, solve problems, and accelerate development. As AI becomes an increasingly important part of the software development process, the ability to program applications and effectively collaborate with AI agents is becoming an essential skill for developers who want to remain competitive.

IMPORTANT

You do not need to use AI agents to write Swift code or develop applications for Apple devices, but it is highly recommended to get used to these tools as soon as possible. Learning how to use AI agents today will give you an advantage when they become essential for any project in the future.

The best way to think about AI agents is as collaborators. If we are learning Swift or exploring a new framework, we can ask for explanations and guidance. If we are developing an application, we can ask an agent to generate code, review our work, suggest improvements, identify errors, write documentation, or help localize our app for different languages and regions. By treating AI agents as collaborators rather than replacements, we remain in control of the development process while benefiting from greater speed and efficiency. We can review their suggestions, refine their output, and ensure that the final result meets our requirements.

This year, Apple recognized the important role that AI agents have begun to play in app development and integrated Xcode with the most popular agents to simplify our work and improve the results we can get from this collaboration. But because there are many options available, AI agents do not come preinstalled; we have to decide which agent we want to work with and install it ourselves. The option is available from Xcode settings. We must click the **Xcode** option at the top of the screen, select **Settings**, and then open the **Intelligence** panel, as shown below.

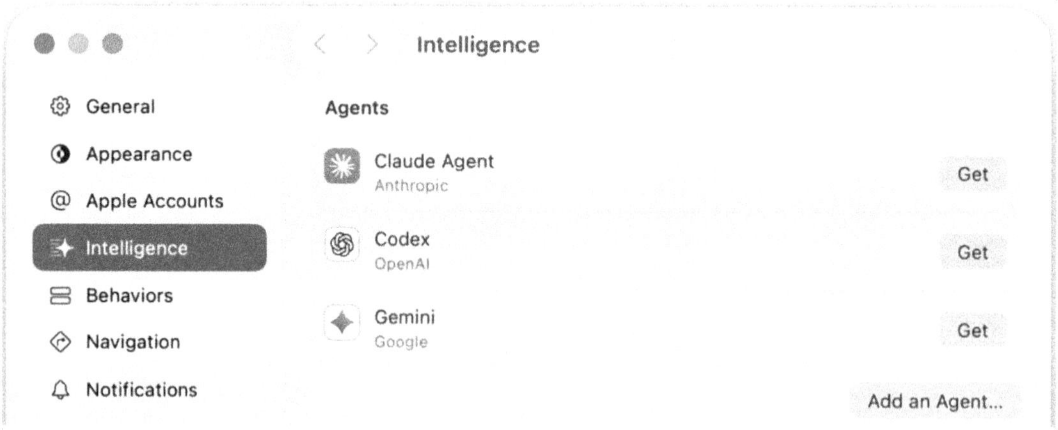

Figure 1-12: *Installing AI Agents*

At the time of this writing, there are three options available: **Claude** from Anthropic, **Codex** from OpenAI, and **Gemini** from Google. **Claude** is only available to paid customers. Currently, a Claude Pro account costs $20 USD per month (check **claude.ai/pricing** for up-to-date information). **Codex** and **Gemini**, on the other hand, are offered for free with limitations. We are limited in the number of requests per minute or per hour, depending on the model, but we can use them for free as long as we want and get a Pro account only when necessary.

To make these agents available, we must install them and sign in with the corresponding account. The first step is to press the **Get** button for the agent we want to install. When we press this button, Xcode downloads all the data and information it needs to run the agent on our computer. After that, we must select the agent and sign in with our account. If we do not have an account, we must create one from each provider's website. In the case of **Claude**, we need to visit **claude.ai/login**, sign up, and then subscribe to the Pro plan. After the account is ready, we must press the Sign In button in Xcode to enter our credentials (Figure 1-13, number 1).

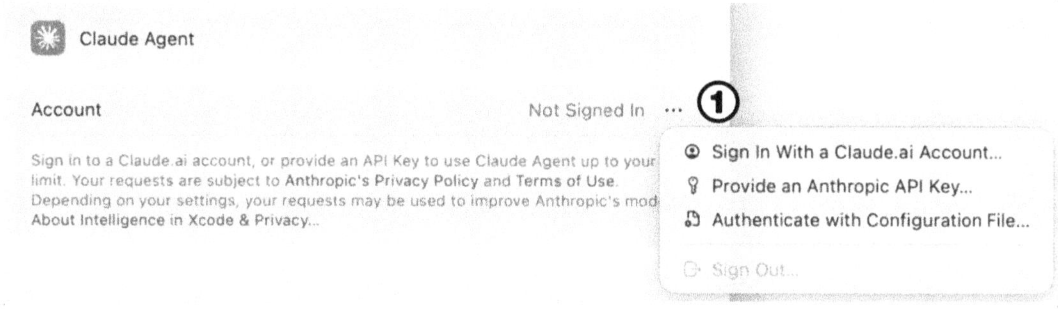

Figure 1-13: *Signing in with Claude*

For **Codex**, the process is similar. We must press the **Get** button to download the agent, and then visit **chatgpt.com/codex/** and click Log In to create our account. Once we have an account with OpenAI, we must select the agent in Xcode and press the Sign In button (Figure 1-14, number 1).

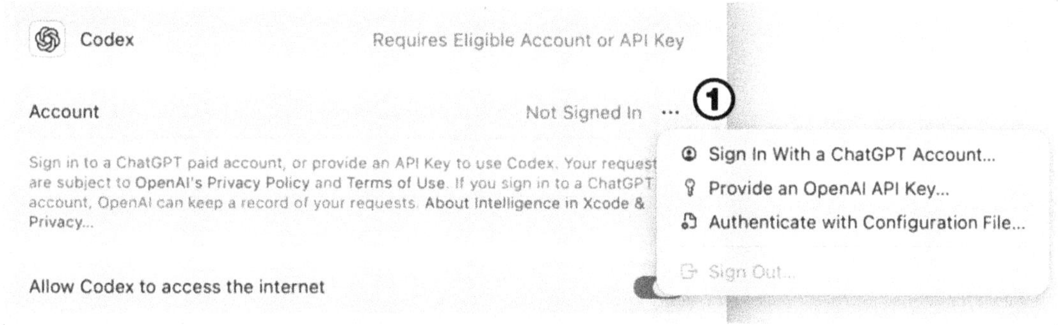

Figure 1-14: *Signing in with OpenAI*

If we prefer to use Google's **Gemini** instead, the process is similar, we must press the **Get** button to download the agent, but rather than signing in with a Google account directly, we must obtain an API key from Google's website. To obtain this key, we need to visit **aistudio. google.com**, press Get Started, and sign in with our Google account. Once inside our account, we must click on **Dashboard -> API Keys** and press the **Create API Key** button. A window opens asking for a name and a project. We must create a new project with any name we want, assign a name to the key, and then press the Create Key button. This generates a new key that we can copy and paste into Xcode. The option to paste the key is also available from the Sign In button (Figure 1-15, number 1).

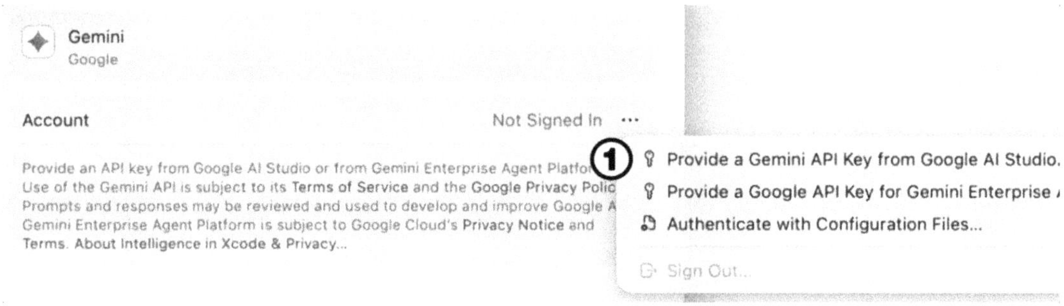

Figure 1-15: *Providing an API key to enable Gemini*

Agents use different artificial intelligence models to perform their tasks. If we use Claude or Codex, the model is set automatically, but if we use a free account with Gemini, we must select the free model ourselves. The option is available when we select the agent. For Gemini, the free models are called Flash (Figure 1-16, number 1).

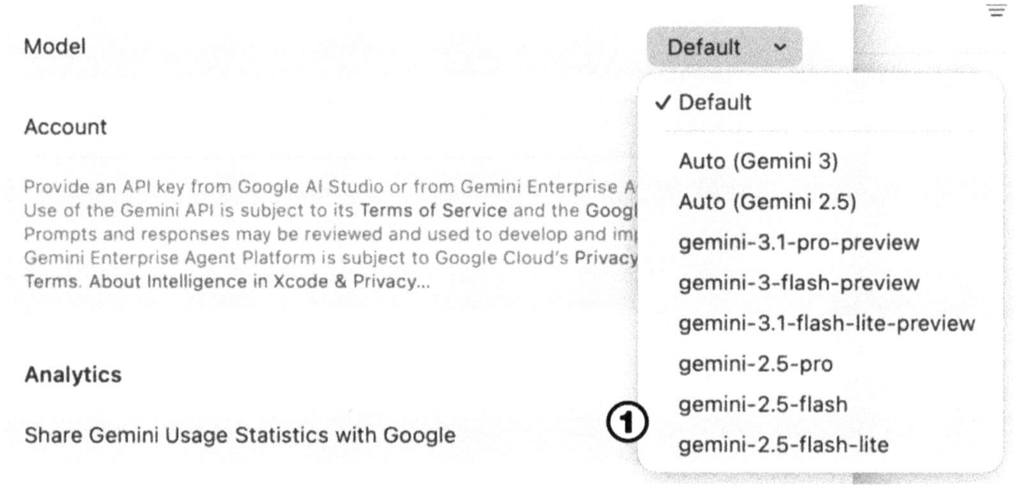

Figure 1-16: *Choosing a model*

Do It Yourself

Go to the menu at the top of the screen, open **Xcode -> Settings**, select the **Intelligence** panel, and press the **Get** buttons to download the agent you want (Figure 1-12). Once the agent finishes downloading, select it and press the Sign In button (Figures 1-11, 1-12 and 1-13). If you do not have an account with the agent provider, visit their websites. For Claude, visit **claude.ai/login**, sign up and subscribe to their Pro plan. For Codex, visit **chatgpt.com/codex/**, click Log In, and follow the instructions to create your account. For Gemini, visit **aistudio.google.com**, sign in with your Google account, click on **Dashboard -> API Keys**, and press the **Create API Key** button to get the key you need to provide to Xcode, as explained before. If you do not find the API Keys option, there is a button with a key icon at the bottom of the main panel to create your keys. After you enable the Gemini agent with the API key, you must select the agent again, and pick a Flash model from the list, as shown in Figure 1-16, number 1.

IMPORTANT

Choosing the right agent is not always straightforward and may change over time. At the moment, we recommend starting with the free **Codex** account and, when possible, upgrading to a Pro account with **Claude**. The models used by **Codex** are quite good, but for programming Apple applications, the **Sonnet** model offered by **Claude** has proven to be more efficient and useful. Try different options, and if you subscribe to a model, always choose monthly billing so you can easily switch to a different model if the current one does not perform as expected.

Once the required data has been downloaded and we have signed in to our account, the agents are ready to use. To start a new conversation with an agent, we can press the New Conversation button on the toolbar (Figure 1-4, number 3), but when multiple agents are available, we must first select the one we want to use from the Coding Assistant panel, as shown below.

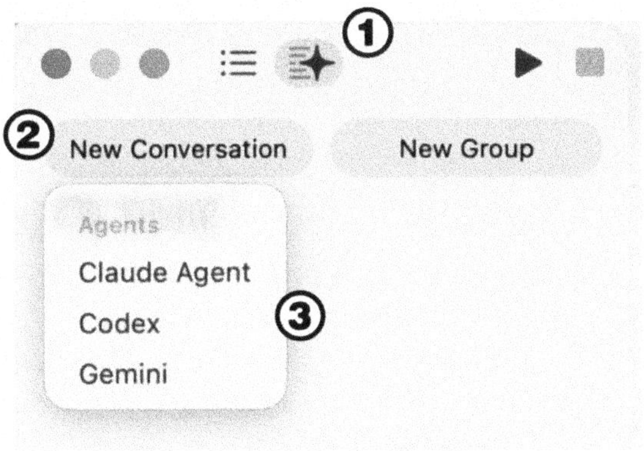

Figure 1-17: *Selecting an agent*

The Coding Assistant panel shows a list of previous conversations and buttons to start a new one. To open it, we press the Coding Assistant button on the toolbar (Figure 1-17, number 1), and to start a new conversation, we click the New Conversation button (Figure 1-17, number 2). This opens a menu to select the agent (Figure 1-17, number 3). After the agent is selected, a new panel opens in the Editor to start the conversation, as shown below.

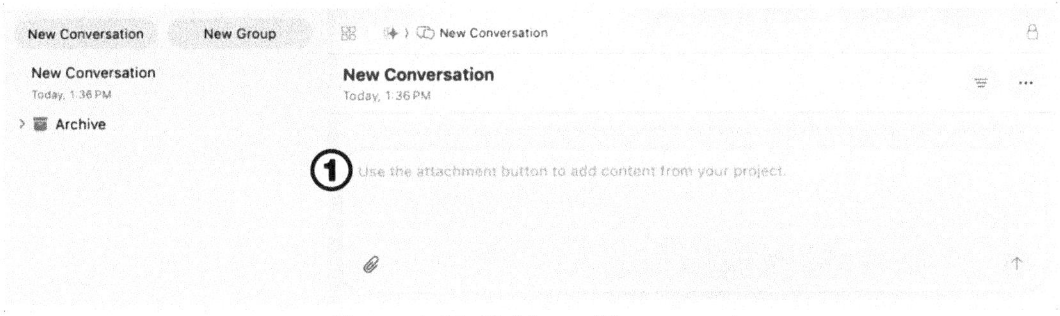

Figure 1-18: *Talking with an agent*

Now, it is all about asking what we need. For example, if we are unsure about the role played by the **#Playground** macro, we can ask "What does the #Playground macro do?" The answer will vary depending on the agent, but they will all describe the macro and how to use it. For example, Codex looks for the macro in the current code and answers according to that reference, as shown below.

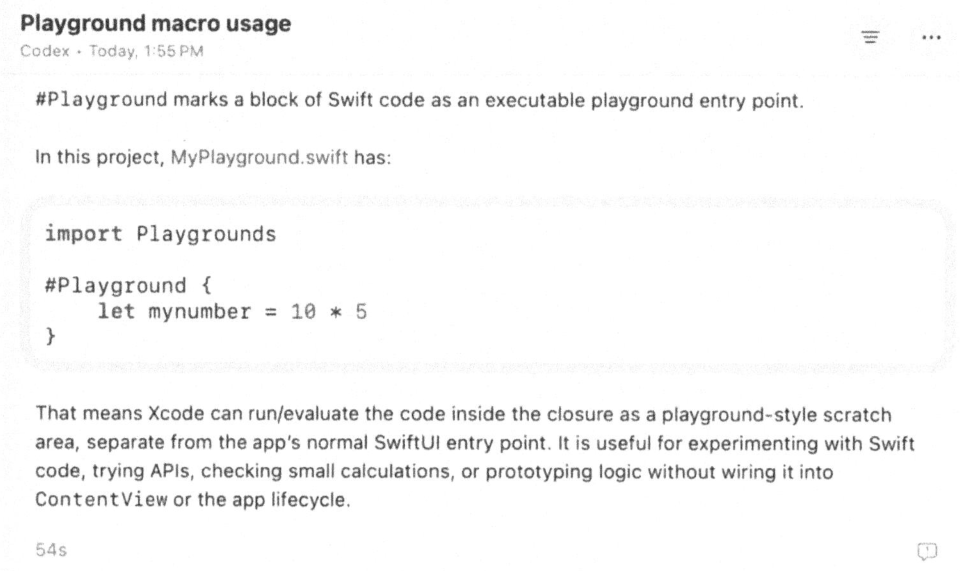

Figure 1-19: *Agent's response*

After the agent produces an answer, we can continue the conversation to ask follow-up questions, request additional information, or clarify anything we do not understand. Because AI agents reason in a way that resembles human thought, we get better results when we communicate with them as we would with another person. For example, earlier we asked a general question about the **#Playground** macro. However, we can be more specific and ask about the **#Playground** macro in the **ContentView.swift** file: "What is the #Playground macro doing in the ContentView.swift file?" By identifying the file or the specific section of code we want to discuss, we give the agent more context, allowing it to better understand our intent and provide a more relevant and useful response.

Do It Yourself

Start a new conversation with your favorite agent from the **Coding Assistant** panel (Figure 1-17) and ask a question about Xcode or the code. For example, you can ask about the code included by the template in the **ContentView.swift** file: "Explain what the code in the ContentView.swift file does." Ask follow-up questions if anything is not clear. Each conversation should focus on a specific topic. If you want to ask about something unrelated, start a new conversation. This keeps the context focused, helps the agent better understand your requests, and reduces the amount of information it has to process, which lowers the risk of exceeding your usage limit.

In the previous example, we used a single panel to talk to the agent, but most of the time we need to ask the agent questions about the code or request changes to a specific file. To work with the code alongside the agent, we must open a second panel. The option is available from the Add Editor Tab button on the toolbar (Figure 1-20, number 1).

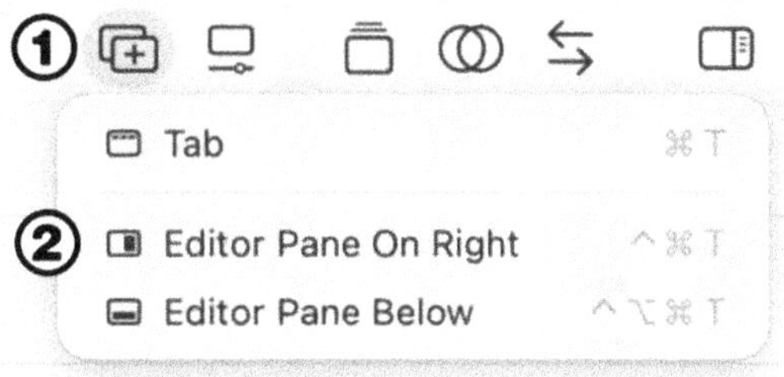

Figure 1-20: *Opening new panels in the Editor*

The button opens a menu with options to create a new tab inside the current panel or open a new panel (Figure 1-20, number 2). When we open a new panel, Xcode loads it with a tab containing the currently selected content, but we can use the Navigator to load any file we want. For example, we can have a conversation in the left panel and the code of our **MyPlayground.swift** file in the right panel, as shown below.

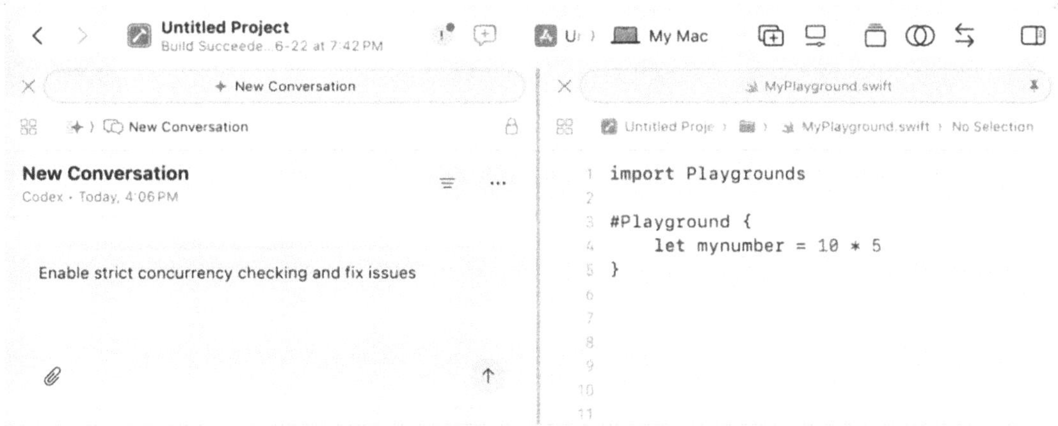

Figure 1-21: *Working with code alongside the agent*

Do It Yourself

If you have already selected the agent you want to work with from the Coding Assistant panel, you can start a new conversation with the same agent by clicking the New Conversation button in the toolbar (Figure 1-4, number 3). The conversation opens in the selected panel, but if you want to open it in a new panel, you can hold the Shift and Option keys while clicking New Conversation. Xcode creates a new panel and starts the conversation there.

IMPORTANT

Developing applications today requires a hybrid set of skills. We need to know how to guide AI agents effectively, but we also need to understand how applications are designed and programmed. The following chapters explain how the Swift programming language works and how to use its features to develop professional applications for Apple devices. Although we have made every effort to present each topic as clearly as possible, some concepts may require additional explanation. Whenever something is unclear, ask your AI agent for clarification and request additional examples when needed. Doing so will help you learn more effectively, become familiar with AI agents, and develop the skills required to interact with them and get the best possible results.

Chapter 2
Introduction to Swift

BASIC

2.1 - Variables

At their core, the function of a programming language is to store, retrieve, and process data. Because data is stored in the computer's memory, it must be managed carefully. If data is not organized properly, it can be accidentally overwritten, corrupted, or lost. To help prevent these problems, programming languages provide a mechanism for storing and organizing data known as variables. Variables are names that represent values stored in memory. Once a variable is defined, its name remains the same, but the value it represents can change over time. Swift provides several built-in data types for storing different kinds of values. Each data type determines the kind of value that can be stored and how much memory is required to store it. The following are some of the most basic data types provided by Swift.

`Int`

This data type defines integer numbers (numbers with no fractional component). It can store values from -9,223,372,036,854,775,808 to 9,223,372,036,854,775,807.

Although it is recommended to use the `Int` data type to store integers, sometimes we may need a more specific type. For this reason, Swift also defines the following.

`Int8`

This data type defines integer numbers of a size of 1 Byte (8 bits). Because of its size, it can store values from -128 to 127.

`Int16`

This data type defines integer numbers of a size of 2 Bytes (16 bits). Because of its size, it can store values from -32,768 to 32,767.

`Int32`

This data type defines integer numbers of a size of 4 Bytes (32 bits). Because of its size, it can store values from -2,147,483,648 to 2,147,483,647.

`Int64`

This data type defines integer numbers of a size of 8 Bytes (64 bits). Because of its size, it can store values from -9,223,372,036,854,775,808 to 9,223,372,036,854,775,807.

These data types store positive and negative values. If we only need to store a positive value, we can use the unsigned versions **UInt**, **UInt8**, **UInt16**, **UInt32**, and **UInt64**.

These data types only store integer values. To store real numbers, like 3.14 or 10.543, Swift includes floating-point data types. The following are the most frequently used.

Float

This data type defines 32 bits floating-point numbers with a precision of 6 digits.

Double

This data type defines 64 bits floating-point numbers with a precision of at least 15 digits.

Floating-point types can handle large numbers using scientific notation, but because of their precision, it is recommended to declare a variable of type **Double** when performing calculations and use **Float** for minor tasks, such as storing coordinates to position graphics on the screen.

BASIC

Declaration and Initialization

If we want to store data in memory, the first thing we need to do is select the right type from the data types provided by the language and then create a variable of that type. This action is called *declaration*, and it is done using the `var` instruction and the syntax `var name: type`.

Listing 2-1: Declaring variables

```
import Playgrounds

#Playground {
    var mynumber: Int
}
```

This example creates a variable called **mynumber** of type **Int**. When the system reads this statement, it reserves space in memory to store it and assigns the name **mynumber** to that space. After the execution of this statement, we can use the variable **mynumber** to store in memory any integer value from -9,223,372,036,854,775,808 to 9,223,372,036,854,775,807.

Do It Yourself

Open the project from the previous chapter or create a new one. Click the `MyPlayground.swift` file to open it, or create the file as explained in Chapter 1, Figure 1-10. Copy the code from Listing 2-1 into this file and open the Canvas. Since the variable does not currently store any value, you should not see anything on the Canvas, but this will change in the following examples.

IMPORTANT

You can use any character you want to declare the name of a variable, except for spaces, mathematical symbols, and some Unicode characters. Also, the name cannot start with a number, and Swift distinguishes between lowercase and uppercase characters (**MyNumber** is considered a different variable than **mynumber**). You must also make sure that the name does not match any reserved word. If you declare a variable with an illegal name, Xcode will show you an error.

Memory is a reusable resource. The space in memory reserved for a variable may have been previously used by another variable. For this reason, after declaring a variable, we must always store a value in it to clear the space. This process is called *initialization*.

Listing 2-2: Initializing variables

```
var mynumber: Int
mynumber = 5
```

In this new example, we first declare the variable as we did before, and then initialize it with the value 5 (we store the number 5 in the space of memory reserved for this variable). To store the value, we use the **=** (equal) symbol and the syntax **name = value**, where **name** is the name of the variable and **value** is the value we want to store in it (once the variable was declared, we do not have to use the **var** instruction or specify its type anymore).

Most of the time, we know what the variable's initial value will be right away. In cases like this, Swift allows us to declare and initialize the variable in just one line of code.

Listing 2-3: Declaring and initializing variables in the same statement

```
var mynumber: Int = 5
```

Do It Yourself

Update the **`#Playground`** macro in the **MyPlayground.swift** file with the code in Listing 2-3. You should see the result on the Canvas (**`mynumber 5`**). Do the same to test the rest of the examples in this chapter.

Variables are called variables because their values are not constant. We can change them any time we want. To store a new value in the space of memory reserved for a variable, we must implement the same syntax used for initialization.

Listing 2-4: Assigning a new value to a variable

```
var mynumber: Int = 5
mynumber = 87
```

The process of storing a value in a variable is called *assignment*. In these terms, we can say that in the example in Listing 2-4 we "initialize the variable **mynumber** with the number 5 and then assign the value 87 to it". The value 87 replaces the value 5 in memory. After that second statement is executed, every time we read the **mynumber** variable from other statements in the code they will return the value 87 (unless another value is assigned to the variable later).

> **IMPORTANT**
>
> Once a variable is declared, the values stored in that variable must be of the same data type. If we declare a variable of type **Int**, we cannot store floating-point values in it later (e.g., 14.129).

Of course, we can create all the variables we want and of the data type we need.

Listing 2-5: Declaring variables of different data types

```
var mynumber: Int = 5
var myfavorite: Float = 14.129
```

The first statement in Listing 2-5 declares an integer variable and initializes it with the value 5. The second statement does the same but for a floating-point variable. When the data type of a value is easy to identify, Swift can infer it and the syntax may be simplified, as shown next.

Listing 2-6: Declaring variables without specifying the data type

```
var mynumber = 5
var myfavorite = 14.129
```

Swift infers the variable's data type from the value we are trying to assign to it. In this last example, the value 5 is clearly an integer and the value 14.129 is clearly a floating-point value, so Swift creates the variable **mynumber** of type **Int** and the variable **myfavorite** of type **Double** (Swift always selects the most comprehensive type).

IMPORTANT

Xcode offers a simple tool you can use to see the data type assigned to a variable and get additional information. All you need to do is click on the name of the variable while holding down the Option key. This opens a popup window with the full declaration of the variable, including its data type, and any information we may need to identify the code's functionality. As we will see later, this not only applies to variables but also other instructions, including properties and methods.

An important feature of variables is that the value of one may be assigned to another.

Listing 2-7: Assigning variables to variables

```
var mynumber = 5
var myfavorite = mynumber
```

The second statement in Listing 2-7 reads the value of the variable **mynumber** and assigns it to the variable **myfavorite**. The data type of **myfavorite** is inferred to be **Int** (the same as that of **mynumber**). After executing this code, we have two integer variables, each with its own space in memory containing the value 5.

Do It Yourself

Update the `#Playground` macro in the **MyPlayground.swift** file with the code in Listing 2-7. You should see two results on the Canvas, one for the `mynumber` variable (`mynumber 5`) and another for the `myfavorite` variable (`myfavorite 5`).

BASIC

Arithmetic Operators

Storing values in memory is what variables allow us to do, but those values do not have to be declared explicitly, they can also be the result of arithmetic operations. Swift supports the operations: **+** (addition), **-** (subtraction), ***** (multiplication), **/** (division) and **%** (remainder).

Listing 2-8: Assigning the result of an operation to a variable

```
var mynumber = 5 + 10  // 15
```

When the system reads the statement in Listing 2-8, it adds 10 to 5 and assigns the result to **mynumber** (15).

IMPORTANT

The text added at the end of the statement in Listing 2-8 is a comment that we use to show the value produced by the statement. Comments are ignored by the Swift compiler but useful for programmers to remember vital information. They are introduced after the characters **//** (e.g., **// comment**) or in between the characters **/* */** (e.g., **/* comment */**). You can write the characters yourself or use Xcode's shortcut by selecting the lines of code you want to turn into a comment and press the keys Command and /.

Of course, we can perform not only addition but any operation we want.

Listing 2-9: Performing operations in variables of different type

```
var mynumber = 2 * 25  // 50
var anothernumber = 8 - 40 * 2  // -72
var myfraction = 5.0 / 2.0  // 2.5
```

The first two statements in Listing 2-9 are easy to read. They perform arithmetic operations on integer numbers that produce an integer value, so the variables `mynumber` and `anothernumber` are of type `Int`. If we want a variable to be of a different type, we must declare it explicitly or help Swift determine the data type. This is why, in the third statement, we explicitly declare the values as floating-point numbers by adding a decimal place (`.0`). This helps Swift to infer the variable's data type as `Double` and produce a result of that type.

When the Swift compiler finds an operation with two or more numbers and has to infer the data type of the result, it converts the number of the less comprehensive type to the most comprehensive type. For example, when we declare an **Int** and a **Double** in the same operation (e.g., `5 + 2.0`), the **Int** value is converted and processed as **Double**, and therefore the result will also be **Double**.

Listing 2-10: Inferring the data type from an operation

```
var myfraction1 = 5.0 / 2.0  // 2.5
var myfraction2 = 5 / 2.0  // 2.5
var myfraction3 = 5 / 2  // 2
```

This example declares and initializes three variables. In the first statement both numbers were declared as floating-point values, so the Swift compiler infers a **Double** and creates the **myfraction1** variable of that data type. In the second statement, we have an integer value and a floating-point value. Because of the floating-point value, the Swift compiler interprets the integer (`5`) as a **Double** (`5.0`) and creates the **myfraction2** variable of type **Double**. But in the last statement there is no clear floating-point value. Both numbers were declared as integers (with no fractional part). In this case, the Swift compiler does not know what we want to do, so it interprets both numbers as integers and creates the **myfraction3** variable of type **Int**. When an operation produces a result that is expected to be an integer, any decimal part is discarded. In this example, the system gets rid of the decimal **5** from the result and only assigns the integer **2** to the variable. If we don't want to lose the decimal part, we must avoid inference and declare the data type explicitly as **Float** or **Double** (e.g. `var myfraction3: Double`).

Dividing integer numbers is pointless most of the time, except in some circumstances when we need to know the remainder. The remainder is the amount left over by a division between two numbers and it is calculated using the **%** symbol.

Listing 2-11: Calculating the remainder

```
var remainder1 = 11 % 3   // 2
var remainder2 = 20 % 8   // 4
var remainder3 = 5 % 2   // 1
```

Each statement in Listing 2-11 calculates the remainder produced by dividing the first number by the second number and assigns the result to the variable. For example, the first statement produces the remainder **2**. The system divides **11** by **3** and finds a quotient of **3**. Then, to get the remainder, it calculates **11** minus the multiplication of **3** times the quotient (**11 – (3 * 3) = 2**).

The second statement produces a remainder of **4** and the third statement produces a remainder of **1**. This last statement is particularly useful because it allows us to determine whether a value is odd or even. When we calculate the reminder of an integer divided by **2**, we get a result according to its parity. If the number is even, the remainder is **0**, and if the number is odd, the remainder is **1** (or **-1** for negative values).

Performing arithmetic operations becomes useful when instead of numbers we use variables.

Listing 2-12: Adding numbers to variables

```
var mynumber = 5
var total = mynumber + 10   // 15
```

This example declares the variable **mynumber** and initializes it with the value **5**. In the next statement, the **total** variable is declared and initialized with the result of the addition of the current value of **mynumber** plus **10** (5 + 10).

In Listing 2-12, we used a new variable to store the result of the operation, but when the old value is not important anymore, we can store the result back into the same variable.

Listing 2-13: Performing operations on the variable's current value

```
var mynumber = 5
mynumber = mynumber + 10   // 15
```

In this example, the current value of **mynumber** is added to **10** and the result is assigned to the same variable. After the execution of the second statement, the value of **mynumber** is 15.

Working with values previously stored in a variable allows our program to evolve and adapt to new circumstances. For instance, we could add 1 to the current value of a variable and store the result in the same variable to create a counter. Every time the statement is executed, the value of the variable is incremented by one unit. Recurrent increments and decrements of the value of a variable are very important in computer programming. Because of this, Swift supports two operators that were specifically designed for this purpose.

+= is a shorthand for **variable = variable + number**, where **number** is the value we want to add to the variable's current value.

-= is a shorthand for **variable = variable - number**, where **number** is the value we want to subtract from the variable's current value.

With these operators, we can easily add or subtract a value to the current value of the variable and assign the result back to the same variable.

Listing 2-14: Modifying the value of a variable using incremental operators

```
var mynumber = 5
mynumber += 4  // 9
```

The process generated by the code in Listing 2-14 is simple. After the value **5** is assigned to the **mynumber** variable, the system reads the second statement, gets the current value of the variable, adds **4** to that value, and stores the result back in **mynumber** (9).

IMPORTANT

Swift also offers overflow operators (**&+**, **&-**, **&***, **&/** and **&%**). These operators are useful when we expect an operation to produce a result that goes over the limit the data type can handle. For more information, visit our website and follow the links for this chapter.

BASIC

Constants

Constants are the same as variables, but their values cannot change. Once a constant is declared and initialized, we cannot change its value. Therefore, constants provide a secure way to store a value and help the system to manage memory. To declare them, we must use the same syntax for a variable but replace the keyword **var** with **let**.

Listing 2-15: Declaring and initializing a constant

```
let mynumber = 5
```

All the rules for variables also apply to constants; with the exception that we cannot assign a new value after the constant was already initialized. The **mynumber** constant declared in Listing 2-15 will always have the value `5`.

> **IMPORTANT**
>
> When you should use constants or variables depends on your application. As a guide, you can use Apple's recommendations: If a stored value will not change in your code, always declare it as a constant with the `let` keyword. Use variables only to store values that must be able to change.

BASIC

2.2 - Swift Data Types

Swift defines additional data types to allow us to work not only with numbers but also more complex values such as logical values (`true` or `false`), characters, and text.

BASIC

Characters

Because of their nature, computers cannot store characters or text, but they can use tables that contain the information necessary to represent those values (numbers, letters, symbols, and more). What the system stores in memory is not the character itself but the value corresponding to the index of the character in the table. For example, if we use the letter A, the value stored in memory will be the decimal number 65 because that is the position of the letter A in the table used by Swift to define these characters.

There are several standard tables of characters available. Swift is compliant with a table called Unicode. This is a comprehensive table that includes all characters from almost all languages in the world, as well as special characters such as emojis. Because of the wide range of characters, the amount of memory needed to store them varies from character to character. For this reason, Swift provides a data type called `Character` to store these values.

Listing 2-16: Declaring and initializing a Character variable

```
var myletter: Character = "A"
```

A character is declared using the **Character** data type and initialized with the value in double quotes. In Listing 2-16, we declare a variable called **myletter** with the value A.

In addition to the characters on the keyboard, Unicode allows us to store emojis and symbols. Xcode offers a handy tool to select the graphics we want. By pressing the combination of keys Control + Command + Space, we can open a popup window and select a graphic with a click of the mouse.

Figure 2-1: *Emojis and symbols*

BASIC

Strings

Individual characters are barely used in computer programming. Instead, we usually store strings of characters. The **String** type was created for this purpose.

Listing 2-17: Declaring and initializing a `String` variable

```
let mytext: String = "My name is John"
```

A string is a sequence of **Character** values. It is declared with the **String** type and the value in double quotes. These types of variables are very flexible; we may replace a string by another one of different length, concatenate two or more, or even modify parts of it. Concatenation is a common operation, and it is done with the **+** and **+=** operators.

Listing 2-18: Concatenating strings

```
var mytext = "My name is "
mytext = mytext + "John"   // "My name is John"
```

In Listing 2-18, the **mytext** variable is created with the value "My name is " and then the string "John" is added at the end of the current value to get the string "My name is John". The **+=** operator works in a similar way, and can be combined with the **+** operators to get the string we want.

Listing 2-19: Concatenating strings with the + and += operators

```
let name = "John"
var mytext = "My name is "
mytext += name  // "My name is John"
```

With the **+** and **+=** operators we can concatenate strings with other strings. To concatenate strings with characters and numbers we must implement a procedure called *String Interpolation*. The variables are enclosed in the string between parentheses and prefixed with a backslash.

Listing 2-20: Including variables in strings

```
let age = 44
let mytext = "I am \(age) years old"  // "I am 44 years old"
```

In this code, we read the **age** variable and add its value to the string. The string "I am 44 years old" is then assigned to **mytext**. Using this tool, we can insert any value we want inside a string, including **Character** and **String** values, numbers, and arithmetic operations. In the following example, the value of **age** is multiplied by 12 and the result is included in the string.

Listing 2-21: Performing operations within strings

```
let age = 44
let mytext = "I am \(age * 12) months old"  // "I am 528 months old"
```

Sometimes we need to insert special characters into the string, like backslashes or quotes. Swift provides two ways to accomplish this. We can prefix the special character with another backslash or enclose the entire string in hash characters, as shown below.

Listing 2-22: Including special characters in a string

```
let text1 = "This is \"my\" age"  // "This is "my" age"
let text2 = #"This is "my" age"#  // "This is "my" age"
```

Another important feature of strings is the ability to create multiple lines of text. Again, Swift offers two alternatives: We can insert the special characters **\n** where we need a new line, or use triple quotes ("""), in which case the Swift compiler will take into account the original format of the text and automatically insert the **\n** characters as needed.

Listing 2-23: Generating multiple lines of text

```
let twolines = "This is the first line\nThis is the second line"
```

```
let multiline = """
This is the first line
This is the second line
"""
```

The **twolines** constant defined in this example includes the **\n** characters between the sentences, prompting the Swift compiler to generate two lines of text. If we look at the result on the Canvas, we will see two lines of text, one on top of the other. Something similar happens with the value of **multiline**, although in this case the """ characters tell the Swift compiler to automatically insert the **\n** characters at the end of each line.

BASIC

Booleans

Boolean variables can only store two values: **true** or **false**. These variables are particularly useful when we want to execute an instruction or a set of instructions only if a condition is met. To declare a Boolean variable, we can specify the data type as **Bool** or let Swift infer it from the value, as in the following example.

Listing 2-24: Declaring a Boolean variable

```
var valid = true
```

The purpose of these types of variables is to simplify the process of identifying a condition. By using a Boolean variable instead of an integer, for example, we just need to check whether the value is equal to **true** or **false** to verify the condition. We will see some practical examples later.

BASIC

Optionals

As mentioned at the beginning of this chapter, after a variable is declared, we must specify its initial value. We cannot use a variable if it has not been initialized. This means that a variable always has a valid value. However, this is not always possible. Sometimes we do not have a value to assign to the variable, or the current one may become invalid. For these situations, Swift defines a modifier that turns any data type into an optional type. This means that the variable marked as optional can have a value or be empty. To declare an optional type, we add a question mark after the type's name.

Listing 2-25: Declaring an optional variable of type Int

```
var mynumber: Int?
```

New values are assigned to optionals as we do with normal variables.

Listing 2-26: Assigning new values to optional variables

```
var mynumber: Int?
mynumber = 5
```

The empty state is represented by the keyword **nil**. Therefore, when an optional variable is declared but not initialized, Swift assigns **nil** to the variable to indicate the absence of a value. This means that if later we need to empty the variable, we can assign **nil** to it, as shown below.

Listing 2-27: Using nil to empty an optional variable

```
var mynumber: Int?
mynumber = 5
mynumber = nil
```

This example declares an optional integer, assigns the value `5` to it, and then sets it to `nil`. Of course, this example is trivial, but setting a variable to `nil` becomes useful in more complex applications.

Although optionals seem to work like regular variables, they do not expose their values. To read the value of an optional, we must first unwrap it by adding an exclamation mark at the end of the name.

Listing 2-28: Unwrapping an optional variable

```
var mynumber: Int?
mynumber = 5
var total = mynumber! * 10  // 50
```

The last statement in Listing 2-28 unwraps **mynumber** to get its value, multiplies this value by `10`, and assigns the result to the **total** variable. This is only necessary when we need to use the value. If we just want to assign an optional to another optional, the process is as always.

Listing 2-29: Assigning an optional to another optional

```
var mynumber: Int?
mynumber = 5
var total = mynumber
```

In this example, the system infers the type of the variable **total** to be an optional of type **Int** and assigns the value of **mynumber** to it. If we want to read the value of **total** later, we must unwrap it as we did with **mynumber** before.

IMPORTANT

Before unwrapping an optional, we need to make sure it contains a value (it is not equal to **nil**). If we try to unwrap an empty optional, the app will return an error and crash. Later in this chapter we will learn how to use conditional statements to check this condition.

There are cases where we know that an optional variable will always have a value, but we do not know what the initial value is. For example, there could be a variable that receives a value from the system as soon as the application is executed. For such situations, Swift includes *Implicitly Unwrapped Optionals*. These are optional variables that are declared with an exclamation mark instead of a question mark. The system treats these variables as optionals until we use them in a statement, as in the following example.

Listing 2-30: Declaring Implicitly Unwrapped Optionals

```
var mynumber: Int!
mynumber = 5
var total = mynumber * 10  // 50
```

In this code, the **mynumber** variable was declared as an implicitly unwrapped optional and it was later initialized with the value **5**. Note that it was not necessary to write the exclamation mark when reading its value anymore. The system unwraps the **mynumber** variable automatically to use its value in the multiplication (this is only available for implicitly unwrapped optionals).

BASIC

Tuples

A tuple is a variable that contains a group of one or more values of equal or different type. It is useful when we need to store values that are somehow related to each other. Tuples are declared with their values and data types in parentheses and separated by comma.

Listing 2-31: Declaring a tuple with two values

```
var myname: (String, String) = ("John", "Doe")
```

In this example, the **myname** variable is a tuple that contains two **String** values. The values of this tuple are of the same type, but we can use any combination of values we want, as shown below.

Listing 2-32: Declaring a tuple with values of different type

```
var myname = ("John", "Doe", 44)
```

To be able to read the values later, an index is automatically assigned to each of the values of the tuple. The first value will be at index **0**, the second at index **1**, and so on. Using the corresponding index and dot notation we can access the value we want to read, as shown below.

Listing 2-33: Reading the values of a tuple

```
var myname = ("John", "Doe", 44)
var mytext = "\(myname.0) is \(myname.2) years old"
// "John is 44 years old"
```

In Listing 2-33, we read the values of the **myname** tuple at index **0** and **2** to include them in a new string and assign the string to **mytext**. The same syntax may be used to modify a value.

Listing 2-34: Modifying the value of a tuple

```
var myname = ("John", "Doe", 44)
myname.0 = "George"
var mytext = "\(myname.0) is \(myname.2) years old"
// "George is 44 years old"
```

The second statement in Listing 2-34 assigns a new string to the first value of the tuple. The data type of the new value must be of the same as the old one or we will get an error. After the code is executed, the value of **mytext** is "George is 44 years old".

Indexes are a quick way to access the values of a tuple, but they do not help us remember what the values represent. To identify the values in a tuple, we can assign a name to each one of them. The name must be declared before the value and separated by a colon, as shown below.

Listing 2-35: Declaring names for the values of a tuple

```
var myname = (name: "John", surname: "Doe", age: 44)
var mytext = "\(myname.name) is \(myname.age) years old"
// "John is 44 years old"
```

Swift also provides a way to copy the values of the tuple into independent variables.

Listing 2-36: Creating multiple variables from the values of a tuple

```
var myname = ("John", "Doe", 44)
var (name, surname, age) = myname
var mytext = "\(name) \(surname) is \(age) years old"
// "John Doe is 44 years old"
```

The names of the variables are declared between parentheses. The values are assigned to the variables in the same order they are declared in the tuple. If only some of the values are required, the rest may be ignored with an underscore, as shown below.

Listing 2-37: Ignoring some of the values of a tuple

```
var myname = ("John", "Doe", 44)
var (name, _, age) = myname
var mytext = "\(name) is \(age) years old"
// "John is 44 years old"
```

Only the variables **name** and **age** are created in this last example. (Note the underscore in the place of the second variable.)

> **IMPORTANT**
>
> Underscores can be used to discard the value produced by an expression. This is what the **`#Playground`** in Xcode's template actually does. If you go back to the **ContentView.swift** file and look at the original code generated for the **`#Playground`** macro, you will find the statement **`_ = 1 + 2`**. This tells the Swift compiler to calculate 1 + 2 but discard the result.

BASIC

2.3 - Conditionals and Loops

Up to this point, we have written the instructions one after the other. In this programming pattern, the system starts with the top statement and continues until it reaches the end of the list, so each statement is executed only once. The purpose of conditionals and loops is to break this sequential flow. Conditionals allow us to execute one or more statements only when a condition is met, and loops execute a group of statements repeatedly.

BASIC

If and Else

A simple but useful conditional statement is **`if`**. With **`if`**, we can check a condition and execute a group of statements only if the condition is met. The statements to be executed are specified after the condition between curly braces.

Listing 2-38: Comparing two values with if

```
var age = 19
var message = "John is old"

if age < 21 {
    message = "John is young"
}
```

Two variables are declared in this code. The **age** variable contains the value we want to check, and the **message** variable is the one we are going to modify depending on the state of the condition. The **if** statement compares the value of **age** with the number 21 using the character **<** (less than). This comparison returns the state of the condition (true or false). If the condition is true (the value of **age** is less than 21), the instruction between braces is executed, so a new value is assigned to the **message** variable, otherwise, the instruction is ignored and the execution continues with the instruction after the braces. In this case, the value of **age** is less than 21 and therefore the string "John is young" is assigned to the **message** variable.

> **IMPORTANT**
>
> One or more lines of code enclosed in curly braces is called *block*. As illustrated by the example in Listing 2-38, the instructions inside a block are displaced to the right. The whitespace on the left is used to help us differentiate the statements in the block from the rest of the statements. This whitespace is automatically generated for you by Xcode, but you can add it yourself, when necessary, by pressing the Tab key on your keyboard.

The **<** character, used in the last example, is part of a group of operators called *Comparison Operators*. The following is the list of comparison operators available in Swift.

== checks whether the value on the left is equal to the value on the right.
!= checks whether the value on the left is different from the value on the right.
> checks whether the value on the left is greater than the value on the right.
< checks whether the value on the left is less than the value on the right.
>= checks whether the value on the left is greater or equal than the value on the right.
<= checks whether the value on the left is less or equal than the value on the right.

All of these operators are applied like the **<** operator. For example, the following code modifies the value of **`message`** if the value of **`age`** is less than or equal to 21.

Listing 2-39: Comparing two values with the <= operator

```
var age = 21
```

```
var message = "John is old"
if age <= 21 {
   message = "John is young"
}
```

When only two results are required, we may define the condition using a Boolean. These values do not need to be compared to any value; they already return a state (true or false).

Listing 2-40: Conditions with Boolean values

```
var underage = true
var message = "John is allowed"
if underage {
   message = "John is underage"
}
```

This code checks whether the value of the **underage** variable is **true** or **false**. If it is **true** (which means the condition is true), a new string is assigned to **message**.

If what we want is to execute the statements when the value is **false**, Swift offers a logical operator to toggle the condition. All we need to do is to precede the condition with an exclamation mark.

Listing 2-41: Using logical operators

```
var underage = true
var message = "John is underage"
if !underage {
   message = "John is allowed"
}
```

The original value of the **underage** variable in the code of Listing 2-41 is **true**, so when the **if** statement toggles the condition, the resulting condition is false and therefore the value of the **message** variable is not modified.

The exclamation mark is part of a group of logical operators provided by Swift. The following are the operators available.

! (logical NOT) toggles the state of the condition. If the condition is true, it returns false, and vice versa.
&& (logical AND) checks two conditions and returns true if both are true.
|| (logical OR) checks two conditions and returns true if one or both are true.

Logical operators work with any kind of conditions, not only Booleans. To work with complex conditions, it is recommended to enclose them between parentheses, as shown below.

Listing 2-42: Using logical operators to check multiple conditions

```
var smart = true
var age = 19
var message = "John is underage or dumb"

if (age < 21) && smart {
   message = "John is allowed"
}
```

The **if** statement in Listing 2-42 compares the value of the **age** variable with 21 and checks the value of the **smart** variable. If **age** is less than 21 and **smart** is **true**, then the overall condition is true, and a new string is assigned to **message**. If any of the individual conditions is false, then the overall condition is false, and the block of instructions is not executed. In this case, both conditions are true and therefore the string "John is allowed" is assigned to **message**.

IMPORTANT

By using **&&** (AND) and **||** (OR) you can create a logical sequence of multiple conditions. The system evaluates one condition at a time from left to right and compares the results. If you want to make sure that the expressions are evaluated in the correct order, you can declare them within parentheses, as in **(true && false) || true**. The expression within the parentheses is evaluated first, and the result is then evaluated against the rest of the expression.

Although we can use comparison operators and logical operators in most of the data types available, optionals are slightly different. Their values are wrapped, so we cannot compare them with other values, or check their state as we do with Booleans. Optionals must be first compared against the **nil** keyword and then unwrapped before working with their values.

Listing 2-43: Checking whether an optional contains a value or not

```
var count = 0
var myoptional: Int? = 5

if myoptional != nil {
   let uvalue = myoptional!
   count = count + uvalue   // 5
}
```

This example shows the process we must follow to safely read the value of an optional variable. The optional is first compared to `nil`. If it is different from `nil` (which means it contains a value), the optional is unwrapped inside the block with an exclamation mark, its value is assigned to a constant, and then the constant is used to perform any operation necessary.

We must always make sure that an optional has a value before unwrapping it. For this reason, Swift introduces a convenient syntax that checks the optional and unwraps its value at the same time. It is called *Optional Binding*, and we can use it in an **if** statement, as shown below.

Listing 2-44: Using Optional Binding to unwrap an optional variable

```
var count = 0
var myoptional: Int? = 5
if let uvalue = myoptional {
   count = count + uvalue   // 5
}
```

This code works the same as the previous example, but it is cleaner and easier to read. The optional is unwrapped as part of the condition. If it is different from **nil**, its value is assigned to the **uvalue** constant and the statements in the block are executed, otherwise, the statements inside the block are ignored (The constant can have any name we want.).

As we will see later, variables and constants declared inside a block are only available to the code in the block. This also means that variables and constants declared in different blocks are independent (their values are stored in different locations in memory). An interesting consequence of this is that we can declare the constant for the Optional Binding with the same name as the variable, and they will be considered by Swift to be different.

Listing 2-45: Using the same name to unwrap a value

```
var count = 0
var myoptional: Int? = 5
if let myoptional = myoptional {
   count = count + myoptional   // 5
}
```

In this case, the **myoptional** constant declared by the **if** statement is only accessible by the code inside the block and therefore is different from the **myoptional** variable declared outside the block. The code can be simplified even more by only declaring the name of the constant, as shown below.

Listing 2-46: Unwrapping an optional value of the same name

```
var count = 0
var myoptional: Int? = 5
if let myoptional {
   count = count + myoptional   // 5
}
```

In this example, Swift looks for an optional variable called **myoptional**, unwraps the value, and assigns it to the constant. The result is the same as before, but the code has been simplified.

IMPORTANT

The constants and variables declared inside and outside blocks have different scopes, which means they are independent and their values are stored in different locations in memory, even when they share the same name. We will learn more about the scope of variables in Chapter 3.

If we want to unwrap several optionals at the same time using Optional Binding, we must declare the expressions separated by comma. This also applies when we want to check for other conditions in the same statement. For instance, the following example unwraps an optional and only executes the code in the block if its value is equal to **5**.

Listing 2-47: Checking multiple conditions with Optional Binding

```
var count = 0
var myoptional: Int? = 5
if let uvalue = myoptional, uvalue == 5 {
   count = count + uvalue  // 5
}
```

The **if** statement in Listing 2-47 unwraps the optional first and, if there is a value, compares it with the number **5**. The statements in the block are executed only if both conditions are true (the variable **myoptional** contains a value and the value is equal to **5**).

Sometimes, a group of instructions must be executed for each state of the condition. For this purpose, Swift includes the **if else** statement. The instructions are declared in two blocks. The first block is executed when the condition is true, and the second block when the condition is false.

Listing 2-48: Using `if else` to respond to both states of the condition

```
var mynumber = 6
if mynumber % 2 == 0 {
   mynumber = mynumber + 2  // 8
} else {
   mynumber = mynumber + 1
}
```

This is a simple example that checks whether a value is odd or even using the remainder operator. The condition gets the remainder of the division between the value of the **mynumber** variable and **2** and compares the result against **0**. If true, it means that the value of **mynumber** is even, so the first block is executed. If the result is different from **0**, it means that the value is odd and the condition is false, so the block corresponding to the **else** instruction is executed instead.

The **if** and **else** statements may be concatenated to check as many conditions as we need. In the following example, the first condition checks whether **age** is less than 21. If false, the second condition checks whether **age** is over 21. And if false, the final **else** block is executed.

Listing 2-49: Concatenating `if else` instructions

```
var age = 19
var message = "The customer is "
if age < 21 {
   message += "underage"   // "The customer is underage"
} else if age > 21 {
   message += "allowed"
} else {
   message += "21 years old"
}
```

If we are using the **`if else`** statements to assign a value to a variable, we can assign the statement directly to the variable, as shown below.

Listing 2-50: Implementing `if else` as an expression

```
var age = 19
var message = if age < 21 {
   "Underage"   // "Underage"
} else {
   "Allowed"
}
```

In this example, the system checks the condition first (**`age < 21`**) and then assigns the corresponding value to the **`message`** variable. If the value of age is less than 21, the value assigned to **`message`** is "Underage"; otherwise, the value assigned to **`message`** is "Allowed". If we are working with simple values, as in this case, we can use a shortcut provided by Swift called *ternary operator*. A ternary operator is a construction composed of a condition and the two values we want to return for each case, separated by the characters **`?`** and **`:`**, as shown below.

Listing 2-51: Implementing a ternary operator

```
var age = 19
var message = age < 21 ? "Underage" : "Allowed"   // "Underage"
```

When the ternary operator is executed, the first value is returned if the condition is true, and the second value is returned if the condition is false. The advantage of using a ternary operator is that it reduces the size of the code significantly, but the result is the same as using an **if else** statement.

Ternary operators can also be implemented to unwrap optionals. For instance, we can check whether an optional variable contains a value and assign it to another variable or give the variable a default value if the optional is empty.

Listing 2-52: Unwrapping an optional with a ternary operator

```
var age: Int? = 19
var realage = age != nil ? age! : 0  // 19
```

This code defines an optional variable called **age** with the value **19**. After the variable is defined, we unwrap it with a ternary operator and assign its value to a new variable called **realage**. If the optional contains a value, it is is assigned to the variable, otherwise, the value **0** is assigned instead.

Assigning values by default when the optional is empty is very common. To simplify our work, Swift offers the *nil-coalescing operator*, which is represented by the characters **??**. This operator works like the ternary operator implemented in Listing 2-52; it unwraps the optional and returns its value or returns another value if the optional is empty. In the following example, we create an empty optional called **age** and use the nil-coalescing operator to assign its value to the **maxage** variable or the value 100 if the optional is empty.

Listing 2-53: Unwrapping an optional with the nil-coalescing operator

```
var age: Int?
var maxage = age ?? 100  // 100
```

BASIC

Switch

We can keep adding **if** and **else** statements to check as many conditions as we need, but this pattern can make the code impossible to read and maintain. When multiple conditions need to be checked, it is better to use the **switch** instruction instead. This instruction compares a value to a list of values and executes the statements of the value that matches. The possible matches are listed between curly braces with the **case** keyword, as in the following example.

Listing 2-54: Checking conditions with `switch`

```
var age = 19
var message = ""
switch age {
   case 13:
      message = "Happy Bar Mitzvah!"
   case 16:
      message = "Sweet Sixteen!"
   case 21:
      message = "Welcome to Adulthood!"
   default:
      message = "Happy Birthday!"  // "Happy Birthday!"
}
```

The cases must be exhaustive. If we do not include a **case** statement for every possible value, we must add a **default** statement at the end that is executed when no match is found. In Listing 2-54, we compare the value of the **age** variable with a small set of values corresponding to special dates. If no **case** matches the value of the variable, the **default** statement is executed and the string "Happy Birthday!" is assigned to **message**.

When we need to execute the same set of instructions for more than one value, we can declare the values separated by comma.

Listing 2-55: Checking multiple conditions per case

```
var age = 6
var message = "You go to "
switch age {
   case 2, 3, 4:
      message += "Day Care"
   case 5, 6, 7, 8, 9, 10, 11:
      message += "Elementary School"   // "You go to Elementary School"
   case 12, 13, 14, 15, 16, 17:
      message += "High School"
   case 18, 19, 20, 21:
      message += "College"
   default:
      message += "Work"
}
```

The **switch** statement can also work with more complex data types, such as strings and tuples. In the case of tuples, **switch** provides additional options to build complex matching patterns. For example, the following code checks the second value of a tuple to determine the difference in age.

Listing 2-56: Matching a tuple in a switch statement

```
var message = ""
var ages = (10, 30)

switch ages {
   case (10, 20):
      message = "Too close"
   case (10, 30):
      message = "The right age"   // "The right age"
   case (10, 40):
      message = "Too far"
   default:
      message = "Way too far"
}
```

This example always compares the first value of the tuple against `10` but checks different matches for the second value. If a value does not matter, we can use an underscore to ignore it.

Listing 2-57: Matching only the second value of a tuple

```
var message = ""
var ages = (10, 30)

switch ages {
   case (_, 20):
      message = "Too close"
   case (_, 30):
      message = "The right age"   // "The right age"
   case (_, 40):
      message = "Too far"
   default:
      message = "Way too far"
}
```

An alternative offered by the **switch** statement to create complex matching patterns is to capture a value in a constant to be able to access it from the instructions of the **case**.

Listing 2-58: Capturing values with constants

```
var message = ""
var ages = (10, 20)

switch ages {
   case (let x, 20):
      message = "Too close to \(x)"   // "Too close to 10"
   case (_, 30):
      message = "The right age"
   case (let x, 40):
      message = "Too far to \(x)"
   default:
      message = "Way too far"
}
```

In this example, when the **switch** statement checks the first and third cases, it creates a constant called **x** and assigns to it the first value, so that we can access and use that value from the statements within the **case**.

There is an even more complex matching pattern that involves the use of a clause called **where**. We can use this clause to check additional conditions. In the following example, we capture the values of the tuple and compare them.

Listing 2-59: Comparing values with `where`

```
var message = ""
var ages = (10, 20)

switch ages {
   case let (x, y) where x > y:
      message = "Too young"
   case let (x, y) where x == y:
```

```
        message = "The same age"
    case let (x, y) where x < y:
        message = "Too old"   // "Too old"
    default:
        message = "Not found"
}
```

Every time the **switch** statement tries to match a **case** in this example, it creates a tuple and assigns the values of **ages** to it. The **where** clause compares the values and when the condition is true, it executes the statements within the **case**.

Like the **if else** statements, the **switch** statement can be used to assign a value to a variable depending on a condition. In the following example, we check the value of **age** and assign the appropriate message to the variable.

Listing 2-60: Implementing the `switch` statement as an expression

```
var age = 19
var message = switch age {
    case 13:
        "Happy Bar Mitzvah!"
    case 16:
        "Sweet Sixteen!"
    case 21:
        "Welcome to Adulthood!"
    default:
        "Happy Birthday!"   // "Happy Birthday!"
}
```

BASIC

While and Repeat While

The conditionals studied in the previous sections execute the statements only once, but sometimes the program requires executing a block of instructions several times until a condition is satisfied. An alternative offered by Swift to create these loops is the **while** statement (and its sibling **repeat while**).

The **while** statement checks a condition and executes the statements in the block while the condition is true. The following example initializes a variable with the value **0** and then checks its value in a **while** statement. If the value of the variable is less than **5**, the statements inside the block are executed. After this, the condition is checked again. The loop keeps running until the condition is false (the value of the **counter** variable is equal or greater than **5**).

Listing 2-61: Using `while` to create a loop

```
var counter = 0
while counter < 5 {
    counter += 1
}
let finalNumber = counter   // 5
```

If the first check of the condition returns false, the statements in the block are never executed. To execute the statements at least once, we must use **`repeat while`**.

Listing 2-62: Using `repeat while` to create a loop

```
var counter = 10
repeat {
   counter += 1
} while counter < 5
let finalNumber = counter  // 11
```

In this case, the initial value of the **counter** variable is declared as **`10`**. This is greater than 5, but since we are using the **repeat while** instruction, the statements in the block are executed before the condition is checked, so the final value of **counter** will be 11. (The value of **`counter`** is incremented once and then the condition returns false, ending the loop.)

IMPORTANT

If the condition is always true, the loop will run indefinitely. Although infinite loops are sometimes useful, they can crash the app. Unless an infinite loop is absolutely necessary, always make sure it has a breaking point.

BASIC

For In

The purpose of the **for in** loop is to iterate over collections of values. During the execution of a **for in** loop, the system reads the elements of the collection one by one in sequential order and assigns their values to a constant that can be used by the statements in the block. In this case, the condition that must be satisfied for the loop to be over is reaching the end of the collection.

The syntax of a **for in** loop is **for constant in collection {}**, where **constant** is the name of the constant that we are going to use to capture the value of each element in the collection, and **collection** is the name of the collection of values that we want to iterate over. For example, we can iterate over the characters in a string, as shown below.

Listing 2-63: Using `for in` to iterate over the characters of a string

```
var mytext = "Hello"
var message = ""

for letter in mytext {
   message += message != "" ? "-" : ""
   message += "\(letter)"
}
```

The code in Listing 2-63 defines two **String** variables: **mytext** with the text "Hello" and **message** with an empty string. After the variables are defined, we use a **for in** loop to iterate over the characters of the string in **mytext** and add each character to the current value of **message**. The code works as follows: in the first cycle, the character "H" is assigned to **letter**. Because at this moment **message** contains an empty string, nothing is added by the first statement in the block. Then, the second statement adds the value of **letter** to the current value of **message** and the next cycle is executed. In this new cycle, the character "e" is assigned to **letter**. This time, the **message** string already contains the letter "H", so the character "-" is added at the end by the first statement ("H-"), and then the second statement adds the letter "e" at the end of this new string ("H-e"). This process continues until all the characters in the **mytext** variable are processed. The final value of **message** is "H-e-l-l-o".

When the constant is not required inside the block, we can replace it with an underscore. For example, the following code includes a loop that iterates over the value of **mytext** to count the number of characters in the string. The value of the **counter** variable is incremented by 1 in each cycle, giving a total of 5.

Listing 2-64: Iterating over a string without reading the characters

```
var mytext = "Hello"
var counter = 0

for _ in mytext {
   counter += 1
}
var message = "The string contains \(counter) letters"
// "The string contains 5 letters"
```

A **for in** instruction may include the **where** clause to perform the next cycle only when a condition is met. For instance, the following code checks the value of **letter** and only performs the cycle when the letter is not an "L". In consequence, only the letters "H", "e", and "o" are counted.

Listing 2-65: Adding a condition to a loop

```
var mytext = "Hello"
var counter = 0

for letter in mytext where letter != "l" {
   counter += 1
}
var message = "The string contains \(counter) letters"
// "The string contains 3 letters"
```

BASIC

Control Transfer Statements

Sometimes loops must be interrupted regardless of the state of their condition. For these situations, Swift provides the following instructions.

continue

This instruction interrupts the current cycle and moves to the next. The system ignores the rest of the statements in the block after the instruction is executed.

break

This instruction interrupts the loop. The rest of the statements in the block and any pending cycles are ignored after the instruction is executed.

The **continue** instruction is applied when we do not want to execute the rest of the statements in the block, but we want to keep the loop running. For instance, the following code counts the letters in a string but ignores the letters "l" (lowercase L).

Listing 2-66: Jumping to the next cycle of the loop

```
var mytext = "Hello"
var counter = 0

for letter in mytext {
   if letter == "l" {
      continue
   }
   counter += 1
}
var message = "The string contains \(counter) letters"
// "The string contains 3 letters"
```

The **if** statement inside the **for in** loop of Listing 2-66 compares the value of **letter** with the letter "l". If the characters match, the instruction **continue** is executed, the last statement inside the loop is ignored, and the loop moves on to the next character in **mytext**. In consequence, the code counts all the characters that are different from "l" ("H", "e", and "o").

Unlike the **continue** instruction, the **break** instruction interrupts the loop completely. The following example only counts the characters before the first letter "l".

Listing 2-67: Interrupting the loop

```
var mytext = "Hello"
var counter = 0

for letter in mytext {
```

```
    if letter == "l" {
        break
    }
    counter += 1
}
var message = "The string contains \(counter) letters"
// "The string contains 2 letters"
```

Again, the **if** statement in Listing 2-67 compares the value of **letter** with the character "l", but this time it executes the **break** instruction when a match is found. If the character currently processed by the loop is "l", the **break** instruction is executed, and the loop is over, no matter how many characters are left in the string. In consequence, only the characters located before the first letter "l" are considered ("H" and "e").

The **break** instruction is also useful to cancel the execution of a **switch** statement. The problem with the **switch** statement in Swift is that the cases must be exhaustive, which means that every possible value must be contemplated. When this is not possible or necessary, we can use the **break** instruction to ignore the values that do not apply. For example, we can declare the cases for the values we need and then break the execution in the **default** case for the rest of the values that we do not care about.

Listing 2-68: Ignoring values in a `switch` statement

```
var age = 19
var message = ""

switch age {
    case 13:
        message = "Happy Bar Mitzvah!"
    case 16:
        message = "Sweet Sixteen!"
    case 21:
        message = "Welcome to Adulthood!"
    default:
        break
}
```

After the execution of this code, the **message** variable is empty because there is no **case** that matches the value of the **age** variable and therefore the code in **default** is executed and the **break** instruction returns the control to the statements after the **switch**.

BASIC

Guard

The **guard** instruction is used to prevent the execution of the code that follows the statement. For example, we can break the execution of a loop when a condition is satisfied, as we do with an **if else** statement.

Listing 2-69: Interrupting a loop with `guard`

```
var mytext = "Hello"
var counter = 0

for letter in mytext {
   guard letter != "l" else {
      break
   }
   counter += 1
}
var message = "The string contains \(counter) letters"
// "The string contains 2 letters"
```

The **guard** instruction works along with the **else** instruction and therefore it is very similar to the **if else** statement, but the code in the block is only executed when the condition is false. In the example of Listing 2-69, the **for in** loop reads the characters of the string in **mytext** one by one, as before. If the characters are different from the letter "l", we increment the value of **counter** by 1, but when the value of **letter** is equal to "l", the condition of the **guard** instruction is false and therefore the **break** instruction is executed, interrupting the loop.

IMPORTANT

The advantage of **guard** over the **if else** statement is that the variable or constant defined in the condition outlives the statement, and therefore we can read its value outside the `else` block. Although you can implement the **guard** instruction to break or continue a loop, as we did in the last example, the instruction was introduced to work along with the **return** instruction to interrupt the execution of a function. We will study the **return** instruction and functions in the next chapter.

Chapter 3
Functions

BASIC

3.1 - Swift Functions

Programs would not be very useful if we could only write them as a continuous sequence of instructions. Originally, this was the only way to write a program, but programming languages soon introduced tools that allowed programmers to group instructions and execute them when needed. One of the most fundamental of these tools is the function. Functions are blocks of code delimited by curly braces and identified by a name. Unlike the blocks used in loops and conditional statements, functions do not require a condition to be satisfied; the statements inside a function are executed every time the function is called. Functions are called by writing their name followed by parentheses. This call can be made from anywhere in the code and as many times as necessary, breaking the sequential flow of a program. When a function is called, execution continues with the statements inside the function and returns to the point of the call only after the function has finished executing.

BASIC

Declaration of Functions

Functions are declared with the **func** keyword followed by a name, parentheses, and the code enclosed in curly braces.

Listing 3-1: Declaring and calling functions

```
import Playgrounds

#Playground {
    func myfunction() {
        let mynumber = 5 * 2  // 10
    }
    myfunction()
}
```

The code in Listing 3-1 declares a function called **myfunction()**. The statements in a function are only processed when the function is called, so after the **myfunction()** function is declared, we call it with the **myfunction()** instruction. In this example, the function multiplies two values and assign the result to a constant, but of course a function can perform more complex tasks, as we will see later.

Do It Yourself

Open your Xcode project. Select the **MyPlayground.swift** file or create a new one. Copy the code in Listing 3-1 into this file. You should see the result of the function's execution on the Canvas (**mynumber 10**). Use this file to test the rest of the examples in this chapter, and remember to ask your AI agent for help whenever you have trouble understanding a topic. For example, ask "How does this code work?" or "What is this code doing?". This will help you get familiar with AI agents and understand how to get the best out of them."

As we already mentioned, once the function is declared, we can call it any time necessary. For example, the following code runs a **while** loop that calls **myfunction()** a total of 5 times (the loop runs while **counter** is less than **5**).

Listing 3-2: Calling functions from a loop

```
func myfunction() {
   let mynumber = 5 * 2  // 10
}
var counter = 0
while counter < 5 {
   myfunction()
   counter += 1
}
```

In this example, the function always performs the same operation, but functions can receive and process different values each time they are called. The types of values a function can receive, and the names they are assigned, are specified inside the function's parentheses. These values are called *parameters*, and they are declared using the same syntax as constants and variables, with the name and data type separated by a colon, as shown below.

Listing 3-3: Sending values to a function

```
func doubleValue(number: Int) {
   let total = number * 2
   let message = "Result: \(total)"  // "Result: 10"
}
doubleValue(number: 5)
```

The values we want to send to a function are specified in the function call. When the function receives these values, it assigns them to constants so they are available to the code inside the function. In Listing 3-3, we define a function with one parameter of type **Int** called **number**, and then call the function with the value **5**. The function receives this value, assigns it to the **number** constant, multiplies it by **2**, and finally includes the result in a string using string interpolation.

We can declare as many parameters as we need separated by comma. The following example multiplies two values and creates a string with the result.

Listing 3-4: Sending multiple values to a function

```
func multiply(number1: Int, number2: Int) {
   let result = number1 * number2
   let message = "The result is \(result)"   // "The result is 80"
}
multiply(number1: 20, number2: 4)
```

Not only can functions be called at any time, but the values we pass to the function when we call it can be different. This makes functions reusable.

Listing 3-5: Sending different values to a function

```
func doubleValue(number: Int) {
   let total = number * 2
   let message = "Result: \(total)"
}
doubleValue(number: 5)  // "Result: 10"
doubleValue(number: 25)  // "Result: 50"
```

By default, the Canvas shows only the latest value produced by each statement. In this case, because we are calling the same function twice, the Canvas shows only the result of the last call. To display all the values produced by the code, we must click the button on the right side of the statement and select Value History (Figure 3-1, number 1). After this, the Canvas shows all the values produced by the calls, as shown below.

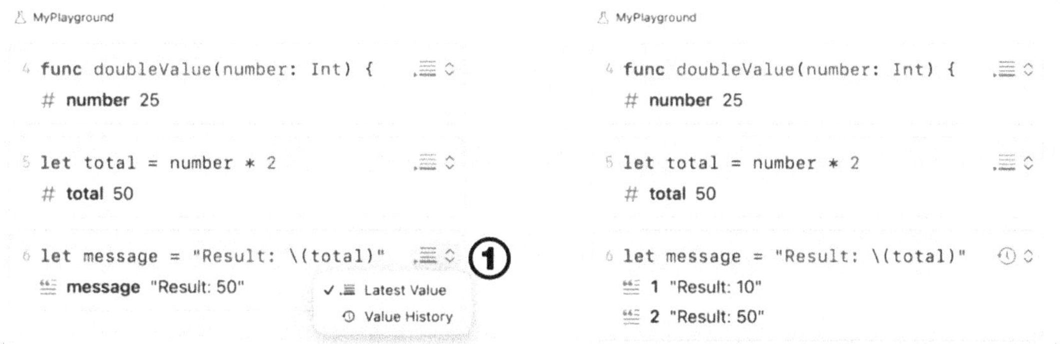

Figure 3-1: *Displaying value history on the Canvas*

The constants and variables declared inside a function, like the **total** and **message** variables used in the previous example, are not accessible from other parts of the code. This means that a function can receive values, but the result produced by processing those values is trapped inside the function. To communicate the result of an operation to the rest of the code, functions can return a value using an instruction called **return**. The **return** instruction finishes the processing of the function, so we must declare it after all the required statements have been processed, as in the following example.

Listing 3-6: Returning a value from a function

```
func doubleValue(number: Int) -> Int {
   let total = number * 2
   return total
}
let result = doubleValue(number: 25)
let message = "The result is \(result)"  // "The result is 50"
```

When we create a function that returns a value, the data type of the value returned is specified in the declaration after the parentheses with the syntax **-> type**, where **type** is just the data type of the value that is going to be returned by the function. A function can only return values of the type specified in its definition. For instance, the function in Listing 3-6 can only return integer values because we declared the returned type as **-> Int**.

When a function returns a value, the system calls the function first and then the value returned is processed inside the statement that made the call. For example, in the code in Listing 3-6, we create the **result** variable and assign to it a call to the **doubleValue()** function. When the system processes this statement, the function is executed first and then the value returned (**50**) is assigned to the **result** variable.

The values received and returned by a function may be of any available data type. The following example takes a string and returns a tuple with a string and an integer.

Listing 3-7: Returning a tuple

```
func sumCharacters(word: String) -> (String, Int) {
   var characters = ""
   var counter = 0
   for letter in word {
      characters += "\(letter) "
      counter += 1
   }
   return (characters, counter)
}
var (list, total) = sumCharacters(word: "Hello")
var message = "There are \(total) characters (\(list))"
// "There are 5 characters (H e l l o )"
```

The **sumCharacters()** function in Listing 3-7 receives a string (**word: String**) and returns a tuple composed of a string and an integer (**-> (String, Int)**). The function adds the characters to the **characters** variable and counts them with the **counter** variable, as we did before (see Chapter 2, Listing 2-64). At the end, the tuple is returned, its values are assigned to the **list** and **total** variables, and then included in a string. The result is "There are 5 characters (H e l l o)".

In addition to returning the result of an operation, the **return** instruction can also be used to interrupt the execution of a function. The **guard** instruction introduced in Chapter 2 is perfectly suited for such cases, as shown in the following example.

Listing 3-8: Interrupting the execution of a function with guard

```
func doubleValue(number: Int) -> Int {
   guard number < 10 else {
      return number
   }
   return number * 2
}
let result = doubleValue(number: 25)
let message = "The result is \(result)"  // "The result is 25"
```

The **doubleValue()** function in Listing 3-8 is similar to previous examples. It receives a number, multiplies it by **2**, and returns the result, but this time we first check that the value received by the function is less than **10**. If the value is equal or higher than **10**, the **guard** instruction calls the **return** instruction with the value received by the function, otherwise, the statements of the function are executed as normal. In this case, the value sent to the function is **25**, therefore the condition is false, and that value is returned.

Note that in the example in Listing 3-8, we simplified our code by performing the multiplication in the **return** instruction. The **return** instruction can take single values or expressions like this. The instruction solves the expression and returns the result. For this reason, we sometimes find functions with only one statement whose sole purpose is to return a value. In this case, we can omit the **return** keyword. For example, the following code sends the number **25** to the function, the function multiplies the value by **2** and returns it, as in the previous examples, but this time we did not need to declare the **return** keyword because there is only one statement inside the function and therefore the Swift compiler knows what to return.

Listing 3-9: Removing the return keyword

```
func doubleValue(number: Int) -> Int {
   number * 2
}
let result = doubleValue(number: 25)
let message = "The result is \(result)"  // "The result is 50"
```

A related keyword is **inout**. This keyword is used to preserve a value after the function finishes processing. When a parameter is marked with **inout**, any changes performed on the value are stored in the original variable. This is useful when we call a function from another function, and we want the modifications introduced by the second function to persist.

Listing 3-10: Modifying external variables from a function

```
func first() {
   var number = 25
   second(value: &number)
   print("The result is \(number)")  // "The result is 50"
}
```

```
func second(value: inout Int) {
   value = value * 2
}
first()
```

The code in this example defines two functions: **first()** and **second()**. The **second()** function receives an **inout** parameter called **value**, which means that any modification on its value is stored in the original variable. The **first()** function defines a variable called **number** and then executes the **second()** function with it, so when the **second()** function multiplies this value times **2**, the result (**50**) is stored in **number**. At the end, we execute the **first()** function to start the process. Note that in the call to the **second()** function we include an ampersand before the variable's name (**&**). This is required to tell the system that the variable is going to be modified by the function.

An important aspect of the definition of a function are the names of the parameters. For example, the function **doubleValue()** of previous examples includes a parameter called **number**. Every time we call this function, we must include the parameter's name (e.g., **doubleValue(number: 50)**). These names are called *argument labels*. Swift automatically generates argument labels for every parameter using their names. Sometimes the names assigned to the parameters of a function may not be descriptive enough. For cases like these, Swift allows us to define our own argument labels; we just need to declare them before the name of the parameter separated by a space.

Listing 3-11: Declaring argument labels

```
func doubleValue(years number: Int) -> Int {
   number * 2
}
let result = doubleValue(years: 8)
let message = "The result is \(result)"  // "The results is 16"
```

The **doubleValue()** function in Listing 3-11 declares an argument label called **years** for the **number** parameter. From now on, the name of the parameter (**number**) is the one used by the statements of the function to access the value received from the call, while the argument label (**years**) is the one used when calling the function.

If what we want instead is to remove an argument label, we can define it with an underscore, as shown below.

Listing 3-12: Removing argument labels

```
func multiply(number1: Int, _ number2: Int) -> Int {
   number1 * number2
}
let result = multiply(number1: 25, 3)
let message = "The result is \(result)"  // "The result is 75"
```

In this example, we preserved the behavior by default for the first parameter and removed the argument label for the second parameter. Now the call only has to include the argument label of the first parameter (**multiply(number1: 25, 3)**).

The functions we have defined so far require that all values be specified in the call. We cannot omit any of the values expected by the function, but Swift allows us to declare a default value for a parameter to get around this requirement.

Listing 3-13: Declaring default values for parameters

```
func sayhello(name: String = "Undefined") -> String {
   return "Your name is " + name
}
let message = sayhello()  // "Your name is Undefined"
```

The code in Listing 3-13 declares the function **sayhello()** with one parameter of type **String** called **name** and with the string "Undefined" as the default value. When the function is called without a value, the string "Undefined" is assigned to **name**.

BASIC

Standard Functions

The advantage of functions is that we can call them from other parts of the code and they always perform the same operations. We don't even need to know how the function works, we just send the function the values we want to process and read the result. Because of this feature, functions can be shared, and programmers can implement pre-programmed functions provided by libraries and frameworks.

All the features of the Swift language we have implemented so far are included in a library called *Standard Library*. The Swift Standard Library includes everything, from operators to data types, as well as predefined functions. The following are some of the most frequently used.

print(String)

This function prints a string on the Xcode's console.

abs(Value)

This function returns the absolute value of an integer.

max(Values)

This function compares two or more values and returns the largest. The values we want to compare are declared separated by commas.

min(Values)

This function compares two or more values and returns the smallest. The values we want to compare are declared separated by commas.

There are also functions available to stop the execution of the application in case of an unrecoverable error.

fatalError(String)

This function stops the execution of the application and prints a message on the console. The argument is a string with the message to be printed.

precondition(Condition, String)

This function stops the execution of the application and prints a message on the console if a condition is false. The first argument is the condition to be checked and the second argument is the message we want to print.

Of all the functions in the Swift Standard Library, **print()** is probably the most useful. Its purpose is to print messages on the Xcode's console that may help us fix bugs in our code. In the following example, we use it to print the result of two operations.

Listing 3-14: Printing values on the console with `print()`

```
let absolutenumber = abs(-25)
let minnumber = min(absolutenumber, 100)
print("The number is: \(minnumber)")  // "The number is: 25"
```

The code in Listing 3-14 implements the **abs()** function to calculate the absolute value of **-25**, then gets the smallest value between **absolutenumber** and the number **100** with the **min()** function, and finally prints a message on the console with the result.

Do It Yourself

Update the code of the **#Playground** macro in your **MyPlayground.swift** file with the code in Listing 3-14. Click the button at the bottom of the interface to open the console (Chapter 1, Figure 1-4, number 9). You should see the message "The number is: 25" printed on the console.

IMPORTANT

Xcode offers two types of consoles: one to display messages from the app when running on a simulator or a device, and another to display messages produced by the Canvas. When testing our code on the Canvas, we must select the Canvas console to see the messages displayed by the **print()** function. The buttons to select the console are labeled Executable and Canvas, and are located at the bottom left corner of the console panel.

As we will see later, sequences and collections of values are very important in computer programming. The strings studied in Chapter 2 are a clear example. A string is a sequence of values of type **Character**. The Swift Standard Library includes a few functions to quickly create sequences of values our application may need to process information. The following are some of the most frequently used.

stride(from: Value, **through:** Value, **by:** Value)

This function returns a collection of values from the value specified by the **from** argument to the value specified by the **through** argument in intervals specified by the **by** argument, including the last value.

stride(from: Value, **to:** Value, **by:** Value)

This function returns a collection of values from the value specified by the **from** argument to the value specified by the **to** argument in intervals specified by the **by** argument, not including the last value.

repeatElement(Value, **count:** Int)

This function returns a collection with the number of elements specified by the **count** argument and with the value specified by the first argument.

zip(Collection, Collection)

This function returns a collection of tuples containing the values of the collections provided by the arguments in sequential order.

The following example applies some of these functions to create a list of tuples that contain a string and an integer.

Listing 3-15: Creating collections of values

```
let sequencetext = repeatElement("Hello", count: 5)
let sequencenumbers = stride(from: 0, to: 10, by: 2)
let finalsequence = zip(sequencetext, sequencenumbers)

for (text, number) in finalsequence {
   print("\(text) - \(number)")
}
```

The code in Listing 3-15 calls the **repeatElement()** function to create a collection of 5 elements, all of them with the string "Hello" ("Hello", "Hello", "Hello", "Hello", "Hello"). Next, the **stride()** function creates another collection with integers from 0 to 10, increased by 2, and without including the last one (0, 2, 4, 6, 8). Next, the **zip()** function merges these two collections in one collection of tuples (the first tuple contains the first value of the **sequencetext** collection along with the first value of the **sequencenumbers** collection, and so on). Finally, we use a **for in** loop to iterate over the values of the **finalsequence** collection and print them on the console. The result is "Hello - 0", "Hello - 2", "Hello - 4", "Hello - 6", "Hello - 8".

BASIC

Scope

The conditionals and loops studied in Chapter 2 and the functions studied in this chapter have a thing in common; they all use blocks of code (statements between curly braces) to enclose their functionality. Blocks are independent processing units; they contain their own statements and variables. To preserve their independence and avoid conflicts between these units and the rest of the code, their variables and constants are isolated. Variables and constants declared inside a block are not accessible from other parts of the code; they can only be used inside the block in which they were created.

The space in the code where a variable is accessible is called *scope*. Swift defines two types of scopes: the global scope and the local scope (also referred to as global space and local space). The variables and constants outside a block have global scope, while those declared inside a block have local scope. The variables and constants with global scope are accessible from any part of the code, while those with local scope are only accessible from the statements inside the block in which they were created (and the statements from blocks created inside their block). We can declare variables in the global scope and then use them in a local scope, but not the other way around, as illustrated by the following example.

Listing 3-16: Using variables and constants of different scopes

```
var multiplier = 1.2
var base = 0

while multiplier < 100 {
   let base = 10.0
   multiplier = multiplier * base
   print(base)  // "10.0"
}
print("Base: \(base)")  // "Base: 0"
print("Total: \(multiplier)")  // "Total: 120.0"
```

This example declares two variables in the global space: **multiplier** and **base**. We use the **multiplier** variable in a **while** loop, but the **base** variable is replaced inside the loop with a constant of the same name. When we assign the value 10.0 to **base** inside the loop, this value is assigned to the **base** constant, not the **base** variable, but when later we print the value of **base** outside the block, the system reads this value from the variable in the global space, not the constant in the local space, because the global space doesn't have access to the **base** constant declared inside the loop.

PRO

Generic Functions

Although creating two or more functions with the same name is not allowed, we can do it if their parameters are not the same. This is called *Overloading* and allows us to define multiple functions with the same name to process different types of values.

Listing 3-17: Declaring different functions with the same name

```
func getDescription(value: Int) -> String {
   let message = "The value is \(value)"
   return message
}
func getDescription(value: String) -> String {
   let message = "The value is \(value)"
   return message
}
let result1 = getDescription(value: 3)
// "The value is 3"
let result2 = getDescription(value: "John")
// "The value is John"
```

The functions in Listing 3-17 have the same name, but one receives an integer and the other a string. We can say that the function that receives the string overloads the function that receives the integer. When we call the **getDescription()** function, the system selects which function is going to be executed depending on the value of the argument.

The advantage of creating functions with the same name is that we only have to remember one name. We call them with the values we want and Swift makes sure that the correct function is executed. However, if the functions perform the same task and differ only in the type of value received, we end up with two or more pieces of code to maintain, which can lead to errors. In such cases, we can declare only one function with a generic data type.

Generic data types act as placeholders for concrete data types. When a function is called, the generic data type is replaced with the data type of the value sent to the function. If we send an integer, the generic data type becomes an `Int`; if we send a string, it becomes a `String`. To define a generic function, we declare the generic data type using a custom name enclosed in angle brackets after the function's name, as shown in the following example.

Listing 3-18: Defining generic functions

```
func getDescription<T>(value: T) -> String {
   let message = "The value is \(value)"
   return message
}
let result1 = getDescription(value: 3.5)  // "The value is 3.5"
let result2 = getDescription(value: "George")  // "The value is George"
```

This function is a generic function. The generic data type was called **T** (this is a standard name for a generic data type, but we can use any name we want). The function performs the same task, and it has the same name than the two functions from the previous example, but now we have reduced the amount of code in our program. When the function is called, the **T** generic data type is converted into the data type received by the function and the value is processed. (The first time the function is called in our example, **T** is turned into a **Double** and the second time into a **String**.)

In our example, we only use one parameter and therefore the function can only work with one data type, but we can declare two or more generic data types separated by commas (e.g., **<T, U>**).

IMPORTANT

Although we can send any value of any type we want to a generic function, the operations we can perform on them are very limited due to the impossibility of the Swift compiler to know the nature of the values received by the function. For example, we can add two integers, but we cannot add two Boolean values. To solve these issues, we can constrain the generic data types with protocols. We will study how to define protocols and how to use them in Chapter 7.

BASIC

3.2 - Closures

Blocks of code, such as those used to create functions, conditionals, and loops, have their own scope and know the variables available to them. Because of this, we can create independent processing units that do not interfere with the operations of other units. This feature is so important in computer programming that Swift allows us to create these units by defining independent blocks called *closures*.

BASIC

Defining Closures

Closures are independent blocks of code with the syntax **{ (parameters) -> Type in statements }**. They are like functions (functions are closures with a name), but they are wrapped with braces and the **in** keyword is included to separate the data types from the statements.

Closures can be assigned to variables and executed using the name of the variable, as we do with functions. The name of the variable becomes the name of the closure, as shown below.

Listing 3-19: Assigning closures to variables

```
let multiplier = { (number: Int, times: Int) -> Int in
   let total = number * times
   return total
}
print("The result is \(multiplier(10, 5))") // "The result is 50"
```

This example defines a closure and assigns it to the **multiplier** constant. After this, the name of the constant can be used to execute the closure. Note that the parameters of the closure and the return type are declared with the same syntax as functions (**(number: Int, times: Int) -> Int**), but the names of the parameters are not turned into argument labels and therefore they are ignored in the call.

An advantage of being able to assign closures to variables is the possibility to initialize the variables with the result of complex operations. A closure is assigned to the variable and executed right away adding parentheses at the end of the declaration. When the system reads the statement, it executes the closure and then assigns the value returned by the closure to the constant or variable, as shown below.

Listing 3-20: Initializing a variable with the value returned by a closure

```
let myaddition = { () -> Int in
   var total = 0
   let list = stride(from: 1, through: 9, by: 1)

   for number in list {
      total += number
   }
   return total
}()
print("The total is \(myaddition)")   // "The total is 45"
```

The closure declared in Listing 3-20 doesn't receive any value and returns an integer (**() -> Int**). The code in the closure adds the values of a collection (1 to 9) and returns the result, but because we included the parentheses at the end of the definition, the value assigned to the **myaddition** constant is the one returned by the closure (**45**), not the closure itself.

If the closure does not receive any parameter, we can simplify the syntax by declaring the constant's data type to be the same than the data type of the value returned by the closure. Note that in this case, the **in** keyword can also be removed.

Listing 3-21: Simplifying a closure

```
let myaddition: Int = {
   var total = 0
   let list = stride(from: 1, through: 9, by: 1)

   for number in list {
      total += number
   }
   return total
}()
print("The total is \(myaddition)")   // "The total is 45"
```

Closures cannot only be assigned to constants and variables but also sent and returned from functions, as any other value. When a function receives a closure, the parameter's data type only has to include the data types the closure receives and returns, as in the following example.

Listing 3-22: Sending a closure to a function

```
let multiplier = { (number: Int, times: Int) -> Int in
   let total = number * times
   return total
}
func processclosure(myclosure: (Int, Int) -> Int) {
   let total = myclosure(10, 2)
   print("The total is: \(total)")  // "The total is: 20"
}
processclosure(myclosure: multiplier)
```

The first statement in Listing 3-22 defines a closure that multiplies two integers and returns the result, and the second statement defines a function that receives this type of closure. Note that the data type of the value received by the function was declared as **(Int, Int) -> Int**. This indicates to the Swift compiler that the **processclosure()** function can receive a closure that in turn receives two integer values and returns another integer. When the **processclosure()** function is called in the last statement, the value of the **multiplier** variable is sent to the function. The function assigns the closure to the **myclosure** constant, and the closure is executed inside the function using this name and the values **10** and **2**, producing the result **20**.

The closure in the previous example was defined in the global space and was executed inside the **processclosure()** function, but we don't need to assign the closure to a variable, we can just define it in the call, as in the following example.

Listing 3-23: Assigning the closure to the function's argument

```
func processclosure(myclosure: (Int, Int) -> Int) {
   print("The total is: \(myclosure(10, 2))")  // "The total is: 20"
}
processclosure(myclosure: { (number: Int, times: Int) -> Int in
   return number * times
})
```

The code in Listing 3-23 works the same way as the previous example, but it was simplified by assigning the closure directly to the function's argument. This can be simplified even further by using a pattern called *Trailing Closures*. When the final argument of a function is a closure, we can declare the closure at the end of the call, as in the following example.

Listing 3-24: Using Trailing Closures

```
func processclosure(myclosure: (Int, Int) -> Int) {
   print("The total is: \(myclosure(10, 2))")  // "The total is: 20"
}
processclosure() { (number: Int, times: Int) -> Int in
   number * times
}
```

When we pass the closure this way, the call does not include the **myclosure** argument anymore. The closure declared after the parentheses is considered to be the last argument of the function and therefore the argument label is not necessary.

In the last example we removed the **return** keyword. As explained before, when the content of a function (or in this case a closure) includes only one statement, the Swift compiler implies that the value produced by that statement is the one to return, and the **return** keyword is not required anymore. But when we are passing the closure to a function, Swift can also infer the data types of the values received by the closure and therefore we don't have to declare that either. Instead, we can represent these values using shorthand argument names. These are special placeholders made up of the **$** symbol and an index starting from **0**. The first value received by the closure is represented by **$0**, the second value by **$1**, and so on.

Listing 3-25: Inferring the closure's data types

```
func processclosure(myclosure: (Int, Int) -> Int) {
   print("The total is: \(myclosure(10, 2))")
   // "The total is: 20"
}
processclosure() { $0 * $1 }
```

Again, the code performs the same task as before, but now the closure is extremely simple. When it is executed from the **processclosure()** function, it receives the values **10** and **2**, assigns them to the placeholders **$0** and **$1**, multiplies their values and returns the result.

Chapter 4

Structures

BASIC

4.1 - Swift Structures

Structures are an essential part of the organizational paradigm proposed by Swift. They are custom data types that include not only data but also the code in charge of processing that data. When we define a structure, what we are doing is declaring a data type that may contain variables and constants (called *properties*) and functions (called *methods*). Later we can declare variables and constants of this type to store information with the characteristics defined by the structure. These values (called *instances*) will be unique, each one with its own properties and methods.

BASIC

Definition of Structures

To define a new structure, we must use the **struct** keyword and enclose the data and functionality in curly braces.

Listing 4-1: Defining a structure

```
import Playgrounds

#Playground {
    struct Item {
        var name: String = "Not defined"
        var price: Double = 0
    }
}
```

Do It Yourself

Update the **MyPlayground.swift** file in your project with the code in Listing 4-1. Since this code only defines a structure, you won't see any results on the Canvas. We will work with this structure and show how to access its values next. As always, ask your AI agent for help whenever you have trouble understanding how any of the following examples work.

The previous example defines a structure called **Item** with two properties: **name** and **price**. The definition delineates the elements of the data type (also known as *members*), like a blueprint. To store values of this new data type, we must declare a variable or constant of this type, as we did for any other data type. In this case, the data type is the name of the structure and the initialization value is a special initializer with the syntax **Name()** (where **Name** is the name of the structure).

Listing 4-2: Declaring a variable of type Item

```
struct Item {
   var name: String = "Not defined"
   var price: Double = 0
}
var purchase: Item = Item()
```

This code creates a variable of type **Item** that stores an instance of the **Item** structure containing the properties **name** and **price**. The instance is created by the **Item()** initializer and then assigned to the **purchase** variable.

In the example in Listing 4-2, the properties of a new instance always take the values declared in the structure's definition (**"Not Defined"** and **0**), but we can modify them as we do with any other variable. The only difference is that the properties are inside a structure, so every time we want to access them, we must mention the structure they belong to. The syntax implements dot notation, as in **variable.property**, where **variable** is the name of the variable that contains the instance of the structure and **property** is the name of the property we want to access.

Listing 4-3: Assigning new values to the properties of a structure

```
struct Item {
   var name = "Not defined"
   var price = 0.0
}
var purchase = Item()
purchase.name = "Lamps"
purchase.price = 10.50

print("Product: \(purchase.name) $ \(purchase.price)")
// "Product: Lamps $ 10.5"
```

In this example, the properties of the **Item** structure and the **purchase** variable are declared as before, but this time we let Swift infer their data types. After the instance is created, new values are assigned to its properties using dot notation. Dot notation is not only used to assign new values but also to read the current ones. At the end, we read the values of the **name** and **price** properties and print them on the console.

IMPORTANT

Note that we have stored the structure in a variable (**var**). This is to be able to assign new values to its properties later. When the values of the properties in a structure are modified, instead of modifying the properties of the current instance, the system creates a new instance and assigns the new values to the properties of that instance. For this to be possible, the structure must be stored in a variable so it can be replaced by the new structure later.

Structures may be instantiated inside other structures, as many times as necessary. The dot notation is extended in these cases to reach every element in the hierarchy.

Listing 4-4: Structures inside structures

```
struct Price {
   var USD = 0.0
   var CAD = 0.0
}
struct Item {
   var name: String = "Not defined"
   var price: Price = Price()
}
var purchase = Item()
purchase.name = "Lamps"
purchase.price.USD = 10.50
```

Listing 4-4 defines two structures: **Price** and **Item**. The `Item` structure contains the same properties as before, but now the data type of the **price** property is **Price**, which means that instead of storing a single value, this property can now store a structure that in turn contains two properties: **USD** and **CAD**. When the **Item** structure is created and assigned to the **purchase** variable, the **Price** structure for the **price** property is also created with its values by default.

By concatenating the names of the variables and properties we can read and modify any value we want. For instance, the last statement in the code of Listing 4-4 accesses the **USD** property of the **price** structure inside the **purchase** structure to assign a price to the item in American Dollars (**purchase.price.USD = 10.50**).

In this example, the **price** structure is created during instantiation, but this is not usually the case. Sometimes the values of the properties containing structures are defined after the instance is created and therefore those properties must be declared as optionals. The problem with optionals is that we always need to check whether the variable or property has a value before we use it. To simplify this task, Swift introduces a tool called *Optional Chaining*.

Optional chaining makes it easy to access properties and methods in a hierarchical chain that contains optional components. As always, these components are accessed using dot notation, but a question mark is added to the names of the properties that have optional values. When the system finds an optional, it checks whether it contains a value and continues reading the expression only in case of success. Here is the same example than before, but with the **price** property turned into an optional.

Listing 4-5: Accessing optional properties

```
struct Price {
   var USD = 0.0
   var CAD = 0.0
}
struct Item {
   var name: String = "Not defined"
   var price: Price?
}
var purchase = Item()
purchase.name = "Lamps"
purchase.price?.USD = 10.50  // nil
```

The **price** property in this code is declared as an optional (its initial value is not defined). Every time we read this property, we must unwrap its value, but if we use optional chaining, we can just concatenate the values with dot notation and add a question mark after the name of the optional property (**purchase.price?.USD**). The system reads every component in the instruction from left to right and checks their values. If any of the optionals have no value, it returns **nil**, but when all the optionals have values, the instruction is interpreted as always. (In this case, the instruction assigns the number 10.50 to the **USD** property.)

PRO

Key Paths

Besides using dot notation to read and write a property, we can use key paths. A key path is a reference to a property. The advantage of using key paths instead of dot notation is that they are stored in structures and therefore we can pass them to other parts of the code and then use them to access the values of the properties they are referencing without even knowing what those properties are. This can be useful when we need to interact with frameworks, or when we are extending code to include our own functionality.

The syntax to define a key path includes a backward slash and the name of the data type followed by the name of the property we want to reference. To access the value of a property using a key path, Swift uses a syntax that includes square brackets after the instance's name and the **keypath** keyword, as illustrated in the following example.

Listing 4-6: Creating key paths

```
struct Item {
   let name: String
   let price: Double
}
var purchase: Item = Item(name: "Lamps", price: 27.50)

let keyPrice = \Item.price
print(purchase[keyPath: keyPrice])  // "27.5"
```

This code defines a structure with two properties: **name** and **price**. Once the structure is defined, we create an instance of it, define a key path that references the **price** property, and finally use this key path to access the property and print its value to the console.

Because in our example the properties are defined as constants (**let**), the key path is created as a read-only key path, but we can easily create a read-and-write key path by defining the properties as variables (**var**). In the following example, we turn the **name** and **price** properties into variables and modify the value of **price** using our **keyPrice** key path.

Listing 4-7: Using read and write key paths

```
struct Item {
   var name: String
   var price: Double
}
var purchase: Item = Item(name: "Lamps", price: 27.50)

let keyPrice = \Item.price
purchase[keyPath: keyPrice] = 30.00
print(purchase.price)  // 30.0
```

BASIC

Methods

Structures can also contain functions. Functions inside structures are called *methods*. The syntax to execute a method inside a structure is **variable.method()**, where **variable** is the name of the variable that contains the instance of the structure and **method** is the name of the method we want to call inside that structure, as shown in the following example.

Listing 4-8: Defining methods

```
struct Item {
   var name = "Not defined"
   var price = 0.0

   func total(quantity: Double) -> Double {
      return quantity * price
   }
}
var purchase = Item()
purchase.name = "Lamp"
purchase.price = 10.50

print("Total: \(purchase.total(quantity: 2))")  // "Total: 21.0"
```

In Listing 4-8, a method is declared as part of the definition of the **Item** structure. The method receives a value representing the number of items sold and calculates the total money spent in the transaction. We could have performed this operation outside the structure by reading the value of the **price** property, but having a method within the structure presents some advantages. First, we don't have to worry about how the method calculates the value; we just call the method with the right value and let it perform the task, no matter how complex it is. And second, we do not have to write the operation over and over again, because it is always part of the instance of the structure we are working with.

A method can read the values of properties but cannot assign new values to them. If we want a method to be able to modify the values of the properties of its own instance, we must prefix the **func** keyword with the **mutating** keyword, as shown below.

Listing 4-9: Assigning new values to properties from the methods in the structure

```
struct Item {
   var name = "Not defined"
   var price = 0.0

   mutating func changename(newname: String) {
      name = newname
   }
}
var purchase = Item()
purchase.changename(newname: "Lamps")

print("Product: \(purchase.name)")  // "Product: Lamps"
```

The **changename()** method of the **Item** structure in Listing 4-9 is declared as a mutating method so it can assign a new value to the **name** property. Therefore, we do not need to modify the **name** property directly, we can call this method with the value we want to store, and the method takes care of assigning the value to the property.

BASIC

Initialization

The initialization of the values of an instance is a very common task and it would be far too cumbersome if we had to assign the values one by one every time a new one is created. For this reason, Swift provides different alternatives to initialize the values of a structure. The one used by default is called *Memberwise Initializer*.

Memberwise initializers detect the properties of the structure and declare their names as argument labels. Using these argument labels, we can provide the values for initialization between the parentheses of the initializer. The following code implements a memberwise initializer to initialize an instance of the **Item** structure introduced in previous examples.

Listing 4-10: Initializing properties

```
struct Item {
   var name = "Not defined"
   var price = 0.0
}
var purchase = Item(name: "Lamp", price: 10.50)
print("Purchase: \(purchase.name) $ \(purchase.price)")
```

Memberwise initializers reduce the amount of code and simplify initialization. Also, if we use the memberwise initializer, we don't need to assign values by default, as shown below.

Listing 4-11: Using memberwise initializers to provide the initial values of a structure

```
struct Item {
   var name: String
   var price: Double
}
var purchase = Item(name: "Lamp", price: 10.50)
print("Purchase: \(purchase.name) $ \(purchase.price)")
```

The two forms of initialization we have seen so far are not customizable enough. Some structures may have multiple properties that require initialization or even methods that must be executed right away to get the proper values for the instance to be ready. To add more alternatives, Swift provides a method called **init()**. The **init()** method is called as soon as the instance is created, so we can use it to initialize the properties any way we want.

Listing 4-12: Initializing properties from the init() method

```
struct Price {
   var USD: Double
   var CAD: Double

   init() {
      USD = 5
      CAD = USD * 1.29
   }
}
var myprice = Price()
```

When the instance is generated by the initializer, the properties are created first and then the **init()** method is executed. Inside this method, we can perform any operation we need to get the properties' initial values. In the example in Listing 4-12, we assign an initial value of **5** to the **USD** property and then multiply this value by the corresponding exchange rate to get the value of the **CAD** property (the same price in Canadian dollars).

As well as with any other method or function, the **init()** method may include parameters. These parameters are used to specify initial values from the initializer.

Listing 4-13: Declaring the parameters to initialize the structure

```
struct Price {
   var USD: Double
   var CAD: Double

   init(americans: Double) {
      USD = americans
      CAD = USD * 1.29
   }
}
var myprice = Price(americans: 5)
```

This is similar to what Swift creates for us in the background when we use memberwise initializers, but the advantage of declaring the **init()** method ourselves is that we can specify only the parameters we need (as in the example in Listing 4-13) or even declare multiple **init()** methods to present several alternatives for initialization, as shown below.

Listing 4-14: Declaring multiple `init()` methods

```
struct Price {
   var USD: Double
   var CAD: Double

   init(americans: Double) {
      USD = americans
      CAD = USD * 1.29
   }
   init(canadians: Double) {
      CAD = canadians
      USD = CAD * 0.7752
   }
}
var myprice = Price(canadians: 5)
```

As explained before, Swift identifies each function by its name and parameters, so we can declare functions with the same name as long as they have different parameters. The example in Listing 4-14 declares two **init()** methods to initialize the instance of the structure. The first method receives a **Double** value with the name **americans** and the second method also receives a **Double** value but with the name **canadians**. The right method will be executed according to the argument included in the initializer. In this case, we use the argument **canadians** with the value **5**, so the instance is initialized by the second **init()** method.

BASIC

Computed Properties

The properties we have declared up to this point are called *Stored Properties*. Their function is to store a value in memory. But there are other types of properties called *Computed Properties*. These properties do not store a value of their own, instead they have access to the rest of the properties of the structure and can perform operations to set and retrieve their values.

Two methods are available for computed properties to be able to set and retrieve a value: **get()** and **set()**. These methods are also called *getters* and *setters* and are declared in curly braces after the name of the property. Although both methods are useful, only the **get()** method is required.

Listing 4-15: Declaring computed properties

```
struct Price {
   var USD: Double
   var ratetoCAD: Double

   var canadians: Double {
      get {
         return USD * ratetoCAD
      }
   }
}
var purchase = Price(USD: 11, ratetoCAD: 1.29)
print("Price in CAD: \(purchase.canadians)")
// "Price in CAD: 14.19"
```

The structure defined in Listing 4-15 contains a stored property called **USD** to store the price in American dollars, a stored property called **ratetoCAD** to store the exchange rate for Canadian dollars, and a computed property called **canadians** that converts the US dollars into Canadian dollars and returns the result. Computed properties are like methods, they calculate the value every time the property is read. No matter if the value of the **ratetoCAD** property changes, the **canadians** property will always return the right price in Canadian dollars.

Computed properties with only a getter are called read-only properties because we can only read their values. When we declare a read-only property, we can omit the **get()** method, so we can simplify our property as follows.

Listing 4-16: Defining read-only properties

```
struct Price {
   var USD: Double
   var ratetoCAD: Double

   var canadians: Double {
      USD * ratetoCAD
   }
}
var purchase = Price(USD: 11, ratetoCAD: 1.29)
print(purchase.canadians)  // "14.190000000000001"
```

By including the **set()** method for the **canadians** property we can, for example, set a new price using the same currency.

Listing 4-17: Adding the set() method to set a new value

```
struct Price {
   var USD: Double
   var ratetoCAD: Double
   var ratetoUSD: Double
```

```
    var canadians: Double {
        get {
            USD * ratetoCAD
        }
        set {
            USD = newValue * ratetoUSD
        }
    }
}
var purchase = Price(USD: 11, ratetoCAD: 1.29, ratetoUSD: 0.7752)

purchase.canadians = 500
print("Price: \(purchase.USD)")  // "Price: 387.6"
```

The new structure defined in Listing 4-17 can retrieve and set a price in Canadian dollars. When we set a new value for the **canadians** property, the value is stored in a constant called **newValue** (the constant is created automatically for us). Using this constant, we can process the new value and perform the operations we need. In this example, the value of **newValue** is multiplied by the exchange rate to get the price in American dollars. The price is always stored in American dollars but using the **canadians** property we can set it and retrieve it in Canadian dollars.

The system automatically assigns the name **newValue** to the value received by the `set()` method, but we can specify a different name between parentheses. In the following example, the parameter is called **CAD** and it is used instead of **newValue** to calculate the value for the **USD** property.

Listing 4-18: Using a different name for the parameter of the set() method

```
struct Price {
    var USD: Double
    var ratetoCAD: Double
    var ratetoUSD: Double

    var canadians: Double {
        get {
            USD * ratetoCAD
        }
        set(CAD) {
            USD = CAD * ratetoUSD
        }
    }
}
var purchase = Price(USD: 11, ratetoCAD: 1.29, ratetoUSD: 0.7752)
```

BASIC

Property Observers

The properties of an instance of a structure may be modified at any moment by different processes, such as in response to user interaction or events triggered by the system. To report that the value of a property has been modified, Swift implements Property Observers. Property Observers are special methods, similar to **get()** and **set()**, that we can include within a property to execute code before and after a value is assigned to it. The methods are called **willSet()** and **didSet()**, and are declared in braces after the property's name.

Listing 4-19: Adding observers to a store property

```
struct Price {
   var increment: Double = 0
   var oldprice: Double = 0
   var price: Double {
      willSet {
         increment = newValue - price
      }
      didSet {
         oldprice = oldValue
      }
   }
}
var product = Price(price: 15.95)
product.price = 20.75
print("New price: \(product.price)")  // "New price: 20.75"
print("Old price: \(product.oldprice)")  // "Old price: 15.95"
```

The **Price** structure in Listing 4-19 includes three properties: **increment**, **oldprice**, and **price**. We use the **price** property to store the value of the item, the **oldprice** property to store the previous price, and the **increment** property to store the difference between the old price and the new one. To set this last value, we declare property observers for the **price** property. Every time a new value is assigned to the property, the **willSet()** and **didSet()** methods are executed.

Swift automatically creates a parameter called **newValue** for the **willSet()** method to provide access to the value that is going to be assigned to the property, and a parameter called **oldValue** for the **didSet()** method to provide access to the property's old value after the new value is assigned. (We can change the names of these parameters as we did for the **set()** method in Listing 4-18.) In our example, when the **willSet()** method is executed, the current value of **price** is subtracted from **newValue** to get the difference, and the result is assigned to the **increment** property. And in the **didSet()** method, we assign the old price provided by **oldValue** to the **oldprice** property to keep a reference to the previous price.

BASIC

Type Properties and Methods

The properties and methods declared in previous examples are accessible on the instances created from the definition of the structure. This means that we must create an instance of the structure to be able to read and modify their values. But there are times when being able to execute properties and methods from the definition itself makes sense. We might need, for example, to get information related to all instances, or call methods to create instances with standard values. In Swift, this is possible by declaring type properties and methods. These are properties and methods accessible from the data type, not the instance created from that type.

Type properties and methods for structures are declared adding the **static** keyword to the definition. Once a property or method is declared with this keyword, they are only accessible from the definition itself. In the following example, we include a type property called **currencies** to inform how many currencies the structures can handle.

Listing 4-20: Defining type properties

```
struct Price {
   var USD: Double
   var CAD: Double

   static let currencies = 2
}
print(Price.currencies)  // 2
```

As illustrated by the code in Listing 4-20, there is no need to create an instance to access a type property or method. After the definition, the **currencies** property is read using the name of the structure and dot notation (**Price.currencies**). If we create an instance from this definition, the only properties accessible from that instance will be **USD** and **CAD**. The **currencies** property is a type property, only accessible from the type itself. The same happens with methods, as shown below.

Listing 4-21: Defining type methods

```
struct Price {
   var USD: Double
   var CAD: Double

   static func reserved() -> Price {
      return Price(USD: 10.0, CAD: 11.0)
   }
}
var reservedprice = Price.reserved()
print("Price in USD: \(reservedprice.USD) CAD: \(reservedprice.CAD)")
// "Price in USD: 10.0 CAD: 11.0"
```

The structure in this example includes a type method called **reserved()**. The method creates and returns an instance of the **Price** structure with standard values. This is a common procedure and another way to create our own initializer. If we use the initializer by default, the values must be provided every time the instance is created, but with a type method all we need to do is to call the method on the type to get in return an instance configured with specific values. In our example, the values correspond to a reserved price. We call the **reserved()** method on the **Price** type, the method creates an instance of the **Price** structure with the values `10.0` and `11.0`, and then this instance is assigned to the **reservedprice** variable. At the end, the values of both properties are printed on the console to confirm that their values were defined by the **reserved()** method. Note that again, the method is not accessible from the instance, only from the data type.

PRO

Generic Structures

In Chapter 3, we explained how to create generic functions. These are functions that can process values of different data types; the function defines a placeholder for the data type and then adopts the data type of the value it receives. But generics data types are not exclusive to functions, we can also turn data types themselves, such as structures, into generic types. The advantage is that we can create independent processing units that can handle different types of values. To create a generic structure, we must declare the generic data type after the name of the structure and between angle brackets, as we did for functions.

Listing 4-22: Defining generic structures

```
struct MyStructure<T> {
   var myvalue:T

   func description() {
      print("The value is: \(myvalue)")  // "The value is: 5"
   }
}
let instance = MyStructure<Int>(myvalue: 5)
instance.description()
```

This example defines a generic structure called **MyStructure** with one generic type called **T**. The structure contains a generic property called **myvalue** and a method that prints a message with the value of the property. After the definition of the structure, we create an instance with an integer. The system replaces the **T** with the **Int** type, creates the instance, and assigns the value **5** to the **myvalue** property. In the last statement, we call the **description()** method to print it.

When we create an instance of a generic structure, the data type we want the structure to work with is included after the name and between angle brackets, but this is only required when the initialization doesn't include any value. For example, the following code creates an instance of the same structure introduced before but with a string and let Swift infer the generic data type from the value.

Listing 4-23: Using generic structures

```
struct MyStructure<T> {
   var myvalue:T

   func description() {
      print("The value is: \(myvalue)")  // "The value is: Hello"
   }
}
let instance = MyStructure(myvalue: "Hello")
instance.description()
```

IMPORTANT

These are basic examples of how to create and work with generic data types. As with functions, generics only become useful when we constrain the data using protocols. We will learn more about generics and protocols in Chapter 7.

BASIC

Type Structures

Including properties and methods inside a structure and then assigning an instance of that structure to a variable is a simple way to wrap data and functionality in a single portable unit of code. Structures are usually used this way, as practical wrappers of code, and Swift takes advantage of this feature extensively. In fact, all the data types defined in Swift are structures. The syntax **variable: Int = value**, for example, is a shortcut provided by Swift for the initializer **variable = Int(value)**. Every time we assign a new value to a variable, we are assigning a structure that contains that value. The following are the initializers of some of the data types studied in Chapter 2.

`Int(Value)`

This is the initializer of the **Int** data type. The argument is the value we want to assign to the instance. If no value is provided, the value 0 is assigned by default. Initializers for similar types are also available (**Int8()**, **Int16()**, **Int32()**, and **Int64()**).

`UInt(Value)`

This is the initializer of the **UInt** data type. The argument is the value we want to assign to the instance. If no value is provided, the value assigned is 0. Initializers for similar types are also available (**UInt8()**, **UInt16()**, **UInt32()**, and **UInt64()**).

`Float(Value)`

This is the initializer of the **Float** data type. The argument is the value we want to assign to the instance. If no value is provided, the value 0.0 is assigned by default.

`Double(Value)`

This is the initializer of the **Double** data type. The argument is the value we want to assign to the instance. If no value is provided, the value assigned is 0.0.

The structures for these data types are defined in the Swift Standard Library. All we need to do to create an instance is to implement the initializer with the value we want to store, as shown below.

Listing 4-24: Initializing variables with standard initializers

```
var mynumber = Int(25)
var myprice = Double(4.99)
```

This is the same as assigning the values directly to a variable (e.g., **`var myPrice = 4.99`**, but these structures include several initializers that can convert values from different types into the type expected by the structure. This process is called *casting*, and we can use it to turn a value of one data type into another. For example, when we divide numbers, the system converts them to the most comprehensive type and then performs the operation, but variables already have a specific type. As a result, they must be explicitly converted before the operation is performed, as shown in the following example.

Listing 4-25: Casting a variable

```
var number1: Int = 10
var number2: Double = 2.5
var total = Double(number1) / number2  // 4.0
```

The variables **number1** and **number2** defined in Listing 4-25 are of type **Int** and **Double**. To perform a division between them we must cast one of them to the data type of the other (arithmetic operations cannot be performed on values of different data types). Using the **Double()** initializer, we create a new value of type **Double** from the value of **number1** and perform the operation. This process can be described as "casting the **number1** variable to a **Double**".

These initializers are also useful when working with **String** values. Sometimes the characters of a string represent numbers that we need to process. The problem is that strings cannot be processed as numbers. We cannot include a string in an arithmetic operation without first converting the string into a value of a numeric data type. Fortunately, the initializers for numeric types such as **Int** and **Double** can convert a value of type **String** into a number. If the operation cannot be performed, the initializer returns **nil**, so we can treat it as an optional value. In the following example, we convert the string **`"45"`** into the integer **`45`** and add the value **`15`** to it.

Listing 4-26: Extracting numbers from strings

```
var units = "45"

if let number = Int(units) {
   let total = number + 15
   print("The total is \(total)")  // "The total is 60"
}
```

The structures defined for data types also have their own properties and methods. This includes type properties and methods. For instance, the following are the most frequently used properties and methods provided by the structures that process integer values.

min

This type property returns the minimum value the data type can handle.

max

This type property returns the maximum value the data type can handle.

random(in: Range)

This type method returns a random number. The value is calculated from a range of integers provided by the **in** argument.

negate()

This method inverts the sign of the value.

isMultiple(of: Int)

This method returns **true** if the value is a multiple of the value provided by the **of** argument.

The **min** and **max** properties are particularly useful because they allow us to determine whether an operation might overflow a variable (produce a result greater or less than the minimum and maximum allowed).

Listing 4-27: Checking the maximum possible value for the `Int8` type

```
var mynumber: Int8 = 120
if (Int8.max - mynumber) >= 10 {  // (127 - 120) >= 10
   print("Operation can be performed")
} else {
   print("Operation overflows the variable")
}
```

This example takes advantage of the **max** property to make sure that incrementing a variable's value will not cause it to overflow (the result will not be greater than the maximum value the type can hold). We calculate how far the current value of a variable called **mynumber** is from the maximum value allowed by the **Int8** type (**Int8.max – mynumber**), and compare this result with the amount we want to add. If the number of units we have left is greater than or equal to the increment, we know the operation can be performed without going over the limit. (In this example, we do not perform the operation, because 120 + 10 produces a result greater than the limit of 127 allowed by **Int8**.)

The type **Double** also includes its own selection of properties and methods. The following are the most frequently used.

pi

This type property returns the value of the constant pi.

infinity

This type property returns an infinite value.

random(in: Range)

This type method returns a random number. The value is calculated from a range of values of type **Double** provided by the **in** argument.

negate()

This method inverts the sign of the value.

squareRoot()

This method returns the square root of the value.

remainder(dividingBy: Double)

This method returns the remainder produced by dividing the value by the value specified by the **dividingBy** argument.

rounded(FloatingPointRoundingRule)

This method returns the value rounded according to the rule specified by the argument. The argument is an enumeration with the values **awayFromZero**, **down**, **toNearestOrAwayFromZero**, **toNearestOrEven**, **towardZero** and **up**.

In this case, the most useful method is probably **rounded()**. With this method, we can round a floating-point value to the nearest integer.

Listing 4-28: Rounding floating-point values

```
var mynumber: Double = 2.890
mynumber = mynumber.rounded(.toNearestOrAwayFromZero)
print("The round number is \(mynumber)")
// "The round number is 3.0"
```

Of course, Boolean values are also structures. Among others, the **Bool** data type offers the following methods.

toggle()

This method toggles the value. If the value is **true**, it becomes **false** and vice versa.

random()

This type method returns a random **Bool** value.

The following example checks the current value of a variable and assigns the value **false** if it is **true**, or vice versa.

Listing 4-29: Modifying the value of a Bool variable

```
var valid: Bool = true
if valid {
   print("It is Valid")
   valid.toggle()
}
print(valid)  // false
```

BASIC

Range Structures

Ranges are collections of values in sequential order. Swift allows us to create open and closed ranges of values. For example, we can create a range from 1 to 5. If the range is open, it will include the values 1, 2, 3, and 4, but if the range is closed, it will include the values 1, 2, 3, 4, and 5. Swift includes two operators to create these ranges.

... (three dots) creates a range from the value on the left to the value on the right, including both values in the range (e.g., 1...5 creates a range that includes the values 1, 2, 3, 4 and 5). The value on the right can be omitted to create a one-sided range. A one-sided range goes from the value on the left to the maximum value allowed for the data type.

..< (two dots and the less than character) creates a range from the value on the left to the value before the value on the right (e.g., 1..<5 creates a range that includes the values 1, 2, 3 and 4).

When we declare a range using these operators, Swift creates a structure to store it. A structure of type **Range** is created for an open range and a structure of type **ClosedRange** is created for a closed range. These structures provide common properties and methods to work with the range. The following are the most frequently used.

`lowerBound`

This property returns the range's lower value (the value on the left).

`upperBound`

This property returns the range's upper value (the value on the right).

`contains``(Element)`

This method returns a Boolean value that determines if the value specified by the argument is within the range.

`clamped(to:`` Range)`

This method compares the original range with the range specified by the **to** argument and returns a new range with the part of the ranges that overlap.

reversed()

This method returns a collection with the values in reversed order.

Ranges are useful in a variety of situations. For instance, if we need a loop with a fixed number of cycles, we can implement a **for in** loop with a range. The following example iterates over a closed range of integers from 0 to 10, generating a total of 11 cycles.

Listing 4-30: Using for in to iterate over a range

```
var total = 0
for value in 0...10 {
   total += value
}
print("The total is \(total)")  // "The total is 55"
```

We can also invert the range with the **reversed()** method.

Listing 4-31: Inverting a range

```
var message = ""
var range = 0..<10

for item in range.reversed() {
   message += "\(item) "
}
print(message)  // "9 8 7 6 5 4 3 2 1 0 "
```

This example creates a range from 0 to 9 with the **..<** operator and then calls the **reversed()** method to invert it. This method creates a collection with the values in reversed order, so we can read it with a **for in** loop. The statement inside the loop adds the values to the **message** string, and this string is printed on the console to confirm that the values were effectively reversed.

Ranges can also simplify **switch** statements that have to consider multiple values per case, as shown below.

Listing 4-32: Using range operators in a `switch` statement

```
var age = 6
var message = "You have to go to "

switch age {
   case 2...4:
      message += "Day Care"
   case 5...11:
      message += "Elementary School"
   case 12...17:
      message += "High School"
```

```
    case 18..<22:
        message += "College"
    case 22...:
        message += "Work"
    default:
        message += "Breastfeeding"
}
print(message)  // "You have to go to Elementary School"
```

In this example, we compare the age with different ranges of values. If the value of **age** is within a range, the instructions for that **case** are executed. As illustrated by this example, we can also declare only one side of a range and let the system determine the other. The last **case** creates a one-sided closed range from the value 22 to the maximum value allowed for the data type.

Ranges are used by the **random()** method to get a random value. The following example generates a loop that calculates multiple random values from 1 to 10. The condition stops the loop when the number returned by the method is equal to 5. In the loop, we also increment the value of the **attempts** variable to calculate the number of cycles required for the **random()** method to return our number.

Listing 4-33: Calculating random numbers

```
var mynumber: Int = 0
var attempts = 0

while mynumber != 5 {
    mynumber = Int.random(in: 1...10)
    attempts += 1
}
print("It took \(attempts) attempts to get the number 5")
```

BASIC

String Structures

As we have seen in Chapter 2, we can initialize a **String** structure by simply assigning a text enclosed in double quotes to a constant or a variable. This is another shortcut. In the background, instances are created from the **String** initializer.

> **String**(Value)
>
> This initializer creates a string from the value provided by the argument. The **String** structure defines multiple versions of this initializer to create strings from different types of values, including other strings, characters, and numbers.

Once the string is created, we can manipulate it with the properties and methods provided by the **String** structure. The following are the most frequently used.

isEmpty

This property returns a Boolean that indicates whether the value is an empty string. This is the same as comparing the string with an empty string (**string ==** "").

count

This property returns the total number of characters in the string.

first

This property returns the first character in the string.

last

This property returns the last character in the string.

lowercased()

This method returns a copy of the string in lowercase letters.

uppercased()

This method returns a copy of the string in uppercase letters.

hasPrefix(String)

This method returns a Boolean value that indicates whether the string begins with the text specified by the argument or not.

hasSuffix(String)

This method returns a Boolean value that indicates whether the string ends with the text specified by the argument or not.

Most of the time, we will assign a string directly to a variable as we have done so far, but the **String()** initializer is useful when we need to convert values into strings. For instance, the following example converts the number 44 into a string and counts the number of digits.

Listing 4-34: Converting a number into a string

```
var age = String(44)
var mytext = "Total digits \(age.count)"  // "Total digits 2"
```

Swift strings are composed of Unicode characters, which occupy different amounts of memory. Because of this, it is not possible to establish the position of a character using integer values. The index of the first character is always 0, but the indexes of the consecutive characters depend on the size of their predecessors. Swift solves this problem by defining a data type called **Index**. This is a structure defined inside the **String** structure that was designed to manage string indexes. The **String** structure includes properties and methods to work with indexes and access the characters of a string. The following are the most frequently used.

```
startIndex
```

This property returns the index of the first character of the string.

```
endIndex
```

This property returns the index of one position after the last character of the string. It is useful to manipulate range of characters, as we will see later.

```
firstIndex(of: Character)
```

This method returns the index where the character specified by the **of** argument appears for the first time in the string.

```
lastIndex(of: Character)
```

This method returns the last index where the character specified by the **of** argument appears in the string.

```
insert(Character, at: Index)
```

This method inserts into the string the character provided by the first argument at the position determined by the **at** argument.

```
insert(contentsOf: String, at: Index)
```

This method inserts into the string the value of the **contentsOf** argument at the position determined by the **at** argument.

```
remove(at: Index)
```

This method removes and returns the character at the position determined by the **at** argument.

```
prefix(Int)
```

This method returns a string created from the first character of the original string to the maximum length determined by the argument.

```
prefix(through: Index)
```

This method returns a string created from the first character of the original string to the character at the index indicated by the **through** argument.

```
prefix(upTo: Index)
```

This method returns a string created from the first character of the original string to the character at the index indicated by the **upTo** argument, but without including this last character.

```
replaceSubrange(Range, with: String)
```

This method replaces the characters in the position determined by the range provided as the first argument with the string provided by the **with** argument.

```
removeSubrange(Range)
```

This method removes the characters in the positions determined by the range specified by the argument.

Strings are collection of values. To access a specific character in a string, we must declare the **Index** structure with the index of the character we want to read after the name of the variable and enclose it in square brackets, as in the following example.

Listing 4-35: Processing the characters of a string

```
var text = "Hello World"
if !text.isEmpty {
   let start = text.startIndex
   let firstChar = text[start]

   print("First character is \(firstChar)")  // "First character is H"
}
```

The first thing we do in this example is to check the value of the **isEmpty** property to make sure the string is not empty and there are characters to read (notice the **!** operator to invert the condition). Once we know that there are characters to work with, we get the index of the string's first character from the **startIndex** property and read the character in that position using square brackets.

If we want to access a character in a different position, we must increment the value returned by **startIndex**. The trick is that, since **Index** values are not integers, we cannot just add a number to them. Instead, we must use the methods provided by the **String** structure. The following are the most frequently used.

index(after: Index)

This method increments the index specified by the **after** argument one unit and returns a new **Index** value with the result.

index(before: Index)

This method decrements the index specified by the **before** argument one unit and returns a new **Index** value with the result.

index(Index, **offsetBy:** Int)

This method increments the index specified by the first argument the amount of units specified by the **offsetBy** argument and returns a new **Index** value with the result.

The following example advances the initial index 6 positions to get a different character.

Listing 4-36: Calculating a specific index

```
var text = "Hello World"
if text != "" {
   let start = text.startIndex
   let newIndex = text.index(start, offsetBy: 6)

   print("The character is \(text[newIndex])")  // "The character is W"
}
```

The **index()** method applied in Listing 4-36 takes an integer to calculate the new index. The original index is incremented the number of units indicated by the integer and the new **Index** value is returned. With this index, we get the character at the position 6 (indexes start from 0).

If we want to obtain the index before the current one, we can specify a negative number of units for the offset value. Another way to move forward and backward is to use the other versions of the **index()** method. The following example gets the next index after the initial index using the **index(after:)** method and prints the corresponding character on the console.

Listing 4-37: Getting the next index

```
var text = "John"
let start = text.startIndex
var next = text.index(after: start)

print("Second letter is \(text[next])")  // "Second letter is o"
```

Once we get the right index, we can call some of the **String** methods to insert or remove characters. The **insert()** method, for instance, inserts a single character at the position indicated by the second argument. In the following example, we call it with the value of **endIndex** to add a character at the end of the string (**endindex** points to the position after the last character).

Listing 4-38: Inserting a character in a string

```
var text = "Hello World"
text.insert("!", at: text.endIndex)

print("New string is \(text)")  // "New string is Hello World!"
```

If we do not know where the character is located, we can find the index with the **firstIndex()** method. The value returned by this method is an optional containing the **Index** value of the first character that matches the argument or **nil** if no character is found. In the following example, we implement it to find the first space character and remove it with the **remove()** method.

Listing 4-39: Removing a character

```
var text = "Hello World"
var findIndex = text.firstIndex(of: " ")

if let index = findIndex {
   text.remove(at: index)
   print("New string is \(text)")  // "New string is HelloWorld"
}
```

If we want to work with groups of characters, we must implement ranges of **Index** values.

Listing 4-40: Getting a range of characters

```
var text = "Hello World"
var start = text.startIndex
var findIndex = text.firstIndex(of: " ")

if let end = findIndex {
   print("First word is \(text[start..<end])")
   //"First word is Hello"
}
```

The **firstIndex()** method in Listing 4-40 looks for a space character and returns its index. With this value, we can create a range from the first character to the space character and get the first word. But we must be careful because the **end** index is pointing to the space character, not to the last character of the word. To get the word without the space, we create an open range with the **..<** operator, so the character on the right is not included.

We can also use ranges to replace or remove parts of the text. For this purpose, the **String** structure offers the methods **replaceSubrange()** and **removeSubrange()**.

Listing 4-41: Working with ranges of characters

```
var text = "Hello World"
var start = text.startIndex
var findIndex = text.firstIndex(of: " ")

if let end = findIndex {
   text.replaceSubrange(start..<end, with: "Goodbye")
   // "Goodbye World"
}
findIndex = text.firstIndex(of: " ")
if let start = findIndex {
   text.removeSubrange(start...)  // "Goodbye"
}
```

In this example, we first implement the **replaceSubrange()** method to replace characters in the **text** variable with the string "Goodbye". To determine the characters to replace, we use a range that starts at the beginning of the string and ends just before the space character ("Hello"). Once this operation is complete, we use an open range with the **removeSubrange()** method to remove the characters in this new string from the space character to the end (" World"). The result is the string "Goodbye". Note that after applying a method to the string, the indexes become invalid and must be recalculated. For this reason, before calling the **removeSubrange()** method, we search again for the position of the space character and update the **findIndex** variable.

The rest of the methods provided by the **String** structure are straightforward. For instance, the following example implements two of them to check if a string contains the word "World" at the end and converts all the letters into uppercase letters.

Listing 4-42: Implementing String methods

```
let text = "Hello World"

if text.hasSuffix("World") {
   print(text.uppercased())  // "HELLO WORLD"
}
```

BASIC

Array Structures

The strings created by the **String** structure and the values we have created in Chapter 3 with functions such as **stride()** or **repeatElement()** are collections of values. Collections do not represent a value; they are containers for other values. A value of type **String** does not contain the string "Hello", it contains a collection of variables of type **Character** with the values "H", "e", "l", "l", and "o". Swift includes several collections like this, some were defined to contain specific values, like **String**, and others are generic (they can store values of any data type we need). One of those collections is **Array**.

Arrays are collections that contain an ordered list of values. They are generic structures that have the capacity to store all the values we need of any data type we want, but with the condition that once a data type is selected, all the values must be of that same type. For example, if we create an array of type **Int**, we will only be able to store values of type **Int** in it. Swift offers multiple syntaxes to create an array, including the following initializers.

Array<Type>()

This initializer returns an empty **Array** structure of the data type indicated by the value of **Type**.

Array(repeating: Value, **count:** Int)

This initializer returns an **Array** structure with copies of the same value. The **repeating** argument determines the value to copy, and the **count** argument determines how many copies the array will contain.

A shortcut to create an array is declaring the data type between square brackets followed by parentheses (e.g., **var list = [Int]()**), but the most frequently used is declaring the array with initial values enclosed in square brackets and separated by comma, as shown below.

Listing 4-43: Declaring arrays

```
var list: [Int] = [15, 25, 35]
```

As with any other variable, Swift can infer the data type from the values, so we can remove it.

Listing 4-44: Declaring arrays with type inference

```
var list = [15, 25, 35]
```

The **list** array declared in this example is initialized with three integer values, 15, 25 and 35. The values of an array are usually called *elements* or *items*. On these terms, we can say that the code in Listing 4-44 declares an array of three elements of type **Int**.

An index is automatically assigned to each value starting from 0, and as with strings, we must specify the index of the value we want to read surrounded by square brackets.

Listing 4-45: Reading the array's elements

```
var list = [15, 25, 35]
print(list[1])  // 25
```

The last statement in Listing 4-45 prints the value of the second element of the **list** array on the console (the element at index 1). We can also use indexes to modify the values.

Listing 4-46: Assigning a new value to an element

```
var list = [15, 25, 35]
list[0] = 400
print(list)  // [400, 25, 35]
```

To add new elements to an array, we can use the **+=** operator.

Listing 4-47: Adding new elements to an array

```
var list = [15, 25, 35]
list += [45, 55]
print(list)  // [15, 25, 35, 45, 55]
```

The **+=** operator concatenates the two arrays and assigns the result back to the same variable. If we want to use two or more arrays to create a new one, we can apply the **+** operator.

Listing 4-48: Concatenating two arrays

```
var list1 = [15, 25, 35]
var list2 = [45, 55, 65]
var final = list1 + list2  // [15, 25, 35, 45, 55, 65]
```

It is possible to declare arrays of arrays. These types of arrays are called *Multidimensional Arrays*. Arrays inside arrays are listed separated by comma.

Listing 4-49: Creating multidimensional arrays

```
var list: [[Int]] = [[2, 45, 31], [5, 10], [81, 12]]
```

This example creates an array of arrays of integers. (Note the declaration of the data type as an array inside another array **[[Int]]**.) To access the values, we must declare the indexes of each level in square brackets, one after another. The following example returns the first value (index `0`) of the second array (index `1`). The instruction looks for the array at index 1 and then gets the number at index 0.

Listing 4-50: Reading values from a multidimensional array

```
var list: [[Int]] = [[2, 45, 31], [5, 10], [81, 12]]
print(list[1][0])  // 5
```

To remove all the elements from an array, we can use one of the initializers introduced before or just assign empty square brackets to the variable.

Listing 4-51: Removing the elements of an array

```
var list = [15, 25, 35]
list = []
```

Arrays are collections of values and therefore we can iterate over their values with a **for in** loop, as we did with strings before.

Listing 4-52: Reading an array with a for in loop

```
var total = 0
let list = [15, 25, 35]

for value in list {
   total += value
}
print("The total is \(total)")  // "The total is 75"
```

The code in Listing 4-52 implements a **for in** loop to add the numbers in the **list** array to the **total** variable. At the end, we print the result. Although this is a legit way to do it, arrays offer multiple properties and methods to read and process their values. The following are the most frequently used properties.

`count`

This property returns the total number of elements in the array.

`isEmpty`

This property returns a Boolean value that indicates if the array is empty.

first

This property returns the first element of the array or **nil** if the array is empty.

last

This property returns the last element of the array or **nil** if the array is empty.

startIndex

This property returns the index of the first element in the array.

endIndex

This property returns the index after the index of the last element in the array.

The following are some of the methods available to add elements to the array.

append(Element)

This method adds the value specified by the argument at the end of the array.

insert(Element, **at:** Int)

This method adds a new element to the array. The first argument is the value we want to assign to the new element, and the **at** argument represents the position of the array where we want to insert the element.

We also have various methods to remove elements from the array.

remove(**at:** Int)

This method removes an element from the array at the index specified by the **at** argument.

removeFirst()

This method removes the first element of the array. It returns the value of the element deleted.

removeLast()

This method removes the last element of the array. It returns the value of the element deleted.

removeAll(**where:** Closure)

This method removes the elements in the array that meet the condition established by the closure assigned to the **where** argument.

removeSubrange(Range)

This method removes a range of elements from the array. The argument is a range of integers representing the indexes of the elements to remove.

dropFirst(Int)

This method removes the number of elements specified by the argument from the beginning of the array. If no amount is declared, only the first element is removed.

dropLast(Int)

This method removes the number of elements specified by the argument from the end of the array. If no amount is declared, only the last element is removed.

The following methods are used to sort the elements in the array.

sorted()

This method returns an array with the elements of the array in ascending order.

sorted(by: Closure)

This method returns an array with the elements of the array in the order determined by the closure provided to the **by** argument.

shuffled()

This method returns an array with the elements of the array in random order.

reversed()

This method returns an array with the elements of the array in reverse order.

swapAt(Int, Int)

This method exchanges the values of the elements at the indexes specified by the arguments.

The following are the methods used to retrieve specific elements from an array.

filter(Closure)

This method filters an array and returns another array with the values that passed the filter. The argument is a closure that processes the elements and returns a Boolean value indicating whether the value passed the filter or not.

map(Closure)

This method returns a new array containing the results of processing each of the values of the array.

compactMap(Closure)

This method returns a new array containing the results of processing each of the values of the array, but ignores the values that produce a **nil** result.

reduce(Value, Closure)

This method sends the values of the array to the closure one by one and returns the result of the operation. The first argument is the value that is going to be processed with the first value of the array.

contains(where: Closure)

This method returns a Boolean that determines if the array contains an element that satisfies the condition in the closure.

allSatisfy(Closure)

This method returns a Boolean value that determines if all the elements in the array comply with the requisites of a closure.

difference(from: Array)

This method returns a **CollectionDifference** structure containing all the changes that have to be performed to synchronize the array with the array provided by the **from** argument. This method can work in conjunction with the **applying()** method to apply all the changes in the array at once.

randomElement()

This method randomly selects an element from the array and returns it. If the array is empty, the value returned is **nil**.

replaceSubrange(Range, **with:** Array)

This method replaces a range of elements with the elements of the array provided by the **with** argument. The first argument is a range of integers corresponding to the indexes of the elements we want to replace.

joined(separator: String)

This method returns a string that includes all the values in an array of strings joined by the string specified by the **separator** argument.

And the following are some of the methods used to obtain information from the array.

count(where: Closure)

This method returns an integer with the number of elements that satisfy the condition determined by the closure.

enumerated()

This method is used to iterate over the elements of the array. It returns a tuple containing the index and the value of the current element.

min()

This method compares the values of the elements and returns the smallest.

max()

This method compares the values of the elements and returns the largest.

In the previous example, we have seen how to iterate over the elements of an array with the **for in** loop, but that iteration only returns the value of the element, not its index. An alternative is provided by the **enumerated()** method, designed to work with these types of loops. Each cycle returns a tuple with the index and the value of the current element.

Listing 4-53: Reading indexes and values of an array

```
let fruits = ["Banana", "Orange", "Apple"]
var message = "My fruits:"

for (myindex, myfruit) in fruits.enumerated() {
   message += " \(myindex + 1)-\(myfruit)"
}
print(message)  // "My fruits: 1-Banana 2-Orange 3-Apple"
```

This example uses the constants **myindex** and **myfruit** to capture the values produced by the **enumerated()** method and generate a string. Note that since the array's indexes start from 0, we added `1` to **myindex** to start counting from 1.

Another useful property is **count**. As mentioned before, we can access each element of the array with the index between square brackets. But trying to read a value in an index that has not yet been defined returns an error. To make sure that the index exists, we can check whether it is greater than 0 and less than the total amount of elements in the array using the `count` property, as shown below.

Listing 4-54: Checking whether an array contains a value in a specific index

```
let ages = [32, 540, 12, 27, 54]
let index = 3
if index > 0 && index < ages.count {
   print("The value is: \(ages[index])")  // "The value is: 27"
}
```

The methods to add and remove elements from an array are straightforward. The following example illustrates how to implement them and the changes they introduce to the array.

Listing 4-55: Adding and removing elements

```
var fruits = ["Banana", "Orange"]
if !fruits.isEmpty {
   fruits.append("Apple")  // ["Banana", "Orange", "Apple"]
   fruits.removeFirst()  // "Banana"
   fruits.insert("Pear", at: 1)  // ["Orange", "Pear", "Apple"]
   fruits.insert(contentsOf: ["Cherry", "Peach"], at: 2)
   // ["Orange", "Pear", "Cherry", "Peach", "Apple"]
}
```

IMPORTANT

Every time an array is modified, its indexes are reassigned. For instance, if you remove the first element of an array of three, the index 0 is reassigned to the second element and the index 1 to the third element. The system always makes sure that the indexes are consecutive and start from 0.

A more complex method is **removeAll(where:)**. This method removes several elements at once, but only those that meet a condition. The condition is established by a closure that processes each of the values in the array and returns **true** or **false** depending on whether the value meets the condition or not. In the following example, we compare each value with the string "Orange" and therefore all the values "Orange" are removed from the array.

Listing 4-56: Removing all the elements that meet a condition

```
var fruits = ["Banana", "Orange", "Apple", "Orange"]
fruits.removeAll(where: { value in
   value == "Orange"
})
print(fruits)  // ["Banana", "Apple"]
```

Another method that requires a closure to process the values is **contains(where:)**. In the following example, we use this method to determine whether an array contains a value greater than 60 or not.

Listing 4-57: Finding if an element meets a condition

```
var list = [55, 12, 32, 5, 9]
let found = list.contains(where: { value in
   value > 60
})
print(found)  // false
```

We can also select a random value with the **randomElement()** method. This method selects a value from the array and returns an optional, so we must compare it against **nil** or use optional binding before processing it, as in the following example.

Listing 4-58: Selecting a random value from an array

```
let fruits = ["Banana", "Orange", "Apple"]
if let randomValue = fruits.randomElement() {
   print("The selected value is: \(randomValue)")
}
```

Another random operation is performed by the **shuffled()** method. With this method we can randomly sort the elements of an array.

Listing 4-59: Changing the order of the elements of an array

```
var fruits = ["Banana", "Orange", "Apple"]
fruits = fruits.shuffled()
print(fruits)  // e.g., ["Orange", "Apple", "Banana"]
```

Besides working with all the elements of an array, we can do it with a range of elements.

Listing 4-60: Reading a range of elements

```
var fruits = ["Banana", "Orange", "Apple", "Cherry"]
var someFruits = fruits[0..<2]  // ["Banana", "Orange"]

print("The new selection has \(someFruits.count) fruits")
// "The new selection has 2 fruits"
```

This example gets the elements at the indexes 0 and 1 from the **fruits** array and assigns them to the new **someFruits** array. Now we have two arrays: **fruits** with 4 elements and **someFruits** with 2.

Arrays created from a range of indexes are of type **ArraySlice**. This is another collection type provided by Swift to store temporary arrays that are composed of elements taken from other arrays. We can iterate over these types of arrays with a loop or read its elements as we do with normal arrays, but if we want to assign them to other array variables or use them for persistent storage, we must cast them as **Array** types using the **Array()** initializer. The initializer takes the values in the **ArraySlice** variable and returns a normal array.

Listing 4-61: Casting arrays of type ArraySlice

```
var fruits = ["Banana", "Orange", "Apple", "Cherry"]
var someFruits = fruits[0..<2]  // ["Banana", "Orange"]
var newArray = Array(someFruits)
```

The **Array** structure also offers the methods **removeSubrange()** and **replaceSubrange()** to remove and replace a range of elements.

Listing 4-62: Removing and replacing elements

```
var fruits = ["Banana", "Orange", "Apple", "Banana", "Banana"]
fruits.removeSubrange(1...2)
fruits.replaceSubrange(0..<2, with: ["Cherry", "Cherry"])
print(fruits)  // "["Cherry", "Cherry", "Banana"]"
```

In Listing 4-62, we call the **removeSubrange()** method to remove the range of elements from index 1 to 2, and then call the **replaceSubrange()** method to replace the elements from index 0 to 1 with another array filled with "Cherries". This is just to illustrate how the methods work, but it shows a recurrent situation in app development where sometimes we need to fill a collection with elements of the same value. When working with arrays, this is easy to achieve. The **Array** structure includes an initializer that takes two arguments, **repeating** and **count**, and generates an array with the number of elements indicated by **count** and the value indicated by **repeating**.

Listing 4-63: Initializing an array with elements of the same value

```
var fruits = ["Banana", "Orange", "Apple"]

let total = fruits.count
let newArray = Array(repeating: "Cherry", count: total)
fruits.replaceSubrange(0..<total, with: newArray)

print(fruits)  // "["Cherry", "Cherry", "Cherry"]"
```

In this example, we create an array with the same amount of elements as the **fruits** array and then use the **replaceSubrange()** method to replace every element with a new one.

The methods to remove and replace elements of an array are not selective enough; they affect the elements in a specific index or a range of indexes without considering their values. If we want to perform a more specific job, we can use the **filter()** method. This method takes a closure and sends each element to the closure for processing. If the closure returns **true**, the element is included in the new array, otherwise it is ignored, as shown below.

Listing 4-64: Filtering the values of an array

```
var fruits = ["Apple", "Grape", "Banana", "Grape"]
var filteredArray = fruits.filter({ $0 != "Grape" })
print(filteredArray)  // "["Apple", "Banana"]"
```

The **filter()** method sends the values one by one to the closure, the closure reads the current value from the placeholder **$0**, compares it with the value "Grape", and returns a Boolean with the result. If the value is **true**, the element is included in **filteredArray**.

If what we need is to modify the elements of an array all at once, we can use the **map()** method. This method sends the values of the array one by one to a closure and returns another array with the results produced by the closure.

Listing 4-65: Mapping an array

```
let list = [2, 4, 8, 16]
let half = list.map({ $0 / 2 })
print(half)  // "[1, 2, 4, 8]"
```

The example in Listing 4-65 defines a list of integers and then calls the **map()** method on the array to divide each value by 2. The **map()** method sends the values of the array to the closure one by one, the closure replaces the placeholder (**$0**) with the current value, divides the number by 2, and returns the result. All the results are stored in a new array and that array is returned by the **map()** method when the process is over.

Of course, we can perform any kind of operations we want on the values in the closure. For instance, the following code implements the `map()` method and the `String()` initializer to convert all the values into strings.

Listing 4-66: Converting the elements of an array into strings

```
let list = [1, 2, 3, 4, 5]
let listtext = list.map({ String($0) })
print(listtext)  // "["1", "2", "3", "4", "5"]"
```

When all we want to do is to initialize a new structure with the value received by the closure, instead of a closure, Swift allows us to provide the structure's initializer. The value received by the closure is sent to the initializer and a new structure of that type is returned.

Listing 4-67: Using a structure initializer with the `map()` method

```
let list = [1, 2, 3, 4, 5]
let listtext = list.map(String.init)
print(listtext)  // "["1", "2", "3", "4", "5"]"
```

This example produces the same result as before, but instead of using a closure, we use the **String** initializer. The **map()** method sends the value to the initializer, the initializer returns a new **String** structure with that value, and the string is assigned to the new array.

Another way to process all the values of an array at once is with the **reduce()** method. This method works like **map()**, but instead of storing the results in an array, it sends the result back to the closure for further processing. For instance, the following code uses the **reduce()** method to get the result of the addition of all the numbers in an array.

Listing 4-68: Reducing an array

```
let list = [2, 4, 8, 16]
let total = list.reduce(0, { $0 + $1 })
print(total)  // "30"
```

The code in Listing 4-68 defines an array of integers and then calls the **reduce()** method on it. This method sends to the closure two values at a time. In the first cycle, the values sent to the closure are the ones provided by the first argument (**0**) and the first value of the array (**2**). In the second cycle, the values sent to the closure are the value returned by the closure in the first cycle (0 + 2 = **2**), and the second value of the array (**4**). The loop goes on until all the values of the array are processed.

When it comes to sorting the elements of an array, there are several options available. The most frequently used are **reversed()** and **sorted()**. The **reversed()** method takes the elements of an array and returns a new array with the same elements in reversed order. The value returned by the method is stored in a structure of type **ReversedCollection**. As we did before with the **ArraySlice** type, we can cast these values as **Array** structures with the **Array()** initializer.

Listing 4-69: Reversing the elements of an array

```
var fruits = ["Apple", "Blueberry", "Banana"]
var array = Array(fruits.reversed())
// ["Banana", "Blueberry", "Apple"]
```

The **sorted()** method sorts the array in ascending order and returns a new array.

Listing 4-70: Sorting the elements of an array

```
var fruits = ["Blueberry", "Apple", "Banana"]
let basket = fruits.sorted()
print(basket)  // ["Apple", "Banana", "Blueberry"]
```

If we want to sort the elements in a custom order, we can use the **sorted(by:)** method. This method takes a function or a closure that receives the value of two elements and returns **true** if the first element should appear before the second element, or **false** otherwise.

Listing 4-71: Sorting the elements of an array in a custom order

```
var fruits = ["Apple", "Raspberry", "Banana", "Grape"]
var newArray = fruits.sorted(by: { $0 > $1 })
print(newArray[0])  // "Raspberry"
```

When the **sorted(by:)** method is executed, it performs a loop. On each cycle, two values of the **fruits** array are sent to the closure. The closure compares the values and returns **true** or **false** accordingly. This indicates to the **sorted()** method which value should appear before the other in the new array, effectively sorting the elements.

Since in our example we are not comparing the argument against a specific value, we can use it to order arrays of any data type. For example, we can use the same closure to sort an array of integers.

Listing 4-72: Sorting an array of integers

```
var numbers = [55, 12, 32, 5, 9]
var newArray = numbers.sorted(by: { $0 < $1 })
print(newArray[0])  // 5
```

If we decide to work with specific data types, we can perform custom tasks. For example, we can count the characters in the strings and sort them according to their length.

Listing 4-73: Sorting strings according to the number of characters

```
var fruits = ["Apple", "Blueberry", "Banana", "Grape"]
var newArray = fruits.sorted(by: { $0.count < $1.count })
print(newArray)  // ["Apple", "Grape", "Banana", "Blueberry"]
```

Arrays also include two powerful methods to compare elements: **min()** and **max()**. These methods compare the values and return the smallest or largest, respectively.

Listing 4-74: Getting the largest element

```
let ages = [32, 540, 12, 27]

if let older = ages.max() {
   let digits = String(older)
   print("The maximum age is \(digits.count) digits long")
   // "The maximum age is 3 digits long"
}
```

The code in Listing 4-74 takes the largest value from an array of integers and counts the number of digits in the value returned. Because the **max()** method returns an optional, we use optional binding to read the value. The rest of the code turns this value into a string and counts its characters to print the number of digits on the console.

Besides selecting the largest or smallest value with the **max()** and **min()** methods, we can also fetch values from the array using the **first** and **last** properties.

Listing 4-75: Getting the first value of an array

```
let ages = [32, 540, 12, 27]

if let firstAge = ages.first {
   print("The first person is \(firstAge) years old")
   // "The first person is 32 years old"
}
```

The value returned by the **first** property is an optional, so we use optional binding to read it and store it in the **firstAge** constant. The **first** and **last** properties only get the first and last values, respectively. To search for any value in the array or its index, the **Array** structure offers the following methods.

firstIndex(of: Element)

This method performs a search from the beginning of the array and returns the index of the first element that matches the value of the **of** argument.

lastIndex(of: Element)

This method performs a search from the end of the array and returns the index of the first element that matches the value of the **of** argument.

`firstIndex(where: Closure)`

This method returns the index of the first value that meets the condition in the closure assigned to the **where** argument.

`lastIndex(where: Closure)`

This method returns the index of the last value that meets the condition in the closure assigned to the **where** argument.

`first(where: Closure)`

This method returns the first value that meets the condition in the closure assigned to the **where** argument.

`last(where: Closure)`

This method returns the last value that meets the condition in the closure assigned to the **where** argument.

If we only need the index of a particular element, we can use the **firstIndex(of:)** method. For instance, we can look for the first appearance of a number in an array and get the index.

Listing 4-76: Getting the index of a specific value

```
let ages = [32, 540, 12, 27, 54]

if let index = ages.firstIndex(of: 540) {
   print("The value is at the position \(index)")
   // "The value is at the position 1"
}
```

If what we need instead is to get the index of a value that meets a condition, we can use methods like **firstIndex(where:)** or **lastIndex(where:)** depending on whether we want to search from the beginning or the end of the array. In the following example, we show how to look for the index of a value and the value itself with the **firstIndex(where:)** and `first(where:)` methods.

Listing 4-77: Getting the index of a value that meets a condition

```
let ages = [32, 540, 12, 27, 54]
let firstIndex = ages.firstIndex(where: { value in value < 30 })
let firstValue = ages.first(where: { value in value < 30 })

if firstIndex != nil && firstValue != nil {
   print("First value is: \(firstValue!)")
   // "First value is: 12"
   print("First value is at index: \(firstIndex!)")
   // "First value is at index: 2"
}
```

The **firstIndex(where:)** method reads every value of the array from the beginning and sends them to the closure assigned to the **where** argument. The closure takes the current value and compares it against the number **30**, if the value is greater than 30, the closure returns **false**, otherwise it returns **true** and the index of that value is assigned to the **first** variable. The **first(where:)** method works exactly the same way, but it returns the value instead of the index. In this case, the first number in the array smaller than 30 is 12, which is at index 2.

The **Array** structure also includes methods to get the indexes of multiple elements and work with those values.

indices(where: Closure)

This method returns a **RangeSet** value with a set of ranges that include all the indexes of the elements that match the condition determined by the closure provided by the **where** argument.

indices(of: Value)

This method returns a **RangeSet** value with a set of ranges that include all the indexes of the elements that match the value provided by the **of** argument.

moveSubranges(RangeSet, **to:** Index)

This method moves the elements at the indexes determined by the first argument to the position determined by the **to** argument.

removeSubranges(RangeSet)

This method removes the elements in the indexes determined by the argument.

The **indices()** method returns a value of type **RangeSet**. This is a structure that stores a set of **Range** values with the indexes of the elements in the array (we will study Sets later in this chapter). Using this method, we can retrieve the indexes of the values that match a condition and then use these values to read or modify the array, as in the following example.

Listing 4-78: Working with a range of indexes

```
var ages = [12, 32, 540, 27, 54]
let listIndexes = ages.indices(where: { $0 < 30 })

for value in ages[listIndexes] {
   print(value)
}
ages.removeSubranges(listIndexes)
print(ages)  // [32, 540, 54]
```

A **RangeSet** value can be used to get elements from an array. In our example, we first implement the **indices()** method to get the indexes of the values that are less than 30 and then read these values with a **for in** loop (**ages[listIndexes]**). At the end, we remove the values in these indexes using the **removeSubranges()** method. As a result, the final array only contains values that are 30 or higher.

BASIC

Dictionary Structures

There is only one way to access the elements of an array and that is through their numeric indexes. Dictionaries offer a better alternative. With dictionaries, we can define the indexes ourselves using any custom value we want. Each index, also known as *key*, must be explicitly declared along with its value. Swift offers multiple syntaxes to create a dictionary, including the following initializers.

Dictionary<Type1: Type2>()

This initializer returns an empty **Dictionary** structure with the keys and values of the data type indicated by **Type1** and **Type2**.

Dictionary(grouping: Collection, **by:** Closure)

This initializer returns a **Dictionary** structure with the values provided by the **grouping** argument grouped in arrays according to the keys returned by the closure provided by the **by** argument.

If the data types are explicitly defined, we can also declare a dictionary with a simplified syntax, as in **var list: [String: String] = Dictionary()**, or use square brackets with a colon, as in **var list: [String: String] = [:]**. The latest is also used to define a dictionary with initial values. In this case, the keys and values are separated by a colon and the elements are separated by commas, as in the following example.

Listing 4-79: Declaring a dictionary with initial values

```
var list: [String: String] = ["First": "Apple", "Second": "Orange"]
```

The first value of each element is the key and the second is the value. Of course, Swift can also infer the data types.

Listing 4-80: Declaring a dictionary with type inference

```
var list = ["First": "Apple", "Second": "Orange"]
```

As with arrays, if we want to read or replace a value, we must declare the key (index) in square brackets after the name of the dictionary.

Listing 4-81: Assigning a new value to an element of a dictionary

```
var list = ["First": "Apple", "Second": "Orange"]
list["Second"] = "Banana"
```

The second statement in Listing 4-81 assigns a new value to the element identified with the "Second" key. Now, the dictionary contains two elements with the values "Apple" and "Banana". If the key used to assign the new value exists, the system updates the value, but if the key does not exist, a new element is created, as shown below.

Listing 4-82: Adding a new element to a dictionary

```
var list = ["First": "Apple", "Second": "Orange"]
list["Third"] = "Banana"
print(list)
// "["Second": "Orange", "First": "Apple", "Third": "Banana"]"
```

Dictionaries return optional values. If we try to read an element with a key that does not exist, the value returned is **nil**.

Listing 4-83: Reading an element that does not exist

```
var list = ["First": "Apple", "Second": "Orange"]
print(list["Third"])  // nil
```

The code in Listing 4-83 tries to read a value with the key "Third" in the **list** dictionary. Since a value with that key doesn't exist, the value **nil** is printed on the console. If the element exists and we want to read its value, we must unwrap it.

Listing 4-84: Reading the value of an element in a dictionary

```
var list = ["First": "Apple", "Second": "Orange"]
if let first = list["First"], let second = list["Second"] {
   print("We have \(first) and \(second)")
   // "We have Apple and Orange"
}
```

Since dictionary elements are optionals, we can assign the value **nil** to remove them. The following example removes the element with the key "First".

Listing 4-85: Removing an element from a dictionary

```
var list = ["First": "Apple", "Second": "Orange"]
list["First"] = nil
```

As with arrays, we can also iterate over the values of a dictionary with a **for in** loop. The value produced by each cycle of the loop is a tuple containing the element's key and value.

Listing 4-86: Using for in to iterate over a dictionary

```
var fruits = ["First": "Apple", "Second": "Orange"]
var message = "My fruits:"

for (mykey, myfruit) in fruits {
   message += " \(mykey)-\(myfruit)"
}
print(message)  // "My fruits: First-Apple Second-Orange"
```

The **for in** loop in Listing 4-86 reads the elements of the **fruits** dictionary one by one, assigns the index and the value to the **mykey** and **myfruit** constants, and adds their values to the **message** variable. At the end, we get a string with all the keys and values in the dictionary.

Of course, dictionaries can also contain arrays as values. The declaration is simple: the key is declared as always, and the single value is replaced by an array.

Listing 4-87: Combining dictionaries with arrays

```
var fruits: [String: [String]] = ["A": ["Apple", "Apricot"], "B":
["Banana", "Blueberries"]]
```

Reading the values of a dictionary like this is a bit more complicated. Because dictionaries return optionals, we cannot just specify the indexes as we do for multidimensional arrays (see Listing 4-50). The array returned by the dictionary must be unwrapped before reading the values, as shown below.

Listing 4-88: Reading arrays inside dictionaries

```
var fruits: [String: [String]] = ["A": ["Apple", "Apricot"], "B":
["Banana", "Blueberries"]]
if let list = fruits["A"] {
   print(list[0])  // "Apple"
}
```

In this example, we create a dictionary with two values. The values are arrays of strings with a string as key. The code gets the array corresponding to the "A" key, unwraps it, and stores it in a constant. The **list** constant now contains the array assigned to the "A" key, and therefore when we read the element at index 0, we get the value "Apple".

What we created in the last example is the same as what the `Dictionary(grouping: by:)` initializer does. This initializer takes the values of a collection and groups them into arrays according to the key returned by the closure, as shown below.

Listing 4-89: Grouping values by a key

```
let list = [15, 25, 38, 55, 42]
let group5 = Dictionary(grouping: list, by: {$0 % 5 == 0 ? "Yes" : "No"})
print(group5)  // "["No": [38, 42], "Yes": [15, 25, 55]]"
```

The **Dictionary** initializer implemented in Listing 4-89 takes the values of the **list** array, sends them to the closure one by one, and creates a new dictionary with the keys returned by the closure. The closure receives the value and returns the strings "Yes" or "No" depending on whether the current value is multiple of 5. If the value is multiple of 5, it is included in an array with the "Yes" key, otherwise it is included in an array with the "No" key.

Dictionaries also include properties and methods to manage the values. The following are the most frequently used.

count

This property returns the total number of elements in the dictionary.

isEmpty

This property returns a Boolean value that indicates if the dictionary is empty.

keys

This property returns a collection with the keys in the dictionary.

values

This property returns a collection with the values in the dictionary.

sorted(by: Closure)

This method returns an array of tuples with each element of the dictionary (key and value) in the order determined by the closure.

randomElement()

This method randomly selects an element from the dictionary and returns a tuple with its key and value. If the dictionary is empty, the value returned is **nil**.

shuffled()

This method returns an array of tuples containing the keys and values of each element of the dictionary in random order.

updateValue(Value, **forKey:** Key)

This method updates the value of an element with the value and key specified by its arguments. If the key does not exist, the method creates a new element. If the key exists, it returns the previous value, otherwise, the value returned is **nil**.

removeValue(forKey: Key)

This method removes the element with the key equal to the value of the **forKey** argument. It returns an optional containing the value of the deleted element or **nil** if no element with the specified key was found.

contains(where: Closure)

This method returns a Boolean value that determines if the dictionary contains an element that meets the condition in the closure.

Some of the methods provided by the **Dictionary** structure are like those included in **Array** structures, but others are more specific. For example, the **updateValue()** and **removeValue()** methods were specifically designed to update and remove values from dictionaries.

Listing 4-90: Adding and removing elements from a dictionary

```
var fruits = ["one": "Banana", "two": "Apple", "three": "Pear"]
fruits.updateValue("Banana", forKey: "three")  // "Pear"
fruits.removeValue(forKey: "one")  // "Banana"
print(fruits)  // "["three": "Banana", "two": "Apple"]"
```

The **updateValue()** method updates the value of an element when there is already an element with that key or creates a new one if the key does not exist. This is the same as assigning a value directly to an element (see Listing 4-81 and 4-82), but the method returns the previous value, which can sometimes be useful.

Because they have custom keys, dictionaries are an unordered collection of values, but we can create an array with their elements in a specific order using the **sorted(by:)** method. This method returns the values as tuples, with the element's key first and the value second.

Listing 4-91: Sorting the values of a dictionary

```
var fruits = ["one": "Banana", "two": "Apple", "three": "Pear"]
var list = fruits.sorted(by: { $0.1 < $1.1 })
print(list)
```

As with arrays, the **sorted(by:)** method sends to the closure two values at a time, but the values in a dictionary are sent as tuples containing the key and value of each element. For instance, the first values sent to the closure in Listing 4-91 are `("one", "Banana")` and `("two", "Apple")`. These values replace the placeholders **$0** and **$1**, so if we want to order the elements according to the names of the fruits, we must compare the values of the tuples at index 1 (**$0.1 < $1.1**). The array returned is a collection of tuples in alphabetical order, with every element containing the keys and values of the dictionary (**[(key: "two", value: "Apple"), (key: "one", value: "Banana"), (key: "three", value: "Pear")]**).

Earlier, we saw how to iterate over the elements of a dictionary with a **for in** loop (see Listing 4-86). The loop gets each element and generates a tuple with the element's key and value. But there are times when we only need the element's key or value. The **Dictionary** structure provides two properties for this purpose: **keys** and **values**. These properties return a collection containing only the keys or the values of a dictionary.

Listing 4-92: Iterating over the dictionary's keys

```
var fruits = ["one": "Banana", "two": "Apple", "three": "Pear"]

for key in fruits.keys {
   if key == "two" {
      print("We have an element with the key 'two'")
   }
}
```

The collections returned by the **keys** and **values** properties are structures of type **Keys** and **Values** defined inside the **Dictionary** structure. As we did before with other collection types, we can turn them into arrays with the **Array()** initializer.

Listing 4-93: Reading the keys of a dictionary

```
var fruits = ["one": "Banana", "two": "Apple", "three": "Pear"]
let keys = Array(fruits.keys)
print(keys)
```

BASIC

Set Structures

When working with arrays and dictionaries, every element has an associated key, which allows us to search for and organize elements based on that value. However, if order is not important, we can use a set. Sets are similar to arrays, but they do not assign an index to their values. As a result, their elements have no defined order, and every value in a set is unique. In Swift, sets are created using the `Set` structure.

> `Set<Type>()`
>
> This initializer returns an empty **Set** structure of the data type indicated by **Type**.

This initializer can be used to create an empty set (e.g., **let myset = Set<Int>()**), but we can also use square brackets, as we do with arrays. The difference with arrays is that we must specify that we are creating a set with the **Set** keyword, as shown below.

Listing 4-94: Creating an empty set of integers

```
var ages: Set<Int> = []
```

If we initialize the set with some values, Swift can infer its type from their data type, simplifying the declaration.

Listing 4-95: Creating a set of integers

```
var ages: Set = [15, 25, 35, 45]
```

To access and process the elements of a set, we can use a **for in** loop, as we did before with strings and arrays, but sets also provide their own properties and methods for this purpose.

`count`

This property returns the number of elements in the set.

`isEmpty`

This property returns a Boolean value that indicates whether the set is empty or not.

`contains(Element)`

This method returns a Boolean value that indicates whether there is an element in the set with the value specified by the argument.

`contains(where: Closure)`

This method returns a Boolean value that determines if the set contains an element that meets the condition in the closure.

`min()`

This method compares the elements in the set and returns the smallest.

`max()`

This method compares the elements in the set and returns the largest.

`sorted()`

This method returns an array with the elements of the set in ascending order.

`sorted(by: Closure)`

This method returns an array with the elements of the set in the order determined by the closure specified by the **by** argument.

`randomElement()`

This method randomly selects an element from the set and returns it. If the set is empty, the value returned is **nil**.

`shuffled()`

This method returns an array with the elements of the set in random order.

`insert(Element)`

This method inserts a new element in the set with the value provided by the argument.

union(Collection)

This method returns a new set created with the values of the original set plus the values provided by the argument (an array or another set).

subtract(Collection)

This method returns a new set created by subtracting the elements provided by the argument to the original set.

intersection(Collection)

This method returns a new set created with the values of the original set that match the values provided by the argument (an array or another set).

remove(Element)

This method removes from the set the element with the value provided by the argument.

isSubset(of: Set)

This method returns a Boolean value that indicates whether or not the set is a subset of the set specified by the **of** argument.

isSuperset(of: Set)

This method returns a Boolean value that indicates whether or not the set is a superset of the set specified by the **of** argument.

isDisjoint(with: Set)

This method returns a Boolean value that indicates whether or not the original set and the set specified by the **with** argument have elements in common.

Using these methods, we can easily access and modify the values of a set. For instance, we can implement the **contains()** method to search for a value.

Listing 4-96: Using `contains()` to find an element in a set

```
var fruits: Set = ["Apple", "Orange", "Banana"]

if fruits.contains("Apple") {
   print("Apple exists!")  // "Apple exists!"
}
```

To insert a new element, we just have to execute the **insert()** method.

Listing 4-97: Inserting a new element in a set

```
var fruits: Set = ["Apple", "Orange", "Banana"]

if !fruits.contains("Grape") {
```

```
    fruits.insert("Grape")
}
print("The set has \(fruits.count) elements")
// "The set has 4 elements"
```

In Listing 4-97, we use the **contains()** method again to check if an element with the value "Grape" already exists in the set, but this is not really necessary. If the value is already part of the set, the **insert()** method does not perform any action.

Of course, we can also remove elements from a set. The structure provides the **remove()** method for this purpose.

Listing 4-98: Removing an element from a set

```
var fruits: Set = ["Apple", "Orange", "Banana"]

if let removed = fruits.remove("Banana") {
    print("\(removed) was removed")  // "Banana was removed"
}
```

The **remove()** method removes the element whose value matches the value of the argument and returns an optional with the value that have been removed or **nil** in case of failure. The code in Listing 4-98 gets the value returned by the method and prints a message if it was successfully removed.

Sets are collections without order. Every time we read a set, the order in which its values are returned is not guaranteed, but we can use the **sorted()** method to create an array with the values of the set in order. The following example sorts the elements of the **fruits** set in alphabetical order, creating a new array we call **orderFruits**.

Listing 4-99: Sorting the elements of a set

```
var fruits: Set = ["Apple", "Orange", "Banana"]
var orderFruits = fruits.sorted()
if let lastItem = orderFruits.last {
    print(lastItem)  // "Orange"
}
```

The rest of the methods available for sets are simple to use. The following example joins two sets with the **union()** method and then subtracts elements from the result with **subtract()**.

Listing 4-100: Combining sets

```
var fruits: Set = ["Apple", "Banana"]
var newSet = fruits.union(["Grapes"])
// "Banana", "Grapes", "Apple"
newSet.subtract(["Apple", "Banana"])
// "Grapes"
```

The **Set** structure also offers methods to compare sets. We can determine if a set is a subset or a superset of another set with the **isSubset()** and **isSuperset()** methods, or check if two sets have elements in common with the **isDisjoint()** method. The following example implements the **isSubset()** method to check if the fruits in a basket come from the store. The code checks if the elements in the **basket** set are found in the **store** set and returns **true** in case of success.

Listing 4-101: Comparing sets

```
var store: Set = ["Banana", "Apple", "Orange", "Pear"]
var basket: Set = ["Apple", "Orange"]

if basket.isSubset(of: store) {
   print("The fruits in the basket are from the store")
}
```

Chapter 5

Enumerations

BASIC

5.1 - Swift Enumerations

Enumerations are a way to create data types with a limited set of values. An enumeration type is like the **Bool** type but with the possible values defined by the programmer. They are declared with the **enum** keyword, and the values are defined in braces with the **case** keyword.

Listing 5-1: Defining an enumeration type

```
import Playgrounds

#Playground {
    enum Number {
        case one
        case two
        case three
    }
}
```

Do It Yourself

Update the **MyPlayground.swift** file in your project with the code in Listing 5-1. Since this code only defines the enumeration, you won't see any results on the Canvas. We will show how to work with this enumeration and access its values next.

The previous example defines an enumeration call **Number** with three possible values: **one**, **two,** and **three**. We can assign any names we want for the enumeration and its values. The values may also be declared just in one **case** statement separated by comma, as shown below.

Listing 5-2: Declaring the enumeration values in one statement

```
enum Number {
   case one, two, three
}
```

Like a structure, an enumeration is a custom data type. To use it, we create a variable of this type and assign one of its possible values using dot notation, as shown below.

Listing 5-3: Initializing an instance of an enumeration

```
enum Number {
   case one, two, three
}
var mynumber: Number = Number.one
```

Variables of this data type can store only the values allowed by the type (`one`, `two`, or `three`), but they can still be modified. Once the data type of a variable is defined, only the dot and the value are needed to change its value.

Listing 5-4: Assigning a new value to a variable of type `Number`

```
enum Number {
   case one, two, three
}
var mynumber = Number.one
mynumber = .two
```

In the last statement of this code, we assign a new value to **mynumber**. The value **.two** may have been written as **Number.two**. Both syntaxes are valid, but Swift infers that the new value is of the same data type as the variable, so it is not necessary to declare the name anymore.

Like Booleans, enumeration types can be used as signals to indicate a state that can later be checked to decide whether a particular task should be performed. For this reason, they are often used with conditionals and loops. In the following example, the value of an enumeration variable is checked with a `switch` statement. This statement is especially useful when working with enumerations because the limited number of values makes it easier to define the cases.

Listing 5-5: Using `switch` with an enumeration type

```
enum Number {
   case one
   case two
   case three
}
```

```
var mynumber = Number.two

switch mynumber {
   case .one:
      print("The number is 1")
   case .two:
      print("The number is 2")   // "The number is 2"
   case .three:
      print("The number is 3")
}
```

In this example, we define the **Number** enumeration, declare the **mynumber** variable of this type, and assign it the value **two**. After that, we check the value of this variable with a **switch** statement that compares it with the three possible values of its type and prints a message on the console.

BASIC

Raw Values

The cases of an enumeration can have values to represent them. These values are called *Raw Values*. Swift assigns values by default to every case, starting from 0, but we can assign our own, as shown below.

Listing 5-6: Assigning raw values to enumeration values

```
enum Number: String {
   case one = "Number One"
   case two = "Number Two"
   case three = "Number Three"
}
var mynumber = Number.one
```

Like structures, enumerations also include their own properties and methods. The most useful property is called **rawValue**, which allows us to read the raw value of each **case**.

Listing 5-7: Reading raw values

```
enum Number: String {
   case one = "Number One"
   case two = "Number Two"
   case three = "Number Three"
}
var mynumber = Number.one
print("The value is \(mynumber.rawValue)")
// "The value is Number One"
```

Enumerations include an initializer to create an instance from a raw value. This means that instead of declaring the variable using the value's name (**one**, **two** or **three**), we can do it with the raw value. The initializer includes the **rawValue** argument to specify the value used to create the instance.

Listing 5-8: Creating an enumeration from a raw value

```
enum Number: String {
   case one = "Number One"
   case two = "Number Two"
   case three = "Number Three"
}
var mynumber = Number(rawValue: "Number Two")

if mynumber == .two {
   print("Correct Value")  // "Correct Value"
}
```

We can read the **case** value or the raw value to identify an instance of an enumeration type. In Listing 5-8, we create an instance of **Number** with the raw value "Number Two" and then check that the variable contains the proper **case** value with an **if** statement.

Enumeration can also include custom methods and computed properties. The following example adds a method to our **Number** enumeration that prints a message depending on the instance's current value.

Listing 5-9: Adding methods to an enumeration

```
enum Number: Int {
   case one
   case two
   case three

   func getMessage() -> String {
      switch self {
         case .one:
            return "We are the best"
         case .two:
            return "We have to study more"
         case .three:
            return "This is just the beginning"
      }
   }
}
var mynumber = Number.two
print(mynumber.getMessage())  // "We have to study more"
```

When we need to check the current value of the instance from inside a method, we must use the **self** keyword. This keyword refers to the instance where the method is being executed (in our case, **mynumber**), and this is how we can check for the instance's current value and return the right message. (We will learn more about the **self** keyword in Chapter 6.)

Associated Values

Enumerations include the possibility to associate values to a case. These are values we can attach to a case when variables of that type are initialized. For instance, in the following example we create an enumeration that can store information about a character, but it differentiates between letters and numbers.

Listing 5-10: Associating values

```
enum MyCharacters {
   case number(Int, String)
   case letter(Character, String)
}
var character = MyCharacters.number(1, "Number One")

switch character {
   case .number(let value, let description):
      print("\(description) - \(value)")  // "Number One - 1"
   case .letter(let letter, let description):
      print("\(description) - \(letter)")
}
```

This example defines an enumeration called **MyCharacters** that includes two cases. The first case is called **number** and it takes two associated values: an integer and a string. The second case is called **letter** and it also takes two associated values: a character and a string. When we create a value of this type, we must select the `case` value, as always, but we must also specify the associated values. If the value of the enumeration is **number**, we must provide an integer and a string, and if the value is **letter**, we must provide a character and a string. The example in Listing 5-10 creates an instance with the value **number** and the associated values 1 and "Number One", and then checks the value with a `switch` statement. Note that in each `case` we test whether the value is **number** or **letter** and extract their associated values with constants between parentheses.

If we need to check a single case, we can use an **if** or a **guard** statement and assign the value only to the case we want to check.

Listing 5-11: Checking the value of an enumeration with an if statement

```
enum MyCharacters {
   case number(Int, String)
   case letter(Character, String)
}
var character = MyCharacters.number(1, "Number One")

if case .number(let number, let text) = character {
   print("Number: \(number)")  // "Number: 1"
   print("Text: \(text)")  // "Text: Number One"
}
```

This syntax includes the **case** keyword and the necessary constants to receive the values. The statement is saying something like "Assign the value to this case, if not possible, return false". In our example, if the **character** variable doesn't contain a **MyCharacters** enumeration with the value **number**, the statement returns **false** and nothing is done; otherwise, the associated values in the **character** variable are assigned to the constants and printed on the console.

Chapter 6
Objects

BASIC

6.1 - Swift Objects

Objects are data types that encapsulate data and functionality in the form of properties and methods, but unlike the structures and enumerations introduced before they are stored by reference, which means that more than one variable can reference the same object in memory.

BASIC

Definition of Objects

Like structures and enumerations, objects are defined first and then instances are created from their definition. The definitions of objects are called *Classes*, and what we called objects are the instances created from those classes. Classes are declared the same way as structures or enumerations, but instead of the **struct** or **enum** keywords we must use the **class** keyword.

Listing 6-1: Defining a class

```
import Playgrounds

#Playground {
    class Employee {
        var name = "Undefined"
        var age = 0
    }
}
```

Do It Yourself

Update the **MyPlayground.swift** file in your project with the code in Listing 6-1. This code only defines a class, so you won't see anything on the Canvas, but you can use it as a starting point to test the rest of the examples in this chapter. As always, ask your AI agent for help whenever you have trouble understanding a topic or how any of the examples work.

The previous example defines a simple class called **Employee** with two properties: **name** and **age**. As always, this does not create anything, it is just defining a new custom data type. To store data in memory in this format, we must assign an instance of this class to a constant or variable.

Listing 6-2: Creating an object from a class

```
class Employee {
   var name = "Undefined"
   var age = 0
}
let employee1 = Employee()
employee1.name = "John"
employee1.age = 32
```

In Listing 6-2, the **Employee()** initializer creates a new instance of the class **Employee**. The words instance and object are synonyms, so we can say that in this example we have created a new object called **employee1** containing two properties, **name** and **age**.

Of course, we can also modify the values of the properties of an object from its methods, but unlike structures, we don't need to declared them as **mutating**, as shown below.

Listing 6-3: Modifying properties from the object's methods

```
class Employee {
   var name = "Undefined"
   var age = 0

   func changename(newname: String, newage: Int) {
      name = newname
      age = newage
   }
}
let employee1 = Employee()
employee1.changename(newname: "Martin", newage: 32)
print("Name: \(employee1.name)")  // "Name: Martin"
```

In Listing 6-3, the **changename()** method is added to the **Employee** class to modify the values of the properties. After the instance is created, we call this method to assign the values "Martin" and 32 to the **name** and **age** properties, respectively.

> **IMPORTANT**
>
> As well as structures, we can create all the objects we need from the same definition (class). Each object will have its own properties, methods, and values. Later we will see how these objects and their values are stored in memory.

BASIC

Type Properties and Methods

We have studied type properties and methods before with structures. These are properties and methods accessible from the data type, not the instances. They work in classes the same way as in structures, but instead of the **static** keyword we must use the **class** keyword to define them.

Listing 6-4: Declaring a type method for a class

```
class Employee {
   var name = "Undefined"
   var age = 0

   class func description() {
      print("This class stores the name and age of an employee")
   }
}
Employee.description()
```

This example defines an **Employee** class with two properties: **name** and **age**. The type method declared next is just describing the purpose of the class. Every time the **description()** method is executed on the class, a description is printed on the console. Again, we don't have to create an instance because the method is executed on the class itself.

> **IMPORTANT**
>
> Classes can also use the **static** keyword to define type properties and methods. The difference between the **static** and **class** keywords is that properties and methods defined with the **static** keyword are immutable and those defined with the **class** keyword can be modified by subclasses. (We will learn about subclasses and inheritance later in this chapter.)

BASIC

Reference Types

Structures and enumerations are value types. This means that every time we assign a variable of any of these data types to another variable, the value is copied. For example, if we create an instance of a structure and then assign that instance to another variable, we end up with two instances of the same structure in memory, as illustrated below.

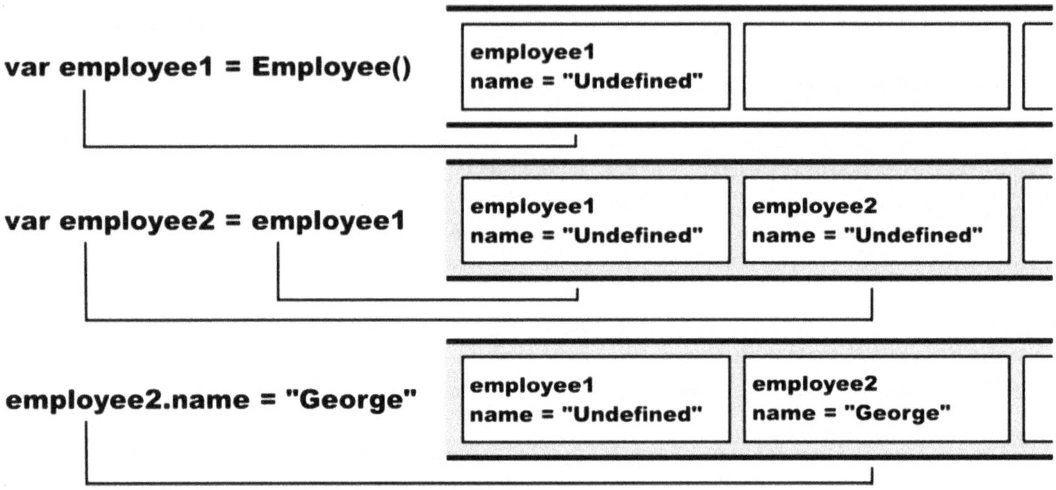

Figure 6-1: *Value types stored in memory*

Figure 6-1 shows how two different copies of the **Employee** structure, one referenced by the variable **employee1** and the other referenced by the variable **employee2**, are stored in memory. Any modification to the values of one of the instances will not affect the other, because they occupy different spaces in memory.

IMPORTANT

Structures and enumerations are copied because they conform to the **`Copyable`** protocol. If you need to create unique copies of values, you can declare the instance as noncopyable. We will learn more about protocols later. For more information about noncopyable types, visit our website and follow the links for this chapter.

Objects, on the other hand, are passed by reference. This means that when we assign an object to a constant or a variable, they store a reference to the object, not the object itself. In the following example, the object in **employee2** is the same as the object in **employee1**. Any change performed on the object from one variable is reflected in the other because both variables point to the same object in memory (they reference the same instance).

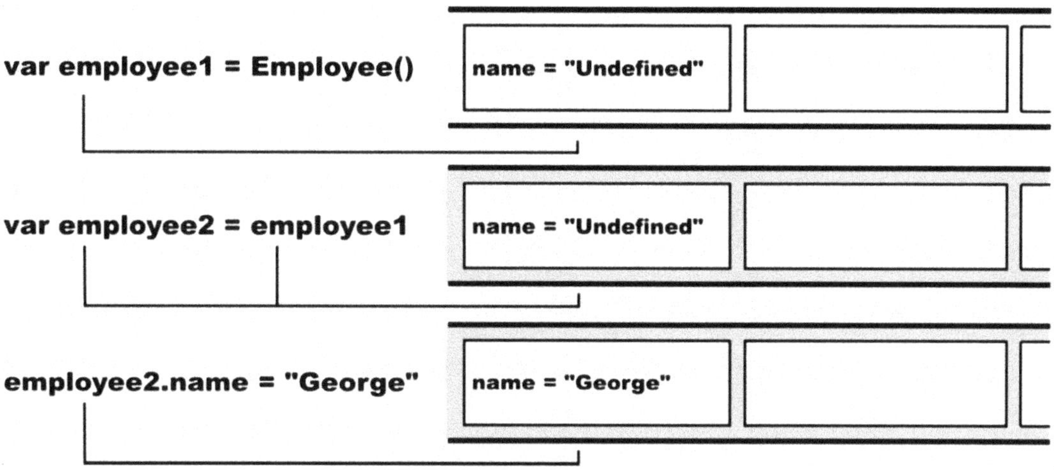

Figure 6-2: *Objects stored in memory*

Constants or variables that were assigned an object do not store the object; they store the value of the memory address where the object is located. When a constant or a variable containing this address is assigned to another constant or variable, only the address is copied, and therefore the object is not duplicated. This is the most important characteristic of objects, and what makes them suitable for situations in which data in memory must be accessed and shared by different parts of the code.

> **IMPORTANT**
>
> Because constants and variables store a reference to an object (a memory address), two or more variables in your code may reference the same object. If you need to know whether this is the case, you can compare the variables with the operators **===** (identical to) and **!==** (not identical to) provided by Swift. If what you need is to know whether two objects contain different information, you can use the basic operators **==** and **!=**, but you can only do this when the objects conform to the **Equatable** protocol (a protocol that determines how the objects are compared). We will study protocols and the **Equatable** protocol in Chapter 7.

BASIC

Self

Because the same object may be referenced by multiple constants or variables, every language that works with objects offers a way for the object to reference itself. In Swift, this is done automatically, but there are situations in which this reference must be declared explicitly. For this purpose, Swift defines a special keyword called **self**. We have introduced this keyword earlier to read the current value of an enumeration from inside the instance (see Chapter 5, Listing 5-9). In structures and objects, the **self** keyword works the same way; it references the instance to which the values belong.

The most common situation requiring the use of this keyword is when the names of the parameters of a method are equal to the names of the properties of the object. If the names are the same, the system does not know whether we are trying to modify the property or the parameter. The `self` keyword clarifies the situation.

Listing 6-5: Referencing the object with self

```
class Employee {
   var name = "Undefined"

   func changename(name: String) {
      self.name = name
   }
}
let employee1 = Employee()
employee1.changename(name: "Martin")

print("Name: \(employee1.name)")  // "Name: Martin"
```

The **self** keyword in the **changename()** method of Listing 6-5 represents the object created from the **Employee** class and helps the system understand what we are trying to access when we use the word **name**. Because we use `self`, when we call the **changename()** method in the **employee1** object, the value of the **name** parameter is assigned to the object's **name** property (**self.name**).

The **self** keyword in this example is a reference to the object stored in the **employee1** variable. This would be the same as declaring **employee1.name**, but since we do not know the name of the variable that is going to store the instance when the class is defined, we must use **self** instead.

Another useful application of the **self** keyword is to reference the data type itself. The value generated by reading the **self** keyword on a data type is called *Metatype*. A metatype refers to the type itself, not an instance of it. For example, the value **Int.self** refers to the definition of the **Int** data type, not an integer number created from that type, as shown in the following example.

Listing 6-6: Referring to the data type with self

```
let reference = Int.self
let newnumber = reference.init(20)
print(newnumber)  // "20"
```

The code in Listing 6-6 stores a reference to the **Int** data type in a constant and then uses that constant to create an instance of **Int** with the value `20`. Note that when working with metatypes we must call the **init()** method implicitly to create an instance. Metatypes are widely used to pass references of data types to methods and initializers of other types, as we will see in further chapters.

PRO

Memory Management

Since objects are stored by reference, they can be referenced by multiple variables at the same time. If a variable is no longer used, the object referenced by that variable cannot be deleted from memory because another variable could still be using it. This could result in memory being filled with objects that are no longer needed by the application. The solution offered by Swift is an automatic system that counts the number of variables that reference an object and does not remove the object from memory until all references have been cleared (all the variables have been deleted, set to **nil**, or are referencing another object). The system is called ARC (Automatic Reference Counting). ARC automatically deletes the objects when there is no longer a constant or a variable referencing that location in memory.

In normal circumstances, this system works automatically by tracking how many references point to the same object and deallocating that object when none of those references remain. However, there are situations in which a strong reference cycle can be created. This occurs when two objects have properties that reference the other object, as shown below.

Listing 6-7: Referencing one object from another

```
class Employee {
   var name: String?
   var location: Department?
}
class Department {
   var area: String?
   var person: Employee?
}
var employee: Employee? = Employee()
var department: Department? = Department()

employee?.name = "John"
employee?.location = department

department?.area = "Mail"
department?.person = employee
```

This example defines two classes: **Employee** and **Department**. Both classes contain a property that references an object of the other class (**location** and **person**). After the definition, objects of each class are created and stored in the **employee** and **department** variables. The reference in the **department** variable is assigned to the **location** property of the **employee** object, and the reference in the **employee** variable is assigned to the **person** property of the **department** object. After this, each object contains a reference to the other.

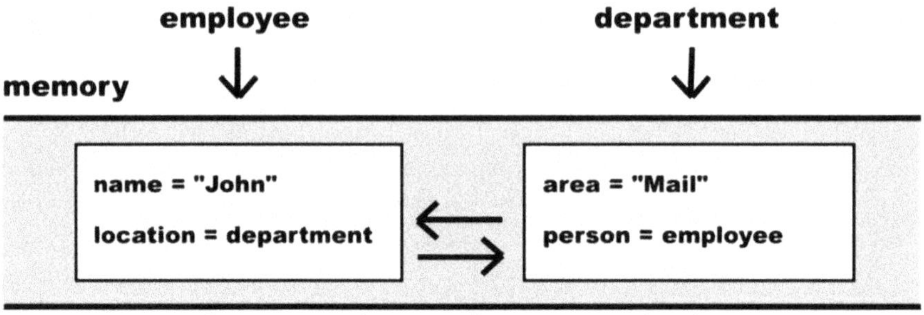

Figure 6-3: *Objects referencing each other*

At this point, each object is referenced by a variable and a property. The object of the **Employee** class is referenced by the **employee** variable and the **person** property, and the object of the **Department** class is referenced by the **department** variable and the **location** property. If, for some reason, we do not need to access these objects from our code anymore and erase or modify the values of the **employee** and **department** variables, ARC will not erase the objects from memory because their properties still have a reference that keeps them alive.

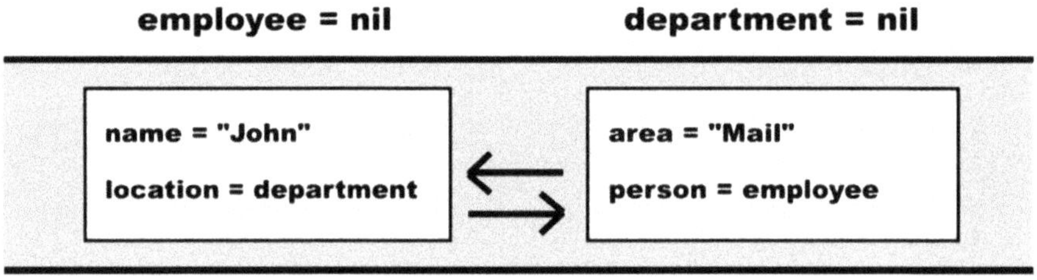

Figure 6-4: *Objects preserved in memory*

In this example, we assume that the value **nil** was assigned to the **employee** and **department** variables, and in consequence the objects are not accessible from code anymore, but they are preserved in memory because ARC has no way to know that they are no longer required.

Swift solves this problem by classifying the references into three categories: strong, weak, and unowned. Normal references are strong; they are always valid and the objects associated to them are preserved in memory for as long as they exist. These are the kind of references we have been using so far, and that is why the cycle created by our example is called *Strong Reference Cycle*. The solution to break this cycle is to define one of the references as **weak** or **unowned**. When ARC encounters one of these types of references to be the last reference to an object, the object is erased from memory as if the reference had never existed.

Listing 6-8: Assigning weak references

```
class Employee {
   var name: String?
   var location: Department?
}
```

```
class Department {
    var area: String?
    weak var person: Employee?
}
var employee: Employee? = Employee()
var department: Department? = Department()

employee?.name = "John"
employee?.location = department

department?.area = "Mail"
department?.person = employee
```

In the code of Listing 6-8, the **person** property was declared as **weak**. Now, when the references from the variables are erased, the object created from the **Employee** class is erased from memory because the only reference left is the weak reference from the **person** property. After this object disappears, the object created from the **Department** class does not have any other strong reference either, so it is also erased from memory.

An **`unowned`** reference works in a similar way, but it differs from a **`weak`** reference in the types of values it applies to. Weak references apply to variables with optional values, since they can become **`nil`** at some point, while unowned references apply to non-optional values, which are expected to always have a value.

IMPORTANT

Closures can create strong reference cycles if we try to access properties or methods defined outside the closure. If we need to reference properties or methods with **self** inside a closure, we can declare the reference to **self** as weak with the syntax **[weak self]** or **[unowned self]**. The expression must be declared before the closure's parameters. For more information on ARC and how to avoid strong reference cycles, visit our website and follow the links for this chapter.

BASIC

Inheritance

One of the main purposes of objects is to define pieces of code that can be reused and shared. The code is defined once and then instances (copies) of that code are created every time they are required. This programming pattern works well when we define our own code but presents some limitations when working with code programmed by other developers and shared through libraries and frameworks. The programmers defining the classes for us cannot anticipate how we are going to use them and all the possible variations required for every application. To provide a solution to this problem, classes incorporate inheritance. A class can inherit properties and methods from another class and then improve it by adding properties and methods of its own. This way, programmers can share classes and developers can adapt them to their needs.

To illustrate how inheritance works, the following examples present a situation in which a class must be expanded to contain additional information that was not initially contemplated.

Listing 6-9: Defining a basic class

```
class Employee {
   var name = "Undefined"
   var age = 0

   func createbadge() -> String {
      return "Employee \(name) \(age)"
   }
}
```

The **Employee** class declared in Listing 6-9 is a normal class, like those we have defined before. It has two properties and a method called **createbadge()** that returns a string with the values of the properties. This class would be enough to create objects that generate the string of text necessary to print a badge for every employee with his or her name and age. But for the sake of argument, let's say that some of the employees require a badge that also displays the department they work in. One option is to define another class with the same properties and methods and add what we need, but this produces redundant code, and it is difficult to do when the class was taken from a library (they are usually not accessible or too complex to modify or duplicate). The solution is to create a new class that inherits the characteristics of the basic class and adds its own properties and methods to satisfy the new requirements.

To indicate that a class inherits from another class, we must write the name of the basic class after the name of the new class separated by a colon, as shown below.

Listing 6-10: Inheriting properties and methods from another class

```
class Employee {
   var name = "Undefined"
   var age = 0

   func createbadge() -> String {
      return "Employee \(name) \(age)"
   }
}
class OfficeEmployee: Employee {
   var department = "Undefined"
}
```

The **OfficeEmployee** class added to our code in Listing 6-10 only has one property called **department**, but it inherits the **name** and **age** properties, and also the **createbadge()** method from the **Employee** class. All these properties and methods are available in any of the objects created from the **OfficeEmployee** class, as shown below.

Listing 6-11: Creating objects from a subclass

```
class Employee {
   var name = "Undefined"
   var age = 0

   func createbadge() -> String {
      return "Employee \(name) \(age)"
   }
}
class OfficeEmployee: Employee {
   var department = "Undefined"
}
let employee = OfficeEmployee()
employee.name = "George"
employee.age = 25
employee.department = "Mail"

var badge = employee.createbadge()
print("Badge: \(badge)")  // "Badge: Employee George 25"
```

A class like **Employee** is called *Superclass*, and a class that inherits from another class like **OfficeEmployee** is called *Subclass*. In these terms, we can say that the **OfficeEmployee** class is a subclass that inherits the properties and methods of the **Employee** superclass. A class can inherit from a superclass that already inherited from another superclass in an infinite chain. When a property is accessed, or a method is called, the system looks for it on the object's class and, if it is not there, it keeps looking in the superclasses up the hierarchical chain until it finds it.

IMPORTANT

Inheritance does not work the other way around. For example, considering the code in Listing 6-11, objects created from the class **OfficeEmployee** have access to the **department** property of this class and the properties and methods of the **Employee** class, but objects created from the **Employee** class do not have access to the **department** property.

Because of this hierarchical chain, sometimes a method does not have access to all the properties available to the object. For example, the **createbadge()** method called on the **employee** object created in Listing 6-11 have access to the properties declared on the **Employee** class but not those declared in the **OfficeEmployee** class. If we want the method to also print the value of the **department** property, we must implement it again in the **OfficeEmployee** class with the appropriate modifications. This is called *Overriding*. To override a method of a superclass, we prefix it with the **override** keyword.

Listing 6-12: Overriding an inherited method

```
class Employee {
   var name = "Undefined"
   var age = 0

   func createbadge() -> String {
      return "Employee \(name) \(age)"
   }
}
class OfficeEmployee: Employee {
   var department = "Undefined"

   override func createbadge() -> String {
      return "Employee \(department) \(name) \(age)"
   }
}
let employee = OfficeEmployee()
employee.name = "George"
employee.age = 25
employee.department = "Mail"

var badge = employee.createbadge()
print("Badge: \(badge)")  // "Badge: Employee Mail George 25"
```

The new **OfficeEmployee** subclass in Listing 6-12 overrides the **createbadge()** method of its superclass to generate a string that includes the value of the **department** property. Now, when the method is called from an object of this class, the system executes the one defined in **OfficeEmployee** (the old method from the superclass is ignored), and therefore the badge includes the values of the three properties.

When we call the **createbadge()** method on the **employee** object created from the **OfficeEmployee** class in Listing 6-12, the method executed is always the one defined in the **OfficeEmployee** class. If we want to execute the method on the superclass instead, we must use a special keyword called **super**. The **super** keyword is like the **self** keyword, but instead of representing the object, **super** represents the superclass. It is often used when we have overridden a method but we still need to execute the method on the superclass, as shown below.

Listing 6-13: Calling a method on the superclass

```
class Employee {
   var name = "Undefined"
   var age = 0

   func createbadge() -> String {
      return "Employee \(name) \(age)"
   }
}
class OfficeEmployee: Employee {
   var department = "Undefined"

   override func createbadge() -> String {
```

```
        let oldbadge = super.createbadge()
        return "\(oldbadge) \(department)"
    }
}
let employee = OfficeEmployee()
employee.name = "George"
employee.age = 25
employee.department = "Mail"

var badge = employee.createbadge()
print("Badge: \(badge)")  // "Badge: Employee George 25 Mail"
```

This is the same as the previous example, but now, when the **createbadge()** method of an object created from the **OfficeEmployee** class is called, the method calls the **createbadge()** method of the superclass first and assigns the result to the **oldbadge** constant. The value of this constant is later added to the value of the **department** property to generate the string to return.

BASIC

Type Casting

Inheritance not only transfers functionality from one class to another but also connects the classes together. The superclasses and their subclasses are linked together in a hierarchical chain. Because of this, whenever we declare a variable of the type of the superclass, objects of the subclasses can be assigned to that variable too. This allows us to do things like creating arrays of objects that are of different classes but belong to the same hierarchy, as shown below.

Listing 6-14: Creating an array of objects from different subclasses

```
class Employee {
    var name = "Undefined"
    var age = 0
}
class OfficeEmployee: Employee {
    var deskNumber = 0
}
class WarehouseEmployee: Employee {
    var area = "Undefined"
}
var list: [Employee] = [OfficeEmployee(), WarehouseEmployee(),
OfficeEmployee()]
```

This example defines a superclass called **Employee** and then two subclasses of **Employee** called **OfficeEmployee** and **WarehouseEmployee**. The purpose is to have the information for every employee in one class and then have classes for specific types of employee. Following this organization, we can create objects that contain the **name**, **age**, and **deskNumber** properties to represent employees working at the office and objects that contain the **name**, **age**, and **area** properties to represent employees working at the warehouse.

No matter the differences between one object and another, they all represent employees of the same company, so sooner or later we will have to include them in the same list. The class hierarchy allows us to do that. We can declare a collection of the data type of the superclass and then store objects of the subclasses in it, as we did in Listing 6-14 with the **list** array.

This is all good until we try to read the array. The array was declared of type **Employee**, so we can only access the properties defined in the **Employee** class. Also, there is no way to know what type of object each element is. We could have an **OfficeEmployee** object at index 0 and later replace it with a **WarehouseEmployee** object. The indexes do not provide any information to identify the objects. Swift solves these problems with the **is** and **as** operators.

is

This operator returns a Boolean value indicating whether the value is of a certain data type.

as

This operator converts a value of one class to another class when possible.

Identifying an object is easy with the **is** operator. This operator returns a Boolean value that we can use in an **if** statement to check the object's class.

Listing 6-15: Identifying the object's data type

```
var countOffice = 0
var countWarehouse = 0

for obj in list {
   if obj is OfficeEmployee {
      countOffice += 1
   } else if obj is WarehouseEmployee {
      countWarehouse += 1
   }
}
print("We have \(countOffice) employees working at the office")  // 2
print("We have \(countWarehouse) employees working at the warehouse") //1
```

In Listing 6-15, we create the **list** array again with objects from the same classes defined in the previous example, but this time we add a **for in** loop to iterate over the array and count how many objects of each class we have found. The **if** statement inside the loop implements the **is** operator to check if the current object stored in the **obj** constant is of type **OfficeEmployee** or **WarehouseEmployee** and increments the counter respectively (**countOffice** or **countWarehouse**).

Counting objects is not really what these operators are all about. The idea is to figure out the type with the **is** operator and then convert the object with the **as** operator to be able to access their specific properties and methods. The **as** operator converts a value of one type to another. The conversions are not always guaranteed, and that is why this operator comes in two more forms: **as!** and **as?**. These versions of the **as** operator work like optionals. The

as! operator forces the conversion and returns an error if the conversion is not possible, and the **as?** operator tries to convert the object and returns an optional with the new object or **nil** in case of failure. The following example illustrates how to use the `as!` operator.

Listing 6-16: Casting an object

```
class Employee {
   var name = "Undefined"
   var age = 0
}
class OfficeEmployee: Employee {
   var deskNumber = 0
}
class WarehouseEmployee: Employee {
   var area = "Undefined"
}
var list: [Employee] = [OfficeEmployee(), WarehouseEmployee(),
OfficeEmployee()]

for obj in list {
   if obj is OfficeEmployee {
      let temp = obj as! OfficeEmployee
      temp.deskNumber = 100
   } else if obj is WarehouseEmployee {
      let temp = obj as! WarehouseEmployee
      temp.area = "New Area"
   }
}
```

When we use the `as!` operator we are forcing the conversion, so we need to make sure that the conversion is possible, otherwise the app will crash. In the code in Listing 6-16, we only use this operator after we have already checked with the **is** operator that the object is of the right class. Once the object is casted (converted) into its original data type, we can access its specific properties and methods. In this example, the objects returned by the **as!** operator are stored in the **temp** constant and then new values are assigned to the **deskNumber** and **area** properties.

Checking for the type before casting is redundant. To simplify the code, we can use the **as?** operator. Instead of forcing the conversion and crashing the app, this version of the **as** operator tries to perform the conversion and returns an optional with the result.

Listing 6-17: Casting an object with the as? operator

```
for obj in list {
   if let temp = obj as? OfficeEmployee {
      temp.deskNumber = 100
   } else if let temp = obj as? WarehouseEmployee {
      temp.area = "New Area"
   }
}
```

In this example, we use optional binding to cast the object and assign the result to the **temp** constant. First, we try to cast **obj** as an **OfficeEmployee** object. If we are successful, we assign the value `100` to the **deskNumber** property, but if the value returned is **nil**, we cast the object to the **WarehouseEmployee** class and modify its **area** property.

If we are sure that the conversion is possible, casting can also be performed on the fly. The statement to cast the object is the same but it must be declared between parentheses, as shown below.

Listing 6-18: Casting an object on the fly

```
let myarea = (list[1] as! WarehouseEmployee).area
print("The area of employee 1 is \(myarea)")
// "The area of employee 1 is New Area"
```

In this example, we do not assign the object to any variable; we just cast the element of the **list** array at index 1 as a **WarehouseEmployee** object inside the parentheses and then read the **area** property. The value of this property is stored in the **myarea** constant and then printed on the console.

IMPORTANT

The **as!** operator is applied when the conversion is guaranteed to be successful, and the **as?** operator is used when we are not sure about the result. But we can also use the basic **as** operator when the Swift compiler can verify that the conversion will be successful, as when we are casting some data types, such as **String** values into **NSString** objects. We will see some examples of these types of casting in Chapter 9.

Because sometimes the objects that require casting are not in the same hierarchy, Swift defines several generic data types to represent values of any kind. The most frequently used are **Any** (structures), **AnyObject** (objects), and **AnyClass** (classes). By taking advantage of these generic types, we can create collections with values that are not associated with each other.

Listing 6-19: Working with objects of AnyObject type

```
class Employee {
   var name = "Undefined"
}
class Department {
   var area = "Undefined"
}
var list: [AnyObject] = [Employee(), Department(), Department()]

for obj in list {
   if let temp = obj as? Employee {
```

```
        temp.name = "New Employee"
    } else if let temp = obj as? Department {
        temp.area = "New Area"
    }
}
```

The **list** array declared in Listing 6-19 is of type **AnyObject** and therefore it can contain objects of any data type. To populate the array, we created two simple and independent classes: **Employee** and **Department**. A few objects are created from these classes and included in the array. The objects are later casted by the **as?** operator inside a **for in** loop and their properties are modified following the same procedure used in previous examples.

BASIC

Extensions

In addition to inheritance, we can add functionality to an existing data type using extensions. Extensions can be used to expand our own structures, enumerations, and classes, and also to extend data types for which we do not have access to the original definition, such as those provided by libraries and frameworks. To define an extension, we prefix the name of the data type with the `extension` keyword. For example, we can extend the `Int` structure to provide a method that prints a description of its value.

Listing 6-20: Extending data types

```
import Playgrounds

extension Int {
    func printdescription() {
        print("The number is \(self)")
    }
}
#Playground {
    let number = 25
    number.printdescription()   // "The number is 25"
}
```

The **Int** data type is a structure defined in the Swift Standard Library. We cannot modify its definition but we can extend it to add more functionality. In this example, we add a method called **printdescription()** to print a message with the current value. This method is not included in the original definition, but it is now available in our code from every instance of the `Int` structure.

Of course, we can also extend our own data types if we consider it appropriate. The following example extends our **Employees** structure to add a new method.

Listing 6-21: Extending custom data types

```
import Playgrounds

struct Employees {
   var name: String
   var age: Int
}
extension Employees {
   func printbadge() {
      print("Name: \(name), Age: \(age)")
   }
}
#Playground {
   let employee = Employees(name: "John", age: 50)
   employee.printbadge()  // "Name: John, Age: 50"
}
```

Extensions can also be conditional. For instance, if we have a generic structure, we can add an extension only for specific types of values. The condition is determined by the **where** clause. The clause works like an **if** statement, so the extension is only applied if the condition is met.

Listing 6-22: Defining a conditional extension

```
import Playgrounds

struct Employees<T> {
   var value: T
}
extension Employees where T == Int {
   func doubleValue() {
      print("\(value) times 2 = \(value * 2)")
   }
}
#Playground {
   let employee = Employees(value: 25)
   employee.doubleValue()  // "25 times 2 = 50"
}
```

In this example, we define a generic structure called **Employees** with a generic property called **value** and then define an extension for this structure with a method called **doubleValue()**, but this method will only be added to the instance if the data type used to create the instance is **Int**. At the end, we create an instance with the value **25** and call the method, which multiplies the value by 2 and prints a string with the result. This works because we created the instance with an integer, but if we try to use another type of value, Xcode will show an error.

Another useful implementation of extensions is the customization of string interpolation. We have introduced string interpolation in Chapter 2 and have been using it in almost every example to insert values in strings (e.g., **print("My name is \(name)")**). What we haven't mentioned is that these values are managed by a structure called **StringInterpolation** (a typealias of **DefaultStringInterpolation**) and that by extending this structure we can customize how the system processes the values. The **StringInterpolation** structure includes the following methods for this purpose.

appendInterpolation(Value)

This method interpolates the value provided by the argument into the final string.

appendLiteral(String)

This method adds the string provided by the argument to the interpolation.

To customize the interpolation, we must extend the **StringInterpolation** structure with an overload of the **appendInterpolation()** method, process the value inside this method, and finally append the result to the interpolation with the **appendLiteral()** method.

Listing 6-23: Customizing string interpolation

```
import Playgrounds

extension String.StringInterpolation {
   mutating func appendInterpolation(celsius value: Double) {
      let fahrenheit = ((value * 9)/5) + 32
      appendLiteral(String(fahrenheit))
   }
}
#Playground {
   print("Temperature in Fahrenheit \(celsius: 25)")
   // "Temperature in Fahrenheit 77.0"
}
```

The **appendInterpolation()** method can take as many parameters as we need. In this example, we define only one parameter with the name **value** and a label called **celsius**. When we create a string with this label and a number, the method is executed. Within the method, we use a formula to turn Celsius degrees into Fahrenheit and then add the result to the interpolation with the **appendLiteral()** method to get the string "Temperature in Fahrenheit 77.0".

BASIC

Initialization

So far, we have initialized the properties of classes in the definition. This is because classes, unlike structures, do not provide memberwise initializers. The properties of a class must be initialized explicitly in the definition or when they are instantiated with the `init()` method.

Listing 6-24: Declaring a Designated Initializer

```
class Employee {
   var name: String
   var age: Int

   init(name: String, age: Int) {
      self.name = name
      self.age = age
   }
}
let employee1 = Employee(name: "George", age: 28)
```

The **init()** method declared for the **Employee** class in Listing 6-24 initializes every property of the class with the values specified by the **Employee()** initializer. This type of initializer is called *Designated Initializer*. When we declare a Designated Initializer, we need to make sure that all the properties are initialized.

If we know that our code will not be able to provide all the values during initialization, we can also declare a Convenience Initializer. A Convenience Initializer is an initializer that offers a convenient way to initialize an object with values by default for some or all of its properties. It is declared with the **init()** method but preceded by the **convenience** keyword. A Convenience Initializer must call the Designated initializer with the corresponding values, as shown below.

Listing 6-25: Declaring a Convenience Initializer

```
class Employee {
   var name: String
   var age: Int

   init(name: String, age: Int) {
      self.name = name
      self.age = age
   }
   convenience init() {
      self.init(name: "Undefined", age: 0)
   }
}
let employee1 = Employee()
```

When we create an instance of **Employee**, the system detects the number and type of arguments we specify and executes the corresponding initializer. For example, if we provide the values for the **name** and the **age** parameters, the system executes the Designated Initializer because this is the initializer that contains the necessary parameters to receive those values, but if the initialization does not include any argument, the Convenience Initializer is executed instead and then the Designated Initializer is called with values by default (**`"Undefined"`** and **`0`**).

Unlike structures, classes can inherit properties and methods from other classes, and this includes the **init()** method. When a subclass does not provide its own Designated Initializer, the initializer of its superclass is used instead.

Listing 6-26: Inheriting the Designated Initializer

```
class Employee {
   var name: String
   var age: Int

   init(name: String, age: Int) {
      self.name = name
      self.age = age
   }
}
class OfficeEmployee: Employee {
   var department: String = "Undefined"
}
let employee1 = OfficeEmployee(name: "George", age: 29)
```

The code in Listing 6-26 defines the subclass **OfficeEmployee** that inherits from the **Employee** class. The **OfficeEmployee** class does not provide any initializer, so the only initializer available is the one provided by its superclass. This initializer only initializes the properties **name** and **age**. The **department** property of **OfficeEmployee** is explicitly initialized with the string "Undefined". To provide an initializer that also includes this property, we must declare a new Designated Initializer in the **OfficeEmployee** class, as shown below.

Listing 6-27: Declaring a Designated Initializer for the subclass

```
class Employee {
   var name: String
   var age: Int

   init(name: String, age: Int) {
      self.name = name
      self.age = age
   }
}
class OfficeEmployee: Employee {
   var department: String

   init(name: String, age: Int, department: String) {
      self.department = department

      super.init(name: name, age: age)
   }
}
let employee1 = OfficeEmployee(name: "John", age: 24, department: "Mail")
```

The Designated Initializer of a subclass must initialize the properties of its own class first and then call the initializer of its superclass. This is done by calling the **init()** method on **super**. The **super** keyword refers to the superclass, so when the system executes the **super.init()** statement in the code in Listing 6-27, the **init()** method of the superclass is executed and the **name** and **age** properties of this class are initialized.

IMPORTANT

There are different ways to combine Designated and Convenience initializers. The possibility of classes to inherit from other classes in an unlimited chain can turn initialization into a very complex process. This book does not explore all the possibilities provided by Swift for initialization. For more information, visit our website and follow the links for this chapter.

PRO

Deinitialization

There is a counterpart of the initialization process called *Deinitialization*. Despite its name, this process is not directly related to the initialization process but rather to the ARC system. ARC, as we studied previously in this chapter, is an automatic system adopted by Swift to manage memory. Letting the system manage the memory and take care of removing the objects our program no longer needs presents a huge advantage, but it also means that we do not always know when an object is going to be removed. There are times when an object is using resources that must be released or information that needs to be stored. Whatever the task, Swift offers the **deinit** method to execute any last-minute instructions we need before the object is erased from memory.

Listing 6-28: Declaring a deinitializer

```
class Item {
   var quantity = 0.0
   var name = "Not defined"
   var price = 0.0

   deinit {
      print("This instance was erased")
   }
}
var purchase: Item? = Item()
purchase = nil
```

This example defines a simple class with a deinitializer. The object is created and assigned to an optional variable. Right after that, the **nil** value is assigned to the same variable to erase the reference and test the **deinit** method, which prints a message on the console.

PRO

Access Control and Modifiers

Swift defines keywords (also called modifiers) that can be applied to entities (classes, structures, properties, methods, and more) to confer them special attributes. We have already seen the **`mutating`** and **`override`** keywords, but there are others, as described below.

`lazy`

This keyword defines a property whose initial value is not assigned until the property is used for the first time.

`final`

This keyword is used on a class when we don't want to allow the code to create subclasses of it. It must be declared before the **class** keyword.

The **`lazy`** keyword is often used when our code needs some time to determine the value of a property and we don't want the initialization of the structure or the class to be delayed. For example, we may have a property that stores a name that is retrieved from a server, which is a resource intensive task that we should only perform when the value is required.

Listing 6-29: Defining lazy properties

```
class Employee {
   lazy var name: String = {
      // Loading name from a server
      print("Loading...")

      return "Undefined"
   }()
   var age = 0
}
let employee = Employee()
```

The **Employee** class in Listing 6-29 defines two properties, **name** and **age**, but this time a closure is assigned to the **name** property to get the employee's name from a server. Because we declared this property as **lazy**, the closure will only be executed when we try to read it. If we execute the example as it is, we get nothing in return, but if we read the **name** property with a statement at the end (e.g., **`print(employee.name)`**), we will see the text "Loading..." printed on the console.

The Swift language also includes keywords that define the level of access for each entity in our code. Access control in Swift is based on modules and source files. Source files are the files we create for our application, while modules are units of related code. For example, a single application and each framework it includes are considered separate modules (We will study frameworks in Chapter 9). Based on this classification, Swift defines five keywords to determine accessibility.

open

This keyword determines that an entity is accessible from the module it belongs to and other modules.

public

This keyword determines that an entity is accessible from the module it belongs to and other modules. The difference between **public** and **open** is that we can't create subclasses of **public** classes outside the module in which they were defined. This also applies to methods and properties (e.g., **public** methods can't be overridden outside the module in which they were declared).

internal

This keyword determines that an entity is accessible only inside the module in which it was created. This is the default access mode for applications. By default, every entity defined in our application is only accessible from inside the application.

private

This keyword determines that an entity is accessible only from the context in which it was created (e.g., a **private** property in a class will only be accessible from methods of the same class).

fileprivate

This keyword determines that an entity is accessible only from the file in which it was declared (e.g., a **fileprivate** property in a class will only be accessible by other entities defined inside the file in which it was declared).

As we will see later, most of these keywords apply to frameworks and are rarely used in single applications. By default, the properties and methods we include in our classes and structures are declared **internal**, which means that our classes and structures are only available from inside our application (module). Unless we are creating our own frameworks, this is all we need, and is the reason why we didn't have to specify any keyword when we defined our structures and classes before, but if we want to have some level of control in our data types or avoid modifying values by mistake, we can declare some of them as **private**, as shown below.

Listing 6-30: Declaring `private` properties

```
class Employee {
   private var name = "Undefined"
   private var age = 0

   func showValues() {
      print("Name: \(name)")
      print("Age: \(age)")
   }
}
let employee = Employee()
employee.showValues()
```

The code in Listing 6-30 defines the **name** and **age** properties of our **Employee** class as **private** and adds a method called **showValues()** to access their values. Due to access control, these properties are only accessible by the method in the class. If we try to read their values from outside the object using dot notation, Xcode will return an error.

If what we want is to be able to read the property from outside the object but not allow assigning new values to it, we can declare it with a public getter but a private setter, as shown below.

Listing 6-31: Declaring a public getter and private setter

```
class Employee {
   private var name = "Undefined"
   public private(set) var age = 0

   func setAge(newAge: Int) {
      age = newAge
   }
}
let employee = Employee()
employee.setAge(newAge: 25)
print(employee.age)
```

The **age** property in the **Employee** class in Listing 6-31 was declared as public, so everyone can read its value, but with a private setter (**private(set)**), so only the methods inside the class can modify it. To change the value, we defined the **setAge()** method. The code creates an instance of the class and calls the method, but this time we can read the value of the **age** property and print it on the console because it was declared with a public getter.

BASIC

Singletons

As already mentioned, we can create as many objects as we want from a single class. These objets are independent from one another; they have their own properties and methods and process their own values. But sometimes our code needs only one object to be created from a class, so every piece of code have access to the same object and works on the same values. To guarantee that only one instance of a class is created and the instance is available from anywhere in our code, the class needs to implement two things: a type property to create the only instance available, and a private initializer that doesn't allow the code to create more, as shown in the following example.

Listing 6-32: Defining a singleton

```
@MainActor
class Employee {
   var name: String
   var age: Int
```

```
    static let shared = Employee(newName: "Undefined", newAge: 0)

    private init(newName: String, newAge: Int) {
        name = newName
        age = newAge
    }
}
let employee1 = Employee.shared
let employee2 = Employee.shared
employee1.name = "George"

print("\(employee1.name) - \(employee2.name)")
// "George - George"
```

The **Employee** class in this example defines a type property called **shared** and initializes it with an instance of the same class, so every time we read this property from anywhere in the code, we get the same **Employee** object in return. For instance, in this example, we define two constants called **employee1** and **employee2**, and initialize them with the instance returned by the **shared** property. Because this is the same object, when we modify a value in the **employee1** object, the same value is returned by the **employee2** object.

Because the purpose of this class is to only allow the creation of one instance (one object), we prefix the initializer with the **private** keyword. As a result, only the single instance created by the **shared** property is available, which is the reason why the object created from this class is called *Singleton*.

IMPORTANT

Note that we have prefixed the definition of the class with the **@MainActor** modifier. This is to prevent the object in the **shared** property from being changed by different threads at the same time and causing an error called *data race*. The **@MainActor** modifier tells the system that objects of this class should only be used in the main thread. We will learn more about this modifier and data races in Chapter 12.

Chapter 7

Protocols

BASIC

7.1 - Swift Protocols

Structures and objects encapsulate data and functionality. Every structure and every object we create contains its own properties and methods to store and process data, and these properties and methods are defined to perform specific tasks. However, there are situations where different structures or objects need to share the same functionality. In these cases, we can define the required functionality in a protocol and then make our structures and classes conform to it.

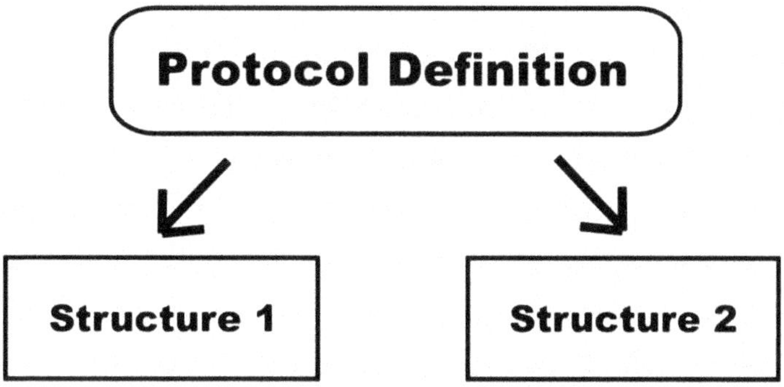

Figure 7-1: *Protocol-Oriented Programming*

Protocols define properties and methods that structures or classes must have in common. The properties and methods that structures or classes share are defined in the protocol and then implemented by the data types. The structures and classes that conform to a protocol remain independent and can provide their own functionality, but they are also guaranteed to implement the functionality specified by the protocol.

BASIC

Definition of Protocols

Protocols are defined with the **protocol** keyword followed by the name and the list of properties and methods between curly braces. No values or statements are assigned or declared inside a protocol, only the names and the corresponding data types. Because of this, methods are defined as always, but they omit the braces and the statements, and properties must include the **get** and **set** keywords between braces to indicate whether they are read-only properties, or we can read and assign values to them. To indicate that the structure conforms to the protocol, we must include the protocol's name after the name of the structure separated by a colon, as shown in the following example.

Listing 7-1: Defining protocols

```
protocol Printer {
   var name: String { get set }
   func printdescription()
}
struct Employees: Printer {
   var name: String
   var age: Int

   func printdescription() {
      print("Description: \(name) \(age)")
      // "Description: John 32"
   }
}
let employee1 = Employees(name: "John", age: 32)
employee1.printdescription()
```

A protocol tells the structure what properties and methods are required, but the structure must implement them. In Listing 7-1, we define a protocol called **Printer** that includes the **name** property and the **printdescription()** method. The **Employees** structure defined next conforms to this protocol, and along with the protocol's property and method it also implements its own property called **age**. Although this property was not defined in the protocol, we can read it inside the **printdescription()** method and print its value.

Do It Yourself

Update the code of the `#Playground` macro in your **MyPlayground.swift** file with the code in Listing 7-1. You should see the message "Description: John 32" printed on the console.

The advantage of using protocols is evident when structures of different types conform to the same protocol, as shown in the following example.

Listing 7-2: Defining multiple structures that conform to the same protocol

```
protocol Printer {
   var name: String { get set }
   func printdescription()
}
struct Employees: Printer {
   var name: String
   var age: Int
```

```
   func printdescription() {
      print("Description: \(name) \(age)")
   }
}
struct Offices: Printer {
   var name: String
   var employees: Int

   func printdescription() {
      print("Description: \(name) \(employees)")
      // "Description: Mail 2"
   }
}
let employee1 = Employees(name: "John", age: 32)
let office1 = Offices(name: "Mail", employees: 2)
office1.printdescription()
```

Although the structures created in Listing 7-2 from the **Employees** and **Offices** definitions are different (they have different properties), they both conform to the **Printer** protocol and provide their own implementation of the **printdescription()** method. The common functionality defined by the protocol ensures that no matter what type of structure we are working with, it will always have an implementation of **printdescription()**.

Protocols are also data types. This allows us to associate structures by their common functionality.

Listing 7-3: Using protocols as data types

```
let employee1 = Employees(name: "John", age: 32)
let office1 = Offices(name: "Mail", employees: 2)

var list: [Printer] = [employee1, office1]
for element in list {
   element.printdescription()
}
```

The code in Listing 7-3 uses the same protocol and structures defined in the previous example, but this time it stores the instances in an array. The type of the array was defined as **Printer**, which means the array can contain structures of any type as long as they conform to the **Printer** protocol. Because of this, no matter the element's data type (**Employees** or **Offices**) we know that they always have an implementation of the **name** property and the **printdescription()** method.

When we process a structure or an object as a protocol type, we can only access the properties and methods defined by the protocol. If we need to access the instance's own properties and methods, we must cast it using the **as** operator as we did with classes before. The following example prints the value of the **age** property if the element of the array is of type **Employees**.

Listing 7-4: Accessing the instance's own properties

```
let employee1 = Employees(name: "John", age: 32)
let office1 = Offices(name: "Mail", employees: 2)

var list: [Printer] = [employee1, office1]
for element in list {
   if let employee = element as? Employees {
      print(employee.age)  // "32"
   }
   element.printdescription()
}
```

Because protocols are data types, we can use them to define variables, or return them from functions. The following example declares a function that returns a value of type **Printer**.

Listing 7-5: Returning values of a protocol type

```
func getFile(type: Int) -> Printer {
   var data: Printer!
   if type == 1 {
      data = Employees(name: "John", age: 32)
   } else if type == 2 {
      data = Offices(name: "Mail", employees: 2)
   }
   return data
}
let file = getFile(type: 1)
file.printdescription()  // "Description: John 32"
```

The **getFile()** function in Listing 7-5 creates an instance of a structure depending on the value received. If the **type** parameter is equal to 1, it returns an instance of **Employees**, but if the value is equal to 2, it returns an instance of **Offices**. But because the value returned by the function is of type **Printer** we know that it will always include the **printdescription()** method, so we can use it.

PRO

Protocol Composition

A data type can conform to two or more protocols at the same time. This is known as *protocol composition*. The protocols the data type must conform to are declared together in its definition, separated by commas. For example, we can make the **`Employees`** structure conform to the **`Printer`** protocol, as before, and also to a new protocol that defines a method for uppercasing all the letters in the name.

Listing 7-6: Conforming to multiple protocols

```
protocol Printer {
   var name: String { get set }
   func printdescription()
}
protocol Highlight {
   func highlightName()
}

struct Employees: Printer, Highlight {
   var name: String
   var age: Int

   func printdescription() {
      print("Description: \(name) \(age)")
   }
   func highlightName() {
      print(name.uppercased())
   }
}
let employee1 = Employees(name: "John", age: 32)
employee1.printdescription()  // "Description: John 32"
employee1.highlightName()  // "JOHN"
```

Now the **Employees** structure must implement two methods: the **printdescription()** method defined by the **Printer** protocol, and the **highlightName()** method defined by the **Highlight** protocol.

As already mentioned, protocols can be used as data types. This allows us to pass and return values from functions based on the protocols they conform to rather than on their concrete types. When a value conforms to a single protocol, we can simply declare that protocol as the return type, as shown in Listing 7-5, but when a value conforms to multiple protocols, we must declare them one after another separated by the **&** symbol. In the following example, we define a function that returns a value that conforms to both the **Printer** and **Highlight** protocols.

Listing 7-7: Returning a data type that conforms to multiple protocols

```
protocol Printer {
   var name: String { get set }
   func printdescription()
}
protocol Highlight {
   func highlightName()
}

struct Employees: Printer, Highlight {
   var name: String
   var age: Int

   func printdescription() {
      print("Description: \(name) \(age)")
   }
```

```
   func highlightName() {
      print(name.uppercased())
   }
}
func getEmployee() -> Printer & Highlight {
   let employee = Employees(name: "John", age: 32)
   return employee
}
let badge = getEmployee()
badge.printdescription()  // "Description: John 32"
badge.highlightName()  // "JOHN"
```

The **getEmployee()** function defined in this example can return any structure or object, as long as it conforms to the **Printer** and **Highlight** protocols. Regardless of the value returned, because it conforms to these two protocols, we know that it provides implementations of the **printDescription()** and **highlightName()** methods, and therefore we can safely use them.

BASIC

Standard Protocols

Swift makes extensive use of protocols. Almost every API includes protocols that define common features and behavior. But there are also important protocols defined in the Swift Standard Library that we can use to improve our custom data types. The following are the most frequently used.

Equatable

This protocol defines a data type which values can be compared with other values of the same type using the operators == and **!=**.

Comparable

This protocol defines a data type which values can be compared with other values of the same type using the operators **>**, **<**, **>=**, and **<=**.

Numeric

This protocol defines a data type that only works with values that can participate in arithmetic operations.

Hashable

This protocol defines a data type that provides the hash value (unique identifier) required for the instance to be included in collections, such as sets and dictionaries.

CaseIterable

This protocol defines a data type, usually an enumeration without associated values, that includes a property called **allCases** that contains the collection of all the cases included in the enumeration.

These protocols are responsible of elemental processes performed by the system and the Swift language. For example, when we compare two values with the == or != operators, the system checks whether the values conform to the **Equatable** protocol and then calls a type method in their data types to compare them and solve the condition (true or false, depending on whether the values are equal or not). Swift data types conform to the **Equatable** protocol and implement its methods by default, but we can also implement them in our own data types to compare their values.

The **Equatable** protocol requires only one method called == to check for equality. (The system infers that if two values are not equal, they are different, and therefore the method for the != operator is optional.) This method must have a name equal to the operator (==), receive the two values to compare, and return a Boolean value to report the result. For instance, we can make our **Employees** structure conform to the **Equatable** protocol and implement a method called == to be able to compare two different instances of the same structure.

Listing 7-8: Conforming to the `Equatable` protocol

```
struct Employees: Equatable {
   var name: String
   var age: Int

   static func == (value1: Employees, value2: Employees) -> Bool {
      return value1.age == value2.age
   }
}
let employee1 = Employees(name: "John", age: 32)
let employee2 = Employees(name: "George", age: 32)

let message = employee1 == employee2 ? "Equal" : "Different"
print(message)  // "Equal"
```

In this example, we use the == method to compare the values of the **age** properties and therefore the structures are considered equal when the employees are the same age. In this case, both instances are created with the value 32 and therefore they are considered equal.

If what we want is to compare each of the properties in the structure, then we can omit the method. When we conform to the **Equatable** protocol, the Swift compiler automatically generates the method for us to compare all the values of the structure (in this case, **name** and **age**).

Listing 7-9: Letting the Swift compiler create the protocol methods for us

```
struct Employees: Equatable {
   var name: String
   var age: Int
}
let employee1 = Employees(name: "John", age: 32)
let employee2 = Employees(name: "George", age: 32)

let message = employee1 == employee2 ? "Equal" : "Different"
print(message)  // "Different"
```

Because in this example we didn't declare the == method, the system creates the method for us and compares the values of all the properties. As a result, the system determines that the objects are different (the ages are the same, but the names are not).

In addition to comparing for equality with the **Equatable** protocol, we can also compare magnitudes with the **Comparable** protocol. This protocol is like **Equatable**, but the system does not offer a default implementation of the type methods, so we must implement them ourselves. The protocol requires four methods to represent the operations >, <, >= and <=. In the following example, we make the **`Employees`** structure conform to the **`Comparable`** protocol to compare the ages of the employees.

Listing 7-10: Conforming to the Comparable protocol

```
struct Employees: Comparable {
   var name: String
   var age: Int
   static func > (value1: Employees, value2: Employees) -> Bool {
      return value1.age > value2.age
   }
   static func < (value1: Employees, value2: Employees) -> Bool {
      return value1.age < value2.age
   }
   static func >= (value1: Employees, value2: Employees) -> Bool {
      return value1.age >= value2.age
   }
   static func <= (value1: Employees, value2: Employees) -> Bool {
      return value1.age <= value2.age
   }
}
let employee1 = Employees(name: "George", age: 32)
let employee2 = Employees(name: "Robert", age: 55)
if employee1 > employee2 {
   print("\(employee1.name) is older")
} else {
   print("\(employee2.name) is older")  // "Robert is older"
}
```

When we compare two instances of the **Employees** structure, the system calls the corresponding type method and returns **true** or **false** depending on the values of the **age** property. Because in this example the value of **age** in the **employee1** structure is not greater than the value of **age** in the **employee2** structure, we get the message "Robert is older".

Of course, we could have compared the properties directly (**employee1.name == employee2.name**) but being able to compare the objects instead simplifies the code and allows us to use our structures (or objects) in APIs that require the values to be comparable. For example, when we created a generic function in Chapter 3, we were not able to perform any operations on the values (see Listing 3-18). Since the data type used in those functions is generic, Swift is incapable of knowing the capabilities of the data type and therefore Xcode returns an error if we try to perform operations on the values, but we can easily solve this problem by making the generic type conform to a protocol. This feature is called *Type Constraint* because it constrains the generic type to a data type with certain capabilities. For instance, the function in the following example receives two generic values, but only of a data type that conforms to the **Equatable** protocol, so they can be compared.

Listing 7-11: Adding a type constraint to a generic function

```
struct Employees: Equatable {
   var name: String
   var age: Int
}
func compareValues<T: Equatable>(value1: T, value2: T) -> String {
   let message = value1 == value2 ? "equal" : "different"
   return message
}
let employee1 = Employees(name: "George", age: 55)
let employee2 = Employees(name: "Robert", age: 55)

let result = compareValues(value1: employee1, value2: employee2)
print("The values are \(result)")  // "The values are different"
```

The conformance to the protocol is specified inside the angle brackets after the name of the generic type. The **compareValues()** function in Listing 7-11 declares the **T** type to conform to **Equatable** and then compares the values with a ternary operator and returns the result. In this case, the ages of the employees are the same (55), but the names are different ("George" and "Robert"), and therefore the system considers the structures to be different.

Another protocol used as a type constraint is **Numeric**. This protocol determines that the data types of the values received by the function must support arithmetic operations.

Listing 7-12: Using the Numeric protocol to set a type constraint

```
func calculateResult<T: Numeric>(value1: T, value2: T) {
   print(value1 + value2)  // 7.5
}
calculateResult(value1: 3.5, value2: 4)
```

The **calculateResult()** function in this example is a generic function and therefore it can receive any value of any type, but because we set a type constraint with the **Numeric** protocol, the function can only receive values of data types that can participate in arithmetic operations.

Another useful protocol is **Hashable**. Every time we include a structure or an object in a set or use them as the index of a dictionary, the system requires the data type to provide a hash value that can be used to uniquely identify each element. This is a random integer that is created based on the values of the properties. The purpose of the **Hashable** protocol is to define properties and methods to handle this value. Most of the data types defined by Swift conform to this protocol and that is why we do not have any issues when including these values in a set or as the index of dictionaries, but for custom structures and objects we must provide the hash value ourselves. Fortunately, if the values in our data type are already hashable, we do not need a specific property to be used to create the hash value, all we need to do is conform to the protocol and the system creates the value for us. The following example makes the **Employees** structure conform to the **Hashable** protocol, so we can include the instances in a set.

Listing 7-13: Conforming to the Hashable protocol

```
struct Employees: Hashable {
   var name: String
   var age: Int
}
let employee1 = Employees(name: "John", age: 32)
let employee2 = Employees(name: "Robert", age: 55)

let list: Set<Employees> = [employee1, employee2]
for item in list {
   print(item.name)
}
```

Hash values are random integers created based on the values of the properties. If we just conform to the protocol, the system uses the values of all the properties in the instance to create it (all the properties must be hashable), but we can specify which properties should be included by implementing the following properties and methods defined by the protocol.

hashValue

This property returns the hash value of the instance. It is of type **Int**.

hash(into: inout Hasher)

This method defines the properties that are going to be included by the hasher to create the hash value.

To calculate the hash value, the Swift Standard Library includes a structure called **Hasher**. This is the structure received by the **hash(into:)** method and it contains a method called **combine()** to tell the hasher which properties should be used to create the value. The following example illustrates how to implement the **hash(into:)** method and call the **combine()** method on the hasher to create a hash value from the value of the **name** property in our structure.

Listing 7-14: Defining our own hash value

```
struct Employees: Hashable {
   var name: String
   var age: Int

   func hash(into hasher: inout Hasher) {
      hasher.combine(name)
   }
}
let employee = Employees(name: "George", age: 32)
print(employee.hashValue)  // e.g., 7722685913545470055
```

IMPORTANT

The last statement in Listing 7-14 prints the value of the **hashValue** property. Since the resulting value is always an integer calculated randomly every time the app is executed, you won't notice any difference from the previous example, but selecting the property to include may be useful when managing sensitive information.

The last protocol from our list is called **CaseIterable**. This is a simple protocol that defines a property called **allCases** to store a collection with all the cases in an enumeration. The system automatically initializes this property, so all we need to do to be able to use it is to conform to the protocol. In the following example, we define an enumeration with three cases and then iterate through the collection in the **allCases** property to print their names.

Listing 7-15: Conforming to the `CaseIterable` protocol

```
enum Departments: CaseIterable {
   case mail
   case marketing
   case managing
}
var message = ""
for department in Departments.allCases {
   message += "\(department) "
}
print(message)  // "mail marketing managing "
```

PRO

Protocol Extensions

Protocols only define the properties and methods that data types have in common, but they do not include any implementation. However, we can implement properties and methods that are shared by all data types conforming to a protocol by extending the protocol itself. As we have already seen, extensions are special declarations that add functionality to an existing data type. We can use them with structures, enumerations, and classes, but they are particularly useful with protocols because they are the mechanism through which protocols can provide their own functionality. As always, the syntax includes the keyword **`extension`** followed by the name of the protocol we want to extend. The following example recreates the **`Printer`** protocol introduced earlier and extends it with a method.

Listing 7-16: Extending a protocol

```
import Playgrounds

protocol Printer {
   var name: String { get set }
}
extension Printer {
   func printdescription() {
      print("The name is \(name)")
   }
}
#Playground {
   struct Employees: Printer {
      var name: String
      var age: Int
   }
   struct Offices: Printer {
      var name: String
      var employees: Int
   }
   let employee = Employees(name: "John", age: 45)
   let office = Offices(name: "Mail", employees: 2)

   employee.printdescription()  // "The name is John"
   office.printdescription()  // "The name is Mail"
}
```

In this example, we define a **Printer** protocol with just the **name** property and then extend it to include a common implementation of the **printdescription()** method. Now, the **Employees** and **Offices** structures in our example share the same implementation and produce the same result when their **printdescription()** methods are executed.

PRO

Delegates

As we have already seen, an instance of a structure or an object can be assigned to the property of another instance. For example, we could have an instance of a structure called **Employees** with a property that contains an instance of a structure called **Offices** to store information about the office where the employee works. This opens the door to new programming patterns where the instances adopt different roles. The most useful pattern is called *Delegation*. A structure or object delegates responsibility for the execution of certain tasks to another structure or object, as shown in the following example.

Listing 7-17: Implementing a delegate

```
struct Salary {
   func showMoney(name: String, money: Double) {
      print("The salary of \(name) is \(money)")
   }
}
```

```
struct Employees {
   var name: String
   var money: Double

   var delegate: Salary

   func generatereport() {
      delegate.showMoney(name: name, money: money)
   }
}
let salary = Salary()
var employee1 = Employees(name: "John", money: 45000, delegate: salary)

employee1.generatereport()  // "The salary of John is 45000.0"
```

The **Employees** structure in Listing 7-17 contains three properties. The properties **name** and **money** store the employee's data, but the **delegate** property stores an instance of the **Salary** structure in charge of printing that data. The code creates the **Salary** instance first and then uses this value to create the **Employees** instance. When we call the **generatereport()** method on the **employee1** structure at the end, the method calls the **showmoney()** method on **delegate**, effectively delegating the task of printing the data to this structure.

This pattern presents two problems. First, the structure that is delegating needs to know the data type of the structure that is going to become the delegate (in our example, the **delegate** property always has to be of type **Salary**). Following this approach, not every structure can be a delegate, only the ones specified in the definition. The second problem is related to how we know which are the properties and methods that the delegate must implement. If the structure is too complex or is taken from a library, we could forget to implement some methods or properties and get an error when the structure tries to access them. Both problems are solved by protocols. Instead of declaring a specific structure as the delegate, we define a protocol and declare the **delegate** property to be of that type, as shown in the following example.

Listing 7-18: Delegating with protocols

```
protocol SalaryProtocol {
   func showMoney(name: String, money: Double)
}
struct Salary: SalaryProtocol {
   func showMoney(name: String, money: Double) {
      print("The salary of \(name) is \(money)")
   }
}
struct Employees {
   var name: String
   var money: Double

   var delegate: SalaryProtocol

   func generatereport() {
      delegate.showMoney(name: name, money: money)
   }
}
```

```
let salary = Salary()
let employee1 = Employees(name: "John", money: 45000, delegate: salary)

employee1.generatereport()  // "The salary of John is 45000.0"
```

The **delegate** property of the **Employees** structure is now of type **SalaryProtocol**, which means that it can store any instance of any type providing that it conforms to the **SalaryProtocol** protocol. As illustrated by this example, the advantage of protocols is that we can use structures of different types to perform the task. It doesn't matter what type they are as long as they conform to the delegate's protocol and implement its properties and methods. For example, we could create two different structures to print the data of our last example and assign to the delegate one instance or another depending on what we want to achieve.

Listing 7-19: Using different delegates

```
protocol SalaryProtocol {
   func showMoney(name: String, money: Double)
}
struct Salary: SalaryProtocol {
   func showMoney(name: String, money: Double) {
      print("The salary of \(name) is \(money)")
   }
}
struct BasicSalary: SalaryProtocol {
   func showMoney(name: String, money: Double) {
      if money > 40000 {
         print("Salary is over the minimum")
      } else {
         print("The salary of \(name) is \(money)")
      }
   }
}
struct Employees {
   var name: String
   var money: Double
   var delegate: SalaryProtocol

   func generatereport() {
      delegate.showMoney(name: name, money: money)
   }
}
let salary = Salary()
var employee1 = Employees(name: "John", money: 45000, delegate: salary)

employee1.delegate = BasicSalary()
employee1.generatereport()  // "Salary is over the minimum"
```

The **BasicSalary** structure added in Listing 7-19 conforms to **SalaryProtocol** and implements its **showMoney()** method, but unlike the **Salary** structure, it produces two different results depending on the employee's salary. The output produced by the execution of the **generatereport()** method on the **Employees** structure now depends on the type of structure we previously assigned to the **delegate** property.

PRO

Generic Protocols

Protocols can also define generic properties and methods, but they work slightly different than the generic types studied before. When we want to define a protocol with a generic property or method, we first must define the name of the generic type with the **associatedtype** keyword.

Listing 7-20: Defining generic protocols

```
protocol Printer {
   associatedtype protype
   var name: protype { get set }
}
struct Employees: Printer {
   var name: String
}
let employee = Employees(name: "John")
print(employee.name)  // "John"
```

This example defines a generic protocol called **Printer** and a structure that conforms to that protocol called **Employees**. The protocol defines a generic type with the name **protype** and then declares a property of that type. The property's real data type is defined by the structure or the class that conforms to the protocol. In this case, the **Employees** structure defines the **name** property as type **String**, and that's the type of values we can use in the instances of this structure, but we could have declared the property as type `Int` or any other necessary.

PRO

Opaque Types

Opaque types are an advanced feature used by frameworks such as SwiftUI to simplify the declaration of complex custom data types. An opaque type hides the returned type from the programmer while still preserving type safety. They are commonly used when working with generic data types, such as the generic structures introduced earlier (see Chapter 4, Listing 4-22). For example, the `reversed()` method provided by arrays returns a `ReversedCollection` structure. Because this structure is generic, its exact type depends on the type of values being processed. An array of strings produces a value of type `ReversedCollection<Array<String>>`, while an array of integers produces a value of type `ReversedCollection<Array<Int>>`, as shown in the following example.

Listing 7-21: Returning values of complex data types

```
struct MyData {
   func reverse(mylist: [Int]) -> ReversedCollection<Array<Int>> {
      let reversed = mylist.reversed()
      return reversed
   }
   func reverseArray() {
      let reversedlist = reverse(mylist: [1, 2, 3, 4, 5])
      print(Array(reversedlist))  // "[5, 4, 3, 2, 1]"
   }
}
let data = MyData()
data.reverseArray()
```

The code in Listing 7-21 defines a structure with two methods: one called **reverse()** to reverse the elements of an array, and another to call this method and print the result on the console. The **reverse()** method receives an array of integers and returns a **ReversedCollection** value with the values in reverse order.

This code runs fine and there are no issues with it, until we decide to work with different value types, such as strings. Instead of **ReversedCollection<Array<Int>>**, the return data type would have to be defined as **ReversedCollection<Array<String>>**. Although in this case it may seem easy to just redefine the function and switch types, the generic data types used in frameworks like SwiftUI can be complex and replacing them repeatedly in generic properties and methods can be time consuming and error prone. But if we know that the values we want to return conform to the same protocol, we can declare the return type as opaque and let the Swift compiler figure out the data type for us. When the compiler finds an opaque type, it takes care of determining the real data type of the value and process it as such.

Opaque types are declared with the **some** keyword followed by the name of the protocol to which the type conforms. For example, collections such as the one returned by the **reversed()** method, conform to a protocol called **Collection**, so we can define the return type as **some Collection** and let the Swift compiler figure out the real data type.

Listing 7-22: Returning opaque types

```
struct MyData {
   func reverse(mylist: [String]) -> some Collection {
      let reversed = mylist.reversed()
      return reversed
   }
   func reverseArray() {
      let reversedlist = self.reverse(mylist: ["One", "Two", "Three",
         "Four", "Five"])
      print(Array(reversedlist))
      // "["Five", "Four", "Three", "Two", "One"]"
   }
}
let data = MyData()
data.reverseArray()
```

This example defines the same **`reverse()`** method as before, but this time the method receives an array of strings and returns the opaque type **`some Collection`**. The value returned by the method is of type **`some Collection`**, but the Swift compiler recognizes that the value's data type is **`ReversedCollection<Array<String>>`**, which means that we are still able to turn it into an **`Array`** and print it on the console.

> **IMPORTANT**
>
> SwiftUI is the framework provided by Apple for creating user interfaces. To learn more about the **`some`** keyword and SwiftUI, read our book *SwiftUI for Masterminds* (**www.formasterminds.com**).

Chapter 8
Error Handling

BASIC

8.1 - Errors

Errors are a natural part of computer programming. Our own code, as well as the code provided by libraries and frameworks, can produce errors. No matter how many precautions we take, success is never guaranteed, and problems often arise even when our code performs the task correctly. For this reason, Swift provides a systematic approach for managing errors.

BASIC

Throwing Errors

When a method produces an error, it is said that it *throws* an error. Several frameworks provided by Apple are already programmed to throw errors, but we can also do it from our own structures and classes. To throw an error, we must use the **throw** and **throws** keywords. The **throw** keyword is used to throw the error and the **throws** keyword is specified in the method's declaration to indicate that the method can throw errors.

Because a method can throw multiple errors, we also must indicate the type of error found with values of an enumeration type. This is a custom enumeration that conforms to the **Error** protocol. For instance, let's consider the following example.

Listing 8-1: Method producing an error

```
struct Stock {
   var totalLamps = 5
   mutating func sold(amount: Int) {
      totalLamps = totalLamps - amount
   }
}
var mystock = Stock()

mystock.sold(amount: 8)
print("Lamps in stock: \(mystock.totalLamps)")
// "Lamps in stock: -3"
```

The code in Listing 8-1 defines a structure called **Stock** that manages the inventory of lamps available in a store. The structure includes the **totalLamps** property, which stores the number of lamps still available, and the **sold()** method, which processes lamp sales. This method updates the inventory by subtracting the number of lamps sold from the value of the **totalLamps** property. If the number of lamps sold is less than the number of lamps in stock, everything works as expected, but when we sell more lamps than we have, as in this example, a clear problem occurs. To report this problem, we can throw an error.

To throw errors from a method, we must define the possible error types, add the **throws** keyword to the method's definition between the parameter list and the return type, detect the error, and throw it using the **throw** keyword, as shown below.

Listing 8-2: Throwing errors

```
enum Errors: Error {
   case OutOfStock
}
struct Stock {
   var totalLamps = 5
   mutating func sold(amount: Int) throws {
      if amount > totalLamps {
         throw Errors.OutOfStock
      } else {
         totalLamps = totalLamps - amount
      }
   }
}
var mystock = Stock()
```

In this example, we declare an enumeration called **Errors** that conforms to the **Error** protocol and includes a case called **OutOfStock**. By declaring **sold()** as a throwing method with the **throws** keyword, we can now throw the **OutOfStock** error every time we try to sell more lamps than we have. If the lamps sold are more than the number of lamps in stock, the method throws the error, otherwise the stock is updated.

BASIC

Handling Errors

Now that we have a method that can throw errors, we must handle the errors when the method is executed. Swift includes the **try** keyword and the **do catch** statements for this purpose. The **do catch** statements create two blocks of code. If the statements inside the **do** block return an error, the statements in the **catch** block are executed. To execute a method that throws errors, we must call the method inside the **do** statement with the **try** keyword in front of it, as shown below.

Listing 8-3: Handling errors

```
enum Errors: Error {
   case OutOfStock
}
```

```
struct Stock {
   var totalLamps = 5
   mutating func sold(amount: Int) throws {
      if amount > totalLamps {
         throw Errors.OutOfStock
      } else {
         totalLamps = totalLamps - amount
      }
   }
}
var mystock = Stock()

do {
   try mystock.sold(amount: 8)
} catch Errors.OutOfStock {
   print("We do not have enough lamps")
}
```

This code expands the previous example to handle the error thrown by the **sold()** method. Because of the addition of the **try** keyword, the system tries to execute the **sold()** method in the **mystock** structure and check for errors. If the method returns the **OutOfStock** error, the statements inside the **catch** block are executed. This pattern allows us to respond every time there is an error and report it to the user or correct the situation without having to crash the app or produce unexpected results.

IMPORTANT

You can add as many errors as you need to the **Errors** enumeration. The errors can be checked later with multiple **catch** statements. Also, you may add all the statements you need to the **do** block. The statements before **try** are always executed, while the statements after **try** are only executed if no error is found.

If the error is not one of the types we are expecting, we can print information about it. The information is stored in a constant called **error** that we can read inside the **catch** block.

Listing 8-4: Getting information about the error

```
enum Errors: String, Error {
   case OutOfStock = "Hello"
}
struct Stock {
   var totalLamps = 5
   mutating func sold(amount: Int) throws {
      if amount > totalLamps {
         throw Errors.OutOfStock
      } else {
         totalLamps = totalLamps - amount
      }
   }
}
```

```
var mystock = Stock()

do {
   try mystock.sold(amount: 8)
} catch {
   print(error)   // OutOfStock
}
```

On the other hand, if we do not care about the error, we can force the **try** keyword to return an optional with the syntax **try?**. If the method throws an error, the instruction returns **nil**, and therefore we can avoid the use of the **do catch** statements.

Listing 8-5: Catching errors with try?

```
enum Errors: Error {
   case OutOfStock
}
struct Stock {
   var totalLamps = 5
   mutating func sold(amount: Int) throws {
      if amount > totalLamps {
         throw Errors.OutOfStock
      } else {
         totalLamps = totalLamps - amount
      }
   }
}
var mystock = Stock()
try? mystock.sold(amount: 8)  // nil
```

Sometimes, we know beforehand that a throwing method is not going to throw an error and therefore we want to avoid writing unnecessary code. In cases like this, we can use the syntax **try!**. For instance, the following code checks if there are enough lamps before calling the **sold()** method, so we know that the instruction will never throw the **OutOfStock** error.

Listing 8-6: Ignoring the errors

```
enum Errors: Error {
   case OutOfStock
}
struct Stock {
   var totalLamps = 5
   mutating func sold(amount: Int) throws {
      if amount > totalLamps {
         throw Errors.OutOfStock
      } else {
         totalLamps = totalLamps - amount
      }
   }
}
var mystock = Stock()
```

```
if mystock.totalLamps > 3 {
   try! mystock.sold(amount: 3)
}
print("Lamps remaining in stock: \(mystock.totalLamps)")
// "Lamps remaining in stock: 2"
```

PRO

Results

Sometimes we need to return more than just an error. For this purpose, the Swift Standard Library defines the **Result** enumeration. This enumeration defines two cases with associated values to use in case of success or failure called **success()** and **failure()**. The **Result** enumeration is generic, which means that the data types of the associated values can be anything we want. For instance, in the following examples we define a **Result** enumeration of type **<Int, Errors>**, so we can return an integer and the **OutOfStock** error defined in the previous example.

Listing 8-7: Returning an error with a Result enumeration

```
enum Errors: Error {
   case OutOfStock
}
struct Stock {
   var totalLamps = 5

   mutating func sold(amount: Int) -> Result<Int, Errors> {
      if amount > totalLamps {
         return .failure(.OutOfStock)
      } else {
         totalLamps = totalLamps - amount
         return .success(totalLamps)
      }
   }
}
var mystock = Stock()

let result = mystock.sold(amount: 3)
switch result {
   case .success(let stock):
      print("Lamps remaining in stock: \(stock)")
   case .failure(let error):
      if error == .OutOfStock {
         print("Error: Out of Stock")
      } else {
         print("Error")
      }
}
```

The **sold()** method in Listing 8-7 now returns a **Result** value of type **<Int, Errors>**, so if an error occurs, the method can return a **failure()** value with the associated value **OutOfStock**, but if we have enough lamps to fulfill the order, we can return a **success()** value with the remaining number of lamps. The result can be processed by a **switch** statement. We check whether the value returned by the method is **failure()** or **success()**, get the associated value with a constant, and proceed accordingly. In this case, there are enough lamps available, so a message is printed on the console with the remaining stock.

Instead of using a **switch** statement, we can use the following method defined by the **Result** enumeration.

`get()`

This method returns the associated value of the **success()** case or throws an error with the associated value of the **failure()** case.

The only purpose of the **get()** method is to simplify the code. Now, instead of a **switch** statement, we can use a **do catch**, as shown below.

Listing 8-8: Processing an error with the get() method

```
enum Errors: Error {
   case OutOfStock
}
struct Stock {
   var totalLamps = 5

   mutating func sold(amount: Int) -> Result<Int, Errors> {
      if amount > totalLamps {
         return .failure(.OutOfStock)
      } else {
         totalLamps = totalLamps - amount
         return .success(totalLamps)
      }
   }
}
var mystock = Stock()

let result = mystock.sold(amount: 2)
do {
   let stock = try result.get()
   print("Lamps in stock: \(stock)")
} catch Errors.OutOfStock {
   print("Error: Out of Stock")
}
```

The result is the same as before, but now all we need to do is call the **get()** method. If the method doesn't return an error, the remaining stock is printed on the console; otherwise, the **catch** block is performed, and a message with the error is printed instead.

Chapter 9
Frameworks

BASIC

9.1 - Introduction to Frameworks

The programming tools introduced in previous chapters are not sufficient to build professional applications. Creating an app requires access to complex technologies and the execution of repetitive tasks that can involve hundreds or even thousands of lines of code. To address this challenge, developers have long relied on prewritten code that performs common operations. These reusable components are organized by purpose into what we call frameworks.

BASIC

Importing Frameworks

There are many frameworks available. Some provide the code needed to manage databases, while others are designed for drawing graphics on the screen, storing files, accessing system resources, and performing many other tasks. To include a framework, we use the `import` instruction at the beginning of a file, followed by the name of the framework, as in `import SwiftUI`. Once a framework is imported, it becomes part of the file, giving our code access to all the structures, classes, functions, and values defined by that framework. We have already used a few frameworks, such as the **Playground** framework to include the functionality needed to test our code and the **SwiftUI** framework to create the basic structures required to run an application, but there are many more, as we will see in this and following chapters.

IMPORTANT

In this book, we will learn about the fundamental frameworks that complement Swift for storing, managing, and displaying data. If you want to explore all the frameworks included in the Software Development Kit provided with Xcode, read our book *SwiftUI for Masterminds* (**www.formasterminds.com**).

BASIC

9.2 - Foundation

Foundation is one of the oldest frameworks provided by Apple. It was written in Objective-C and developed by Steve Jobs's second company NeXT. It was created to manage basic tasks and store data. The framework provides its own data types (structures and classes) to store any value we want, including numbers, strings, arrays and dictionaries, and a primary class called **NSObject** with basic functionality that every other class inherits from. Most of these definitions are now obsolete, replaced by Swift data types, but others remain useful, as we will see next.

BASIC

Standard Functions

As we have seen in Chapter 3, the Swift Standard Library includes a few standard functions, such as **print()** and **abs()**, but others are provided by external frameworks. The following are some of the basic functions available when we import the **Foundation** framework.

pow(Float, Float)

This function returns the result of raising the first value to the power of the second value. The arguments may be numbers of type **Float** or **Double**.

sqrt(Float)

This function returns the square root of the value of its argument. The argument may be of type **Float** or **Double**.

log(Float)

This function returns the natural logarithm of a value. Similar functions are **log2()**, **log10()**, **log1p()**, and **logb()**. It can take a value of type **Float** or **Double**.

sin(Float)

This function returns the sine of a value. Similar functions are **asin()**, **sinh()**, and **asinh()**. The argument may be of type **Float** or **Double**.

cos(Float)

This function returns the cosine of a value. Similar functions are **acos()**, **cosh()**, and **acosh()**. The argument may be of type **Float** or **Double**.

tan(Float)

This function returns the tangent of a value. Similar functions are **atan()**, **atan2()**, **tanh()**, and **atanh()**. The argument may be of type **Float** or **Double**.

The application of these functions is straightforward, as shown in the following example.

Listing 9-1: Applying math functions

```
import Foundation
import Playgrounds

#Playground {
    let square = sqrt(4.0)
    let power = pow(2.0, 2.0)
    let maximum = max(square, power)

    print("The maximum value is \(maximum)")
    // "The maximum value is 4.0"
}
```

The first thing we do in the code in Listing 9-1 is to import the **Foundation** framework. After this, we can implement any of the tools defined inside the framework, including the basic functions introduced above. This example gets the square root of 4.0, calculates 2.0 to the power of 2.0, and compares the results using the **max()** function from the Swift Standard Library.

Do It Yourself

Update the **MyPlayground.swift** file in your project with the code in Listing 9-1. You should see the message "The maximum value is 4.0" printed on the console.

BASIC

Strings

Foundation defines a class called **NSString** to store and manage strings of characters. The **String** structure offered by the Swift Standard Library for this same purpose adopts most of its functionality, turning the class obsolete, but because Swift coexists with old frameworks and data types, **NSString** objects are still required in some circumstances. The **NSString** class includes several Initializers to create these objects. The one usually implemented in Swift takes an argument called **string** with the string of characters we want to assign to the object, as shown below.

Listing 9-2: Creating an `NSString` object

```
var text: NSString = NSString(string: "Hello")
print(text)  // "Hello"
```

If we already have a **String** value in our code, we can cast it into an **NSString** object with the **as** operator.

Listing 9-3: Casting a `String` value into an `NSString` object

```
var text = "Hello World"
var newText = text as NSString
print(newText)  // "Hello World"
```

A **String** structure can be turned into an **NSString** object with the **as** operator because they are interconnected. It is said that the **String** structure bridges with the **NSString** class. This means that, once we import the **Foundation** framework, we can access the functionality offered by the **NSString** class from a **String** structure, including the following properties and methods.

`capitalized`

This property returns a string with the first letter of every word in uppercase.

`length`

This property returns the number of characters in the string of an **NSString** object. (For **String** values, we should use the **count** property instead.)

`localizedStringWithFormat``(String, Values)`

This type method creates a string from the string provided by the first argument and the values provided by the second argument. The first argument is a template used to create the string, and the second argument is the list of values we want to include in the string separated by comma.

`contains``(String)`

This method returns a Boolean value that indicates whether or not the string specified by the argument was found inside the original string.

`localizedStandardContains``(String)`

This method returns a Boolean value that indicates whether or not the character or string specified by the argument is present in the string. It works like **`contains()`**, but the search is case-insensitive and local conventions, such as language, are taken into account.

`components(separatedBy:` `String)`

This method divides the string by the separator specified by the **separatedBy** argument and returns an array with all the parts.

`replacingOccurrences(of:` `String,` **`with:`** `String)`

This method returns a new string with all the strings that match the value specified by the **of** argument replaced by the string specified by the **with** argument.

trimmingCharacters(in: CharacterSet)

This method erases the characters indicated by the **in** argument at the beginning and the end of the string and returns a new string with the result. The argument is a **CharacterSet** structure with type properties to select the type of characters to remove. The most frequently used are **whitespaces** (spaces) and **whitespacesAndNewlines** (spaces and new line characters).

compare(String, **options:** CompareOptions, **range:** Range?, **locale:** Locale?)

This method compares the original string with the string provided by the first argument and returns an enumeration of type **ComparisonResult** with a value corresponding to the lexical order of the strings. The **orderedSame** value is returned when the strings are equal, the **orderedAscending** value is returned when the original string precedes the value of the first argument, and the **orderedDescending** value is returned when the original string follows the value of the first argument. The **options** argument is a property of the **CompareOptions** structure. The properties available are **caseInsensitive** (it considers lowercase and uppercase letters to be the same), **literal** (performs a Byte-to-Byte comparison), **diacriticInsensitive** (ignores diacritic marks such as the visual stress on vowels), **widthInsensitive** (ignores the width difference in characters that occurs in some languages), and **forcedOrdering** (the comparison is forced to return **orderedAscending** or **orderedDescending** values when the strings are equivalent but not strictly equal). The **range** argument defines a range that describes the portion of the original string we want to compare. Finally, the **locale** argument is a **Locale** structure that defines localization. Only the first argument is required.

caseInsensitiveCompare(String)

This method compares the original string with the string provided by the argument. It works exactly like the **compare()** method but with the option **caseInsensitiveSearch** set by default.

range(of: String, **options:** CompareOptions, **range:** Range?, **locale:** Locale?)

This method searches for the string specified by the first argument and returns a range to indicate where the string was found or **nil** in case of failure. The **options** argument is a property of the **CompareOptions** structure. The properties available for this method are the same we have for the **compare()** method, with the difference that we can specify three more: **backwards** (searches from the end of the string), **anchored** (matches characters only at the beginning or the end, not in the middle), and **regularExpression** (searches with a regular expression). The **range** argument defines a range that determines the portion of the original string where we want to search. Only the first argument is required.

Some of these methods are like those offered by the **String** structure but they perform additional operations on the values. For instance, we can incorporate values into strings with string interpolation, but the **localizedStringWithFormat()** method offers a different approach. This method takes a string with placeholders and replaces them with a list of values. The placeholders are declared with the `%` symbol followed by a character that represents the type of value we want to include. For example, if we want to replace the placeholder with an integer, we must use the characters **`%d`**.

Listing 9-4: Creating a formatted string

```
var age = 44
var mytext = String.localizedStringWithFormat("My age is %d", age)
print(mytext)  // "My age is 44"
```

There are different placeholders available. The most frequently used are **%d** for integers, **%f** for floating-point numbers, **%g** to remove redundant 0 (zeros), and **%@** for objects and structures. We can use any of these characters and as many times as necessary. This is like what we would get with string interpolation, but with this method we can also format the values. For instance, we can determine the number of digits a value will have by adding the amount before the letter.

Listing 9-5: Formatting numbers

```
let length = 12.3472
let total = 54
let decimals = String.localizedStringWithFormat("Decimals: %.2f", length)
let digits = String.localizedStringWithFormat("Digits: %.5d", total)
print(decimals)  // "Decimals: 12.35"
print(digits)  // "Digits: 00054"
```

The code in Listing 9-5 formats two numbers: a **Double** and an **Int**. The double value is processed with the **%.2f** placeholder, which means that the value is going to be rounded to two decimals after the point, and the integer is processed with the **%.5d** placeholder, which means that the number in the string is going to contain a total of five digits. If there are not enough digits in the original number, the rest of the spaces are filled with zeros.

Other methods perform operations that are already available for **String** values, but they produce a more comprehensive result. For example, the **compare()** method compares strings like the == operator, but the returned value is not just **true** or **false**, as shown in the following example.

Listing 9-6: Comparing String values

```
var fruit = "Orange"
var search = "Apple"

var result = fruit.compare(search)
switch result {
   case .orderedSame:
      print("Fruit and Search are equal")
   case .orderedDescending:
      print("Fruit follows Search")  // "Fruit follows Search"
   case .orderedAscending:
      print("Fruit precedes Search")
}
```

The **compare()** method takes a string, compares it to the original string, and returns a **ComparisonResult** value to indicate the order. The **ComparisonResult** enumeration contains three values: **orderedSame**, **orderedDescending**, and **orderedAscending**. After comparing the values of the **fruit** and **search** variables in our example, the **result** variable contains one of these values according to the lexical order of the strings. In this case, the value "Orange" assigned to **fruit** is larger (follows alphabetically) the value "Apple" assigned to **search**, so the value returned is **orderedDescending** (the order is descending from **fruit** to **search**).

The **compare()** method implemented in Listing 9-6 and the == operator studied in Chapter 2 distinguish a lowercase string from an uppercase string. By adding an option to the **compare()** method, we can compare two strings without considering lowercase or uppercase letters.

Listing 9-7: Comparing `String` values with options

```
var fruit = "Orange"
var search = "ORANGE"

var result = fruit.compare(search, options: .caseInsensitive)
switch result {
   case .orderedSame:
      print("The values are equal")  // "The values are equal"
   case .orderedDescending:
      print("Fruit follows Search")
   case .orderedAscending:
      print("Fruit precedes Search")
}
```

The strings stored in the **fruit** and **search** variables in Listing 9-7 are different, but because of the **caseInsensitive** option, they are considered equal.

> **IMPORTANT**
>
> This type of comparison is very common, which is why the class includes the **caseInsensitiveCompare()** method that all it does is calling the **compare()** method with the **caseInsensitive** option already set.

We can make a more precise comparison by specifying the range of characters we want to compare, as shown below.

Listing 9-8: Comparing only a range of characters

```
var phone = "905-525-6666"
var search = "905"

var start = phone.startIndex
var end = phone.firstIndex(of: "-")
```

```
if let endIndex = end {
   let result = phone.compare(search, options: .caseInsensitive, range:
      start..<endIndex)
   if result == .orderedSame {
      print("The area code is the same")
      // "The area code is the same"
   } else {
      print("The area code is different")
   }
}
```

This example compares only the initial characters of a string to check the area code of a phone number. The code defines a range that goes from the first character of the **phone** variable to the position before the - character. This range is provided to the **compare()** method and in consequence the value of the **search** variable is compared against the first three characters in the string.

We can also use ranges to search for strings using the **range()** method. This method searches for a string inside another string and returns a range that determines where the string was found.

Listing 9-9: Searching and replacing characters in a string

```
var text = "The Suitcase is Black"
var search = "black  "
search = search.trimmingCharacters(in: .whitespacesAndNewlines)

var range = text.range(of: search, options: .caseInsensitive)
if let rangeToReplace = range {
   text.replaceSubrange(rangeToReplace, with: "Red")
}
print(text)  // "The Suitcase is Red"
```

The **range()** method returns an optional value that contains the range where the string was found or **nil** in case of failure. In Listing 9-9, we search for the value of the **search** variable inside the **text** variable and check the optional value returned. When we have a range to work with (which means that the value was found) we use it to call the **replaceSubrange()** method of the **String** structure to replace the characters in the range with the word "Red" (see Chapter 4, Listing 4-41). Note that because search values are usually provided by the user, we trim the value of the **search** variable with the **trimmingCharacters()** method to make sure that there are no space characters at the beginning or the end of the string (the two spaces after the word "black" are removed).

If what we want is to process the components of a string, like the area code in a phone number, we can divide the string with the **components(separatedBy:)** method. In the following example, we get the line number from a phone number by reading the last element of the array returned by the method.

Listing 9-10: Getting the components of a string

```
let phone = "905-525-6666"
let elements = phone.components(separatedBy: "-")
print(elements.last!)  // "6666"
```

BASIC

Ranges

Although Swift includes structures to store ranges of values, some frameworks programmed in Objective-C still implement an old **Foundation** class called **NSRange**. The **NSRange** class is slightly different than the **Range** structure. Instead of storing the initial and final values of the range, **NSRange** objects store the initial value and the length of the range. The following are some of the initializers provided by the `NSRange` class, as well as the initializers included in the `Range` structure to convert the values.

NSRange(Range)

This initializer creates an **NSRange** object from a **Range** value.

NSRange(Range, **in:** String)

This initializer creates an **NSRange** object to represent a **Range** structure with string indexes.

Range(NSRange)

This initializer creates a **Range** structure from an **NSRange** value.

Range(NSRange, **in:** String)

This initializer creates a **Range** structure to represent an **NSRange** object with string indexes.

The **NSRange** class includes two properties to retrieve the values: **location** and **length**. The following example initializes an **NSRange** object from a Swift range and prints its values.

Listing 9-11: Creating and reading an NSRange value

```
let range = NSRange(4..<10)
print("Initial: \(range.location)")  // "Initial: 4"
print("Length: \(range.length)")  // "Length: 6"
```

The initializer implemented in this example is for countable ranges. If we work with string indexes, we must use the initializer defined for strings. This is because the **String** structure works with Unicode characters while **NSString** objects work with a less comprehensive character encoding called *UTF-16*. Working with different character encodings means that the space the characters occupy in memory varies. The following example illustrates how to work with this initializer.

Listing 9-12: Converting a range of string indexes

```
let text = "Hello World"
if let start = text.firstIndex(of: "W") {
   let newRange = NSRange(start..., in: text)
   print("Initial: \(newRange.location)")  // "Initial: 6"
   print("Length: \(newRange.length)")  // "Length: 5"
}
```

BASIC

Numbers

Foundation offers a class called **NSNumber** to represent and store numbers. With the introduction of the Swift's data types, the use of this class is no longer necessary, but there are a few old frameworks that still require these types of values. The class includes the following initializer.

NSNumber(value: Value)

This initializer creates an **NSNumber** object with the value specified by the **value** argument. The argument may be a value of any of the data types available in Swift for numbers.

The class also provides properties for retrieving Swift data types from **NSNumber** objects. The following are the most frequently used.

intValue

This property returns an **Int** value with the object's number.

floatValue

This property returns a **Float** value with the object's number.

doubleValue

This property returns a **Double** value with the object's number.

The following example shows how to create **NSNumber** objects and how to get them back as Swift data types to perform operations.

Listing 9-13: Working with `NSNumber` objects

```
var mynumber = NSNumber(value: 35)
var mydouble = mynumber.doubleValue * 2  // 70
```

In addition to the data type, **Foundation** also provides the means to format numbers. Every time we print a number, all the digits are shown on the screen, including all the decimal digits. In Listing 9-5, we explained how to specify how many digits of a number we want to include in a string using placeholders (e.g., **%.2f**), but this is not customizable enough. To provide a better alternative, the framework includes the following formatting method that we can use with our Swift data types.

`formatted(``FormatStyle)`

This method formats the number according to the styles provided by the argument.

To format a number, we must call this method from the instance with the styles we want to apply to it. The styles are defined by structures that conform to the **FormatStyle** protocol. The following are the methods define by the structures to style a number.

`precision(``Precision)`

This method defines the number of digits included in the integer and decimal parts of the number. The argument is a **Precision** structure, which includes the **integerLength(Int)** and **fractionLength(Int)** methods to specify the number of digits in the integer and decimal parts, and the **integerAndFractionLength(integer: Int, fraction: Int)** method to specify both.

`rounded(rule:``FloatingPointRoundingRule)`

This method rounds the number to the nearest value. The **rule** argument is an enumeration with the values **up**, **down**, **awayFromZero**, **toNearestOrAwayFromZero**, **toNearestOrEven**, and **towardZero**.

`grouping(``Grouping)`

This method determines if the digits of a number are going to be separated in groups (e.g., 9,000,000). The argument is a structure with the properties **automatic** (default) and **never**.

`notation(``Notation)`

This method determines the notation. The argument is a structure with the properties **automatic** (default), **compactName**, and **scientific**.

`sign(strategy:``SignDisplayStrategy)`

This method determines if the sign will be included (+ and -). The **strategy** argument is a **SignDisplayStrategy** structure, which includes the **automatic** (default) and **never** properties, and also the **always(includingZero: Bool)** method to determine if the sign is displayed or not.

`decimalSeparator(strategy:``DecimalSeparatorDisplayStrategy)`

This method determines if a separator is going to be included after the number. The **strategy** argument is a structure with the properties **automatic** (default) and **always**.

The **FormatStyle** protocol defines the **number** property to return the instance of the structure that represents the styles for a number. From this instance, we can apply all the styles we want, as shown below.

Listing 9-14: Formatting a number

```
let mynumber: Double = 32.56789
let text = mynumber.formatted(.number.precision(.fractionLength(2)))
print(text)  // "32.57"
```

The styles are provided one by one with dot notation. We first get the styling structure from the **number** property. Next, we call the **precision()** method, and send to this method the value returned by the **fractionLength()** method, which formats the number with 2 decimal digits. As a result, we get a string with the value "32.57" (the value is rounded up).

Styles can be concatenated, one after another, with dot notation. For instance, in the previous example, the number was rounded up by default, but we can change this behavior by applying the **rounded(rule:)** method, as shown below.

Listing 9-15: Rounding a number

```
let mynumber: Double = 32.56789
let text = mynumber.formatted(.number.precision(.fractionLength(2)).
rounded(rule: .down))
print(text)  // "32.56"
```

In this example, the **rounded(rule:)** method is called after the number is formatted with 2 decimal digits, so the rest of the digits are rounded down.

The grouping, notation, and decimal separator styles usually apply to large numbers. For instance, by default, the digits of large numbers are separated in groups using commas, as in 32,000,000, but we can change this behavior with the **grouping()** method.

Listing 9-16: Disabling grouping

```
let mynumber: Int = 32000000
let text = mynumber.formatted(.number.grouping(.never))
print(text)  // "32000000"
```

We can also show the sign in front of the number (+ or -). In the following example, we always show the sign except when the number is equal to 0.

Listing 9-17: Adding the sign

```
let mynumber: Int = 32000000
let text = mynumber.formatted(.number.sign(strategy:
.always(includingZero: false)))
print(text)  // "+32,000,000"
```

In addition to **number**, the **FormatStyle** protocol defines the **percent** property to style the number as a percentage, and the **currency(code:)** method to format monetary values. The **percent** property is a **Percent** structure that all it does is to add the % sign to the number.

Listing 9-18: Formatting the number as a percentage value

```
let mynumber: Int = 32
let text = mynumber.formatted(.percent)
print(text)  // "32%"
```

On the other hand, the **currency(code:)** method can produce a number with any format and currency symbol we want. The currency is defined by the string assigned to the argument. There are values for any currency available. For instance, the USD string is for American Dollars, the CAD string is for Canadian Dollars, and the EUR string is for Euros. The following example gets the number expressed in Canadian dollars.

Listing 9-19: Formatting currency values

```
let mynumber: Double = 32.55
let text = mynumber.formatted(.currency(code: "CAD"))
print(text)  // "CA$32.55"
```

BASIC

Decimals

With the **formatted()** method, we can round and format numbers for display on the screen. However, in some cases, rounding must be performed during the calculation itself to produce the correct results. This is especially important in financial applications, where values must be rounded consistently throughout the entire calculation process, usually to two decimal places. To perform this type of precise arithmetic, the **Foundation** framework provides the **Decimal** structure. The following are some of the initializers available to create these values.

Decimal(Value)

This initializer creates a **Decimal** structure with the value specified by the argument.

Decimal(string: String)

This initializer creates a **Decimal** structure by parsing the numeric representation contained in a string. The **string** argument is a string with the decimal number to be converted, expressed using base-10 notation.

To create a **Decimal** structure, we can use any Swift numeric values, as shown below.

Listing 9-20: Creating Decimal values

```
var amount = Decimal(19.498743)
print(amount)  // 19.49874300000000512
```

In this example, we create a **Decimal** value using the number **19.498743**, but the value stored internally becomes **19.49874300000000512**. This happens because the number is first converted to a floating-point representation before being used to initialize the **Decimal** structure. To avoid intermediate floating-point conversion and ensure the accurate results we need for financial applications, we can provide the value as a string, as shown below.

Listing 9-21: Creating Decimal values for financial applications

```
var amount = Decimal(string: "19.498743")!
print(amount)  // 19.498743
```

Although this approach preserves the values exactly as they are provided to the structure, numbers used in financial applications must be limited in the number of decimal digits they contain. To round **Decimal** values, the **Foundation** framework provides the following method.

```
NSDecimalRound(UnsafeMutablePointer<Decimal>,
UnsafePointer<Decimal>, Int, NSDecimalNumber.RoundingMode)
```

This method rounds a **Decimal** value according to the arguments. The first argument is a pointer to the **Decimal** value where the result will be stored, the second argument is a pointer to the **Decimal** value to be rounded, the third argument specifies the number of digits to keep in the decimal portion of the value, and the fourth argument defines the rounding behavior to apply. This is an enumeration with the values **plain**, **down**, **up**, and **bankers**.

This is an older method provided by the **Foundation** framework and, as a result, it stores the output directly into the variables passed to it using pointers. A pointer is created by prefixing the variable name with the **&** symbol. In this case, we need two pointers: one referring to the value to be rounded and another referring to the variable where the rounded result will be stored. In the following example, we use this method to round the value introduced before.

Listing 9-22: Rounding Decimal values to two digits

```
var amount = Decimal(string: "19.498743")!
var rounded = Decimal()
NSDecimalRound(&rounded, &amount, 2, .plain)
print(rounded)  // 19.5
```

In this example, the **NSDecimalRound()** method takes the **Decimal** value stored in the **amount** variable and rounds its decimal portion to two digits using the **plain** rounding mode. The **plain** mode rounds to the nearest value based on the digit being removed. If that digit is 5 or greater, the value is rounded up; otherwise, it is rounded down (e.g., 2.346 -> 2.35, 2.344 -> 2.34). Other modes work in similar ways. The **down** mode always rounds toward zero (e.g., 2.349 -> 2.34), the **up** mode always rounds away from zero (e.g., 2.341 -> 2.35), and the **bankers** mode also rounds to the nearest value, but when the value is exactly halfway, it rounds to the nearest even digit (e.g., 2.345 -> 2.34, 2.355 -> 2.36).

Although the previous value was rounded to two decimal digits, printing it to the console displays only one digit in the decimal portion. This happens because the system automatically removes trailing zeros from the value. If we want to display all decimal digits to the user, we must format the final value using the **formatted()** method introduced before. In the following example, we format the value as an amount in U.S. dollars.

Listing 9-23: Formatting a Decimal value

```
var amount = Decimal(string: "19.498743")!
var rounded = Decimal()
NSDecimalRound(&rounded, &amount, 2, .plain)
print(rounded.formatted(.currency(code: "USD")))  // US$19.50
```

Decimal numbers can be used in arithmetic operations like any other numeric type. In this case, we must round values during the calculation process whenever required, and format the final result only at the end before presenting it to the user. In the following example, we show how to calculate taxes from a value, and format the final amount in U.S. dollars.

Listing 9-24: Performing calculations with Decimal values

```
var amount = Decimal(string: "19.498743")!
var rate = Decimal(string: "2.1743")!

var taxes = amount * rate / 100
var rounded = Decimal()
NSDecimalRound(&rounded, &taxes, 2, .plain)
print(rounded.formatted(.currency(code: "USD")))  // US$0.42
```

BASIC

Dates

Foundation defines multiple classes and structures to create and process dates, including **Date**, **Calendar**, **DateComponents**, **DateInterval**, **Locale**, and **TimeZone**. The data type in charge of creating the structure to store the actual date is **Date**. The following are some of the initializers.

`Date()`

This initializer creates a **Date** structure with the current date.

`Date(timeIntervalSinceNow:` `TimeInterval)`

This initializer creates a **Date** structure with a date calculated from the addition of the current date plus the time specified by the **timeIntervalSinceNow** argument. The argument is a value of type **TimeInterval** that indicates how many seconds the date is from the initial date.

`Date(timeInterval:` `TimeInterval,` **`since:`** `Date)`

This initializer creates a **Date** structure with a date calculated from the addition of the date specified by the **since** argument plus the time specified by the **timeInterval** argument in seconds.

`Date(timeIntervalSinceReferenceDate:` `TimeInterval)`

This initializer creates a **Date** structure with a date calculated from a reference date in the past plus the time interval in seconds specified by the argument.

The following example shows different ways to initialize a date.

Listing 9-25: Storing dates with `Date` structures

```
var currentdate = Date()
var nextday = Date(timeIntervalSinceNow: 24 * 60 * 60)
var tendays = Date(timeInterval: -10 * 24 * 3600, since: nextday)
```

As shown in this example, time intervals are expressed in seconds. A simple way to calculate an interval is by multiplying each time component. For example, the **`Date`** structure assigned to the **`nextday`** variable in our example is created by adding one day to the current date. This is done by multiplying the 24 hours in a day by the 60 minutes in an hour and by the 60 seconds in a minute (**`24 * 60 * 60`**). The same approach is used for the **`Date`** assigned to the **`tendays`** variable. In this case, the initializer adds the interval to the date in the **`nextday`** variable. The number of seconds is calculated using the same components as before, but the result is multiplied by **`-10`** to obtain a date that is ten days before **`nextday`**.

IMPORTANT

The interval is declared as a value of type **Double**, but instead of **Double** the framework calls it **TimeInterval**. This is a typealias (an alternative name for an existing type). Once defined, aliases are used exactly like regular data types. To create your own type aliases, you can use the instruction **typealias** (e.g., **typealias Myinteger = Int**).

Besides the initializers, the structure also includes type properties that return special dates. Some of these properties produce values that are useful to set limits and sort lists. The following are the most frequently used.

`distantFuture`

This type property returns a **Date** structure with a value that represents a date in a distant future.

`distantPast`

This type property returns a **Date** structure with a value that represents a date in a distant past.

The **Date** structure also includes properties and methods to calculate and compare dates. The following are the most frequently used.

`timeIntervalSinceNow`

This property returns a **TimeInterval** value representing the difference in seconds between the date in the **Date** structure and the current date.

`timeIntervalSinceReferenceDate`

This property returns a **TimeInterval** value representing the difference in seconds between the current date and a reference date in the past (In modern systems, this is January 1st, 2001). The structure also includes the **`timeIntervalSince1970`** property to return the interval between the current date and January 1st 1970.

`compare``(Date)`

This method compares the date in the **Date** structure with the date specified by the argument and returns an enumeration of type **ComparisonResult** with a value corresponding to the order of the dates. The possible values are **orderedSame** (the dates are the same), **orderedAscending** (the date is earlier than the value), and **orderedDescending** (the date is later than the value).

`timeIntervalSince``(Date)`

This method compares the date in the **Date** structure with the date specified by the argument and returns the interval between both dates in seconds.

`addingTimeInterval``(TimeInterval)`

This method adds the seconds specified by the argument to the date and returns a new **Date** structure with the result.

`addTimeInterval``(TimeInterval)`

This method adds the seconds specified by the argument to the date and stores the result in the same **`Date`** structure.

Comparing dates and calculating the intervals between dates is a constant requirement in app development. The following example compares the current date with a date calculated from a specific number of days. If the resulting date is later than the current date, the code prints a message on the console to show the time remaining in seconds.

Listing 9-26: Comparing two dates

```
var days = 7
var today = Date()
var event = Date(timeIntervalSinceNow: Double(days) * 24 * 3600)

if today.compare(event) == .orderedAscending {
   let interval = event.timeIntervalSince(today)
   print("We have to wait \(Int(interval)) seconds")
   // "We have to wait 604800 seconds"
}
```

The dates in **Date** structures are not associated to any calendar. This means that to get the components in a date, such as the year, month, or day, we must decide first in the context of which calendar the date is going to be interpreted. The calendar for a date is defined by the **Calendar** structure. This structure provides properties and methods to process a date according to a specific calendar, such as Gregorian, Buddhist, or Chinese. To initialize a **Calendar** structure, we have the following initializer and type property.

`Calendar(identifier:` `Identifier)`

This initializer creates a **Calendar** structure with the calendar specified by the argument. The **identifier** argument is a property of a structure called **Identifier** defined inside the **Calendar** structure. The properties available are **gregorian**, **buddhist**, **chinese**, **coptic**, **ethiopicAmeteMihret**, **ethiopicAmeteAlem**, **hebrew**, **ISO8601**, **indian**, **islamic**, **islamic-Civil**, **japanese**, **persian**, **republicOfChina**, **islamicTabular** and **islamicUmmAlQura**.

`current`

This type property returns a structure with the current calendar set in the system.

A **Calendar** structure includes the following properties and methods to manage the calendar and to get and set new dates.

`identifier`

This property returns the value that identifies the calendar.

`locale`

This property sets or returns the **Locale** structure used by the **Calendar** structure to process dates. The value by default is the **Locale** structure set by the system.

`timeZone`

This property sets or returns the **TimeZone** structure used by the **Calendar** structure to process dates. The value by default is the **TimeZone** structure set by the system.

```
dateComponents([Calendar.Component], from: Date)
```

This method returns a **DateComponents** structure with the components indicated by the first argument from the date indicated by the **from** argument. The first argument is a set of enumeration values that represent the components we want to extract from the date. The values available are **era**, **year**, **yearForWeekOfYear**, **quarter**, **month**, **weekOfYear**, **weekOfMonth**, **weekday**, **weekdayOrdinal**, **day**, **hour**, **minute**, **second**, and **nanosecond**.

```
dateComponents([Calendar.Component], from: Date, to: Date)
```

This method returns a **DateComponents** structure with the components indicated by the first argument. These components represent the difference between the dates specified by the **from** and **to** arguments. The first argument is a set of enumeration values that represent each component. The values available are **era**, **year**, **yearForWeekOfYear**, **quarter**, **month**, **weekOfYear**, **weekOfMonth**, **weekday**, **weekdayOrdinal**, **day**, **hour**, **minute**, **second**, and **nanosecond**.

```
date(byAdding: DateComponents, to: Date)
```

This method returns a **Date** structure with the value obtained by adding the components indicated by the **byAdding** argument to the date indicated by the **to** argument.

```
date(from: DateComponents)
```

This method returns a date created from the components provided by the **from** argument.

The **Calendar** structure works along with the **DateComponents** structure to read and return components from a date. The instances created from the **DateComponents** structure include the properties **era**, **year**, **yearForWeekOfYear**, **quarter**, **month**, **weekOfYear**, **weekOfMonth**, **weekday**, **weekdayOrdinal**, **day**, **hour**, **minute**, **second**, and **nanosecond** to read and set the values of the components. The following example combines these tools to get the year of the current date.

Listing 9-27: Extracting components from a date

```
var today = Date()
let calendar = Calendar.current
var components = calendar.dateComponents([.year], from: today)
print("The year is \(components.year!)")
// "The year is 2026"
```

In Listing 9-27, we get a reference to the calendar set in the system from the **current** property and then use the **dateComponents()** method to get the year from the current date, but we can get as many components as we need by adding the corresponding values to the set. The following example gets the year, month, and day from the current date.

Listing 9-28: Extracting multiple components from a date

```
var today = Date()
let calendar = Calendar.current
var comp = calendar.dateComponents([.year, .month, .day], from: today)
print("Today is \(comp.day!)-\(comp.month!)-\(comp.year!)")
// "Today is 02-01-2026"
```

The **DateComponents** structure is used to retrieve the components of existing dates and to set the values for new dates. In the following example, a new **Date** structure is created from the values of a **DateComponents** structure.

Listing 9-29: Creating a new date from single components

```
let calendar = Calendar.current
var comp = DateComponents()
comp.year = 1970
comp.month = 8
comp.day = 21

var birthday = calendar.date(from: comp)
// "Aug 21, 1970, 12:00 AM"
```

The **date(from:)** method of the **Calendar** structure returns a new date with the values provided by the **DateComponents** structure. The components which values are not explicitly defined take values by default. In our example, since we didn't specify the hours and minutes, those values were set to 12:00 AM.

Generating a new date requires a specific calendar. For example, in the code of Listing 9-29, the component values are declared using the format established by the Gregorian calendar. In this case, we rely on the calendar provided by the system (`current`), but if we want to use the same calendar regardless of where the app is running, we must set it explicitly using the `Calendar` initializer, as shown below.

Listing 9-30: Using a Gregorian calendar

```
let id = Calendar.Identifier.gregorian
let calendar = Calendar(identifier: id)

var comp = DateComponents()
comp.year = 1970
comp.month = 8
comp.day = 13
var birthday = calendar.date(from: comp)
// "Aug 13, 1970 at 12:00 AM"
```

Declaring a specific calendar is not only recommended when creating new dates but also when calculating dates by adding components, as in the following example.

Listing 9-31: Adding components to a date

```
let id = Calendar.Identifier.gregorian
let calendar = Calendar(identifier: id)
var comp = DateComponents()
comp.day = 120

var today = Date()
// "27 Dec 2025 at 8:29 PM"
var appointment = calendar.date(byAdding: comp, to: today)
// "26 Apr 2026 at 8:29 PM"
```

The **date()** method implemented in Listing 9-31 adds components to a date and returns a new **Date** structure with the result. The component **day** was set to 120. The **date()** method takes this value, adds it to the date in the **today** structure, and returns a date that is 120 days from the current date.

A common task when working with multiple dates is calculating the time between them, such as the number of hours remaining for a process to complete or the number of days remaining before an event begins. The **Calendar** structure provides a version of the **dateComponents()** method that allows us to compare two dates and obtain the difference expressed in a specific component.

Listing 9-32: Comparing dates

```
let calendar = Calendar.current
var comp = DateComponents()
comp.year = 1970
comp.month = 8
comp.day = 21

var today = Date()
var birthdate = calendar.date(from: comp)

if let olddate = birthdate {
   let components = calendar.dateComponents([.day], from: olddate, to:
today)
   print("Days between dates: \(components.day!)")
   // "Days between dates: 20217"
}
```

This example calculates the days between a date of birth and the current date. The value returned by the **date()** method used to generate the date of birth returns an optional, so we unwrap it before calculating the difference. We assign this value to the **olddate** constant and then compare it with the current date. The number of days between dates is returned and printed on the console.

Another way to specify intervals between dates is with the **DateInterval** structure. This structure allows us to create an interval with **Date** values. The following are the initializers.

`DateInterval(start: Date, end: Date)`

This initializer creates a **DateInterval** structure with the interval between the values provided by the **start** and **end** arguments.

`DateInterval(start: Date, duration: TimeInterval)`

This initializer creates a **DateInterval** structure with an interval that starts at the date specified by the **start** argument and last as long as the time specified by the **duration** argument.

The **DateInterval** structure also offers the following properties and methods.

`start`

This property sets or returns the initial **Date** of the interval.

`end`

This property sets or returns the final **Date** of the interval.

`duration`

This property sets or returns the duration of the interval in seconds.

`contains(Date)`

This method returns a Boolean value that indicates whether the date specified by the argument is inside the interval or not.

`intersects(DateInterval)`

This method returns a Boolean value that indicates if the interval intersects with the interval specified by the argument.

`intersection(with: DateInterval)`

This method returns a **DateInterval** value with the interval in which the original interval and the one provided by the **with** argument overlap.

A typical use of the **DateInterval** structure is to create an interval from two dates and check if a specific date falls within the interval, as in the following example.

Listing 9-33: Finding a date in an interval

```
let calendar = Calendar.current

var components = DateComponents()
components.year = 1970
components.month = 8
components.day = 21
var birthday = calendar.date(from: components)

components.year = 2027
```

```
components.month = 8
components.day = 21
var future = calendar.date(from: components)

if birthday != nil && future != nil {
   let today = Date()
   let interval = DateInterval(start: birthday!, end: future!)
   if interval.contains(today) {
      print("You still have time")  // "You still have time"
   }
}
```

The code in Listing 9-33 creates two dates, **birthday** and **future**, and then generates an interval from one date to another. The **contains()** method is used next to check whether the current date is within the interval or not.

As with numbers, the **Foundation** framework also provides tools to format dates. The **Date** structure defines two versions of the **formatted()** method.

formatted(date: DateStyle, **time:** TimeStyle)

This method formats the date with the styles specified by the arguments. The **date** argument defines the style for the date. It is a structure with the type properties **abbreviated**, **complete**, **long**, **numeric**, and **omitted**. And the **time** argument defines the style for the time. It is a structure with the type properties **complete**, **omitted**, **shortened**, and **standard**.

formatted(FormatStyle)

This method formats the date with the styles specified by the argument.

If all we need is a standard format, we can call the **formatted(date:, time:)** method with the styles we want for the date and time. The method takes these values and returns a string with a date in the format defined by the current locale (the user's language and location).

Listing 9-34: Formatting dates

```
let mydate = Date.now
let text = mydate.formatted(date: .abbreviated, time: .omitted)
print(text)  // "27 Dec 2025"
```

The code in Listing 9-34 gets the current date from the **now** property and then calls the method with the **abbreviated** and **omitted** values. This creates a string that contains an abbreviated date and no time ("27 Dec 2025").

Standard styles include all the components of the date, but the **Date** structure includes an additional version of the **formatted()** method that takes a **FormatStyle** structure to format the date any way we want. The following are some of the methods included for customization.

day(Day)

This method includes the day. The argument defines the style for the day. It is a structure with the properties **defaultDigits**, **ordinalOfDayInMonth**, and **twoDigits**.

month(Month)

This method includes the month. The argument defines the style for the month. It is a structure with the properties **abbreviated**, **defaultDigits**, **narrow**, **twoDigits**, and **wide**.

year(Year)

This method includes the year. The argument defines the style for the year. It is a structure with the properties **defaultDigits** and **twoDigits**.

hour(Hour)

This method includes the hour. The argument defines the style for the hour. It is a structure with the properties **defaultDigitsNoAMPM** and **twoDigitsNoAMPM**.

minute(Minute)

This method includes the minutes. The argument defines the style for the minutes. It is a structure with the properties **defaultDigits** and **twoDigits**.

second(Second)

This method includes the seconds. The argument defines the style for the seconds. It is a structure with the properties **defaultDigits** and **twoDigits**.

weekday(Weekday)

This method includes the weekday. The argument defines the style for the day. It is a structure with the properties **abbreviated**, **narrow**, **oneDigit**, **short**, **twoDigits**, and **wide**.

The **FormatStyle** structure includes the following properties to configure the parameters used to format the date.

calendar

This property sets or returns the calendar used to format the date. It is of type **Calendar**.

locale

This property sets or returns the locale used to format the date. It is of type **Locale**.

timeZone

This property sets or return the time zone used to format the date. It is of type **TimeZone**.

Although we can create our own **FormatStyle** structure, the structure includes a type property called **dateTime** to return an instance with the calendar and standard values set by the device. If the configuration by default is enough, we can use this property to format the date.

Listing 9-35: Specifying a custom format

```
let mydate = Date.now
let text = mydate.formatted(.dateTime.weekday(.wide))
print(text)  // "Friday"
```

The code in Listing 9-35 calls the **weekday()** method from the **FormatStyle** structure returned by the **dateTime** property to get the day of the week. In this case, we call the method with the value **wide**, which returns the day's full name ("Friday"). Only one component is included in this example, but we can add more by concatenating the methods with dot notation, as shown below.

Listing 9-36: Including multiple date components

```
let mydate = Date.now
let text = mydate.formatted(.dateTime.day().hour().month(.wide))
print(text)  // "27 December at 9 PM"
```

In this code, we implement the **day()**, **month()**, and **hour()** methods. Note that the order in which the methods are called doesn't matter. The result is a string with a date that includes the month (full name), the day, and the hour ("27 December at 9 PM").

Dates and times are always formatted using a standard format that depends on the user's locale (language and region). As a result, the same date can appear differently depending on the settings of the device. For example, the same date will look like this "27 Dec 2026" for a user in the United States and like this "2026年12月27日" for a user in China. The user's locale is determined by an instance of the `Locale` structure. Every device has a default `Locale` assigned to it, and our code uses it unless we explicitly specify a different one. To access the current locale or create a new one, the `Locale` structure provides the following initializer and type property.

`Locale(identifier: String)`

This initializer creates a **Locale** structure configured for the region specified by the argument. The argument is a string that represents a language and a region, such as en_ US for the United States or zh_CN for China.

`current`

This type property returns the **Locale** structure assigned by default to the device or specified by the user in the Settings app.

The **FormatStyle** structure includes the following method to format a date for a locale.

`locale(Locale)`

This method specifies the locale to use by the formatter.

While it is recommended to use the `Locale` structure set by the system and keep the values by default, there are cases where our application must present the information with a specific configuration. For example, we may need to create an application that always displays dates in Chinese, regardless of where the user is located. We can do this by defining a `Locale` structure and then using that structure in the `locale()` method, as shown below.

Listing 9-37: Specifying a different locale

```
let mydate = Date.now
let chinaLocale = Locale(identifier: "zh_CN")
let text = mydate.formatted(.dateTime.locale(chinaLocale).day().month().
year())
print(text)  // "2026年6月27日"
```

This example creates a new **Locale** structure with the zh_CN identifier, which corresponds to China and the Chinese language, and then formats the date with this locale and the **day()**, **month()**, and **year()** methods. The result is a string with the date in Chinese ("2026年6月27日").

IMPORTANT

The list of identifiers you can use to create a **Locale** structure is extensive. You can print the type property **availableIdentifiers** from the **Locale** structure to get an array with all the values available (`print(Locale.availableIdentifiers)`).

The date stored in a **Date** structure is not a date but the number of seconds between the date represented by the structure and an arbitrary date in the past (January 1st, 2001). To process these values and get the actual date, the **Calendar** structure needs to know the user's time zone. The **Foundation** framework includes the **TimeZone** structure to manage these values. A **TimeZone** structure is assigned by default to the system with the time zone where the device is located, but we can define a different one as we did with the **Locale** structure. To get a reference to the current structure or create a new one, the **TimeZone** structure includes the following initializer and type property.

`TimeZone(identifier: String)`

This initializer creates a **TimeZone** structure configured for the time zone determined by the value of the **identifier** argument. The argument is a string that represents the name of the time zone, such as "Europe/Paris" or "Asia/Bangkok".

`current`

This type property returns the **TimeZone** structure assigned by default to the device or specified by the user in the Settings app.

The **FormatStyle** structure does not include a method to provide a specific time zone to format the date. For this purpose, we must create a custom instance and then assign the time zone to the structure's **timeZone** property, as in the following example.

Listing 9-38: Working with different time zones

```
if let tokyoTimeZone = TimeZone(identifier: "Asia/Tokyo"),
   let madridTimeZone = TimeZone(identifier: "Europe/Madrid") {
   let mydate = Date.now
   let mytime = mydate.formatted(.dateTime.hour().minute().second())

   var dateTimeStyle = Date.FormatStyle()
   dateTimeStyle.timeZone = tokyoTimeZone
   let tokyoTime = mydate.formatted(dateTimeStyle.hour().minute()
      .second())
   dateTimeStyle.timeZone = madridTimeZone
   let madridTime = mydate.formatted(dateTimeStyle.hour().minute()
      .second())

   print("My Time: \(mytime)")
   // "My Time: 9:25:19 PM"
   print("Tokyo Time: \(tokyoTime)")
   // "Tokyo Time: 10:25:19 AM"
   print("Madrid Time: \(madridTime)")
   // "Madrid Time: 3:25:19 AM"
}
```

The code in Listing 9-38 creates two **TimeZone** structures, one for Tokyo and another for Madrid. If successful, we initialize a **FormatStyle** structure and format the date twice, first for Tokyo and then for Madrid. Note that the **TimeZone** structure is assigned to the **timeZone** property of the **FormatStyle** structure before using it to format each date.

IMPORTANT

The list of names for the time zones is stored in a database. The **TimeZone** structure offers the **knownTimeZoneIdentifiers** type property that you can print to see all the values available (`print(TimeZone.knownTimeZoneIdentifiers)`).

BASIC

Measurements

Some applications require the use of units of measurement, such as pounds, miles, liters, and others. Defining our own units present some challenges, but the **Foundation** framework includes the **Measurement** structure to simplify our work. This structure includes two properties: one for the value and another for the unit. The initializer requires these two values to create the structure.

```
Measurement(value: Double, unit: Unit)
```

This initializer creates a **Measurement** structure with the values specified by the **value** and **unit** arguments. The **unit** argument is a property of a class that inherits from the **Dimension** class.

The value of a `Measurement` structure represents the magnitude of the measurement, such as **55** in 55 km, while the unit is defined by the `Dimension` class and represents the unit of measurement, such as **km** in 55 km. The `Dimension` class provides the basic functionality required to describe a measurement, but the specific units are defined by its subclasses. The **Foundation** framework includes several subclasses for this purpose. The following are the most frequently used.

```
UnitDuration
```

This subclass defines the units of measurement for duration (time). It includes the following properties to represent the units: **seconds**, **minutes**, and **hours**, with **seconds** defined as the basic unit.

```
UnitLength
```

This subclass defines the units of measurement for length. It includes the following properties to represent the units: **megameters**, **kilometers**, **hectometers**, **decameters**, **meters**, **decimeters**, **centimeters**, **millimeters**, **micrometers**, **nanometers**, **picometers**, **inches**, **feet**, **yards**, **miles**, **scandinavianMiles**, **lightyears**, **nauticalMiles**, **fathoms**, **furlongs**, **astronomicalUnits**, and **parsecs**, with **meters** defined as the basic unit.

```
UnitMass
```

This subclass defines the units of measurement for mass. It includes the following properties to represent the units: **kilograms**, **grams**, **decigrams**, **centigrams**, **milligrams**, **micrograms**, **nanograms**, **picograms**, **ounces**, **pounds**, **stones**, **metricTons**, **shortTons**, **carats**, **ouncesTroy**, and **slugs**, with **kilograms** defined as the basic unit.

```
UnitVolume
```

This subclass defines the units of measurement for volume. It includes the following properties to represent the units: **megaliters**, **kiloliters**, **liters**, **deciliters**, **centiliters**, **milliliters**, **cubicKilometers**, **cubicMeters**, **cubicDecimeters**, **cubicMillimeters**, **cubicInches**, **cubicFeet**, **cubicYards**, **cubicMiles**, **acreFeet**, **bushels**, **teaspoons**, **tablespoons**, **fluidOunces**, **cups**, **pints**, **quarts**, **gallons**, **imperialTeaspoons**, **imperialTablespoons**, **imperialFluidOunces**, **imperialPints**, **imperialQuarts**, **imperialGallons**, and **metricCups**, with **liters** defined as the basic unit.

The **Measurement** structure includes the following properties and methods to access the values and convert them to different units.

```
value
```

This property sets or returns the structure's value. It is of type **Double**.

unit

This property sets or returns the structure's unit of measurement. It is represented by a property of a subclass of the **Dimension** class.

convert(to: Unit)

This method converts the values of the **Measurement** structure to the unit specified by the **to** argument.

converted(to: Unit)

This method converts the values of the **Measurement** structure to the unit specified by the **to** argument and returns a new **Measurement** structure with the result.

The initialization of a **Measurement** structure is simple, we just need to provide the value for the magnitude and the property that represents the unit of measurement we want to use. The following example creates two structures to store a measurement of 30 centimeters and another of 5 pounds.

Listing 9-39: Initializing `Measurement` structures

```
var length = Measurement(value: 30, unit: UnitLength.centimeters)
// 30.0 cm
var weight = Measurement(value: 5, unit: UnitMass.pounds)
// 5.0 lb
```

If the measurements are of the same dimension, such as length, we can perform operations with their values. The **Measurement** structure allows the operations **+**, **-**, *****, **/**, and also the use of the comparison operators **==**, **!=**, **<**, **>**, **<=**, and **>=** to compare values. The following example adds two measurements in centimeters.

Listing 9-40: Adding the values of two `Measurement` structures

```
var length = Measurement(value: 200, unit: UnitLength.centimeters)
var width = Measurement(value: 800, unit: UnitLength.centimeters)

var total = length + width  // 1000.0 cm
```

If the units are different, the **Measurement** structure returned by the operation is defined with the dimension's basic unit. For example, if we are working with lengths, the basic unit is meters. The following example adds two lengths of different units (meters and kilometers). The system converts kilometers to meters and then performs the addition, returning a **Measurement** structure with a value in meters (the basic unit).

Listing 9-41: Adding two values of different units

```
var length = Measurement(value: 300, unit: UnitLength.meters)
var width = Measurement(value: 2, unit: UnitLength.kilometers)
var total = length + width  // 2300.0 m
```

If we want everything to be performed in the same unit, we can convert a value to a different unit using the methods **convert()** or **converted()**. In the following example, we convert the unit of the **length** variable to kilometers and perform the addition again in kilometers.

Listing 9-42: Converting units

```
var length = Measurement(value: 300, unit: UnitLength.meters)
var width = Measurement(value: 2, unit: UnitLength.kilometers)
length.convert(to: UnitLength.kilometers)
var total = length + width  // 2.3 km
```

The values of a **Measurement** structure are displayed as they are stored, but this is usually not what we need to show to users. To prepare the value for display, the **Measurement** structure includes its own **formatted()** method.

formatted(FormatStyle**)**

This method formats the measurement with the styles specified by the argument.

This method requires a **FormatStyle** structure to format the value. The structure includes the following initializer and type method to create an instance for every type of unit.

FormatStyle(width: UnitWidth, **locale:** Locale, **usage:** MeasurementFormatUnitUsage, **numberFormatStyle:** FloatingPointFormatStyle**)**

This initializer creates a **FormatStyle** structure with the format set by the arguments. The **width** argument specifies how the unit is going to be displayed. It is a structure with the properties **abbreviated**, **narrow**, and **wide**. The **locale** argument specifies the locale. The **usage** argument specifies the purpose of the measurement. The structure to declare this value includes properties for any type of measurement, including **asProvided** (UnitType), **food** (UnitEnergy), **general** (UnitType), **person** (UnitLength), **personHeight** (UnitLength), **personWeight** (UnitMass), **road** (UnitLength), **weather** (UnitTemperature), and **workout** (UnitEnergy). Finally, the **numberFormatStyle** argument specifies the format of the value.

measurement(width: UnitWidth, **usage:** MeasurementFormatUnitUsage, **numberFormatStyle:** FloatingPointFormatStyle**)**

This method returns a **FormatStyle** structure with the format set by the arguments. The arguments are the same required by the initializer.

The **FormatStyle** structure also includes an additional initializer and method specifically designed to format temperatures.

FormatStyle(width: UnitWidth, **locale:** Locale, **usage:** MeasurementFormatUnitUsage, **hidesScaleName:** Bool, **numberFormatStyle:** FloatingPointFormatStyle)

This initializer creates a **FormatStyle** structure with the format set by the arguments. The **width** argument specifies how the unit is going to be displayed. It is a structure with the properties **abbreviated**, **narrow**, and **wide**. The **locale** argument specifies the locale. The **usage** argument specifies the purpose of the measurement. The structure to declare this value includes properties for any type of measurement. The ones available at the moment are **asProvided** (UnitType), **food** (UnitEnergy), **general** (UnitType), **person** (UnitTemperature), **personHeight** (UnitLength), **personWeight** (UnitMass), **road** (UnitLength), **weather** (UnitTemperature), and **workout** (UnitEnergy). The **hidesScaleName** argument determines if the name of the unit is going to be displayed, and the **numberFormatStyle** argument specifies the format of the value.

measurement(width: UnitWidth, **locale:** Locale, **usage:** MeasurementFormatUnitUsage, **hidesScaleName:** Bool, **numberFormatStyle:** FloatingPointFormatStyle)

This method returns a **FormatStyle** structure with the format set by the arguments. The arguments are the same required by the initializer.

Most of the arguments in these initializers and methods are optional. If an argument is not declared, the formatter uses values by default. For instance, if we just want to show the full name of the unit, we can implement the **measurement()** method with the **width** argument and the value **wide**.

Listing 9-43: Formatting a measurement

```
let length = Measurement(value: 40, unit: UnitLength.kilometers)
let text = length.formatted(.measurement(width: .wide, usage:
.asProvided))
print(text)  // "40 kilometers"
```

In this example, we have also included the **usage** argument with the **asProvided** value to tell the formatter to use the original units (kilometers). If this argument is not declared, the formatter uses the value by default, which formats the measurement with the configuration and locale set in the device. For example, if we specify the **road** value instead, the formatter will format the value to represent a distance using the device's locale, which for a device running in the United States means that the original value will be expressed in miles.

Listing 9-44: Formatting a measurement for a specific purpose

```
let length = Measurement(value: 40, unit: UnitLength.kilometers)
let text = length.formatted(.measurement(width: .wide, usage: .road))
print(text)  // "25 miles"
```

By default, the formatter rounds the number. That's why in this example the result of converting 40 kilometers to miles is 25, when it should've been 24.8548. If we want to specify a different format, we can add the **numberFormatStyle** argument and implement the methods introduced before. For instance, we can specify a precision of 2 digits for the decimal part with the **fractionLength()** method, as shown below.

Listing 9-45: Formatting the measurement value

```
let length = Measurement(value: 40, unit: UnitLength.kilometers)
let text = length.formatted(.measurement(width: .wide, usage: .road,
numberFormatStyle: .number.precision(.fractionLength(2))))
print(text)  // "24.85 miles"
```

The **formatted()** method in this example includes the **width** argument to get the unit's full name, the **usage** argument to format the value to represent a distance, and the **numberFormatStyle** argument to format the value. If we are located in the United States, the value is expressed in miles again, but with better accuracy.

If our application must always display a value with the same unit of measurement independently of the device's location, we can set a specific locale. The **formatted()** method doesn't include an argument to designate a locale, but the initializers included in the **FormatStyle** structure do. The following example formats the measurements in Chinese, no matter where the device is located.

Listing 9-46: Formatting a measurement for a specific locale

```
func calculate() -> String {
   let length = Measurement(value: 40, unit: UnitLength.kilometers)
   let chinaLocale = Locale(identifier: "zh_CN")
   var format = Measurement<UnitLength>.FormatStyle(width: .wide, locale:
      chinaLocale, usage: .asProvided)
   let text = length.formatted(format)
   return text
}
print(calculate())  // "40.00公里"
```

The code in Listing 9-46 defines a method called `calculate()` to format the measurement. The method initializes a **FormatStyle** structure with the locale configured for China and then calls the **formatted()** method with this structure to format the value. Note that the **FormatStyle** structure is defined inside the **Measurement** structure, which is a generic structure and therefore we must specify the type of values the structure is going to process. In this case, we are working with units of length so we must specify the **UnitLength** data type.

BASIC

Timer

Timers are objects that perform an action after a specific period of time. There are two types of timers: repeating and non-repeating. Repeating timers perform the action and then reschedule themselves to do it again in an infinite loop. Non-repeating timers, on the other hand, perform the action one time and then invalidate themselves. The **Foundation** framework defines the **Timer** class to create these timers. The class includes the following properties and methods.

isValid

This property returns a Boolean value that indicates if the timer can still be fired or it was invalidated.

timeInterval

This property returns the time interval in seconds for repeating timers.

tolerance

This property sets or returns a period of tolerance in seconds to provide the system with more flexibility. It is a value of type **TimeInterval**. The value by default is 0.

scheduledTimer(withTimeInterval: TimeInterval, **repeats:** Bool, **block:** Closure)

This type method returns repeating and non-repeating timers depending on the values of its arguments. The **withTimeInterval** argument represents the seconds the timer must wait before performing the action, the **repeats** argument is a Boolean value that determines if the timer is repeating (**true**) or non-repeating (**false**), and the **block** argument is the closure to be execute when the time is up.

fire()

This method fires the timer without considering the time remaining.

invalidate()

This method invalidates the timer (stops the timer).

The **scheduledTimer()** method creates a timer according to the value of the arguments and automatically adds it to an internal loop that processes the timer when the time is up. The time is set in seconds with a **TimeInterval** value (a typealias of **Double**), and we can declare the closure as a trailing closure to simplify the code, as in the following example.

Listing 9-47: Creating a non-repeating timer

```
print("Wait 5 seconds...")
Timer.scheduledTimer(withTimeInterval: 5.0, repeats: false) { (timer) in
   print("The time is up")
}
```

The code in Listing 9-47 creates a non-repeating timer. It prints a message and then initializes a timer with the **scheduleTimer()** method. The timer is set to 5 seconds, non-repeating, and the closure just prints a message on the console. When we execute the code, the first message appears on the console and 5 seconds later the message "The time is up" is printed below.

The closure receives a reference to the **Timer** object that we can use to access the timer's properties. It was not required in the last example because the timer invalidated itself, but it may be useful when working with repeating timers, as in the following example.

Listing 9-48: Creating a repeating timer

```
nonisolated(unsafe) var counter = 0

func startTimer() {
   Timer.scheduledTimer(withTimeInterval: 1.0, repeats: true) {
      (timerref) in
      report(timer: timerref)
   }
}
func report(timer: Timer) {
   print("\(counter) times")
   counter += 1
   if counter > 10 {
      print("Finished")
      timer.invalidate()
   }
}
startTimer()
```

In this code, we define two functions. The **startTimer()** function schedules the timer, and the **report()** function is executed when the time is up. In this last function, we count how many times the code was executed with the **counter** variable and print a message on the console with the result. If the value is greater than 10, we print the text "Finished" and invalidate the timer, so the function is not executed anymore.

IMPORTANT

Global variables can be modified from anywhere in the code, including different threads, which can produce a bug called data race. A data race is an error that occurs when two or more pieces of code try to modify a value at the same time. In this example, we know that the variable is only going to be modified from the closure assigned to the timer, so we prefix it with the `nonisolated(unsafe)` keyword to tell the system that we are going to take care of the issue ourselves. We will learn more about data races and how to avoid them in Chapter 12.

BASIC

9.3 - Core Graphics

Core Graphics is a long-standing framework written in the C programming language. It was designed to provide a two-dimensional drawing engine for Apple platforms. The framework includes a comprehensive set of drawing tools along with its own specialized data types. Rather than being replaced over time, the **Core Graphics** framework was integrated into newer frameworks, which is why it remains an essential part of Apple's graphics stack today.

BASIC

Data Types

What modern applications rely on most from this long-standing framework are its data types. In Swift, Core Graphics data types are implemented as structures, each with its own initializers, properties, and methods. These structures store values that describe attributes of on-screen elements, such as position and size. For example, the following structure is used to represent coordinate values.

`CGFloat`

This structure is used to store values of type **Double** for drawing purposes.

A more complex structure is **CGSize**, designed to store values that represent dimensions (width and height). This data type includes the following initializer and properties.

`CGSize(width: CGFloat, height: CGFloat)`

This initializer creates a **CGSize** structure with the values specified by the **width** and **height** arguments. The structure defines initializers to create instances from values of type **Int**, **CGFloat**, and **Double**.

`zero`

This type property returns a **CGSize** structure with its values set to zero.

`width`

This property sets or returns the structure's width.

`height`

This property sets or returns the structure's height.

Another structure included in the framework is **CGPoint**, which is used to define points in a two-dimensional coordinate system. It includes the following initializer and properties.

`CGPoint(x: CGFloat, y: CGFloat)`

This initializer creates a **CGPoint** structure with the coordinates specified by the **x** and **y** arguments. The structure defines initializers to create instances from values of type **Int**, **CGFloat**, and **Double**.

`zero`

This type property returns a **CGPoint** structure with its values set to zero.

`x`

This property sets or returns the structure's x coordinate.

`y`

This property sets or returns the structure's y coordinate.

There is also a more complex structure called **CGRect** that we can use to define and work with rectangles. This data type includes the following initializers and properties.

`CGRect(origin: CGPoint, size: CGSize)`

This initializer creates a **CGRect** structure to store the origin and size of a rectangle. The **origin** argument is a **CGPoint** structure with the coordinates of the rectangle's origin, and the **size** argument is a **CGSize** structure with the rectangle's width and height.

`CGRect(x: CGFloat, y: CGFloat, width: CGFloat, height: CGFloat)`

This initializer creates a **CGRect** structure to store the origin and size of a rectangle. The **x** and **y** arguments define the coordinates of the rectangle's origin, and the **width** and **height** arguments its size. The structure defines initializers to create instances from **Int**, **CGFloat**, and **Double** values.

`zero`

This type property returns a **CGRect** structure with its values set to zero.

`origin`

This property sets or returns a **CGPoint** structure with the coordinates of the rectangle's origin.

`size`

This property sets or returns a **CGSize** structure with the rectangle's width and height.

`midX`

This property returns the value of the rectangle's **x** coordinate located at the horizontal center of the rectangle. The framework also include the **minX** and **maxX** properties to return the smallest and largest value in the x-coordinate for the rectangle.

`midY`

This property returns the value of the rectangle's **y** coordinate located at the vertical center of the rectangle. The framework also include the **minY** and **maxY** properties to return the smallest and largest value in the y-coordinate for the rectangle.

The structures provided by the **Core Graphics** framework are declared and initialized as any other structures in Swift, but we must import the framework first for the types to be recognized.

Listing 9-49: Initializing Core Graphics' structures

```
import CoreGraphics
import Playgrounds

#Playground {
    var myfloat: CGFloat = 35
    var mysize: CGSize = CGSize(width: 250, height: 250)
    var mypoint: CGPoint = CGPoint(x: 20, y: 50)
    var myrect: CGRect = CGRect(origin: mypoint, size: mysize)
}
```

> **IMPORTANT**
>
> To access the features of the `Core Graphics` framework, we normally need to import it explicitly, as shown in this example. However, higher-level frameworks such as `Foundation` and `SwiftUI` import Core Graphics automatically. As a result, when we are working with these frameworks, there is no need to import Core Graphics separately.

The **CGSize** and **CGPoint** structures may be initialized with their member initializers, but the **CGRect** structure provides an additional initializer to create the instance from the values of its internal structures.

Listing 9-50: Using the CGRect convenience initializer

```
var myrect = CGRect(x: 30, y: 20, width: 100, height: 200)

print("The origin is at \(myrect.origin.x) and \(myrect.origin.y)")
// "The origin is at 30.0 and 20.0"
print("The size is \(myrect.size.width) by \(myrect.size.height)")
// "The size is 100.0 by 200.0"
```

The **origin** and **size** properties of a **CGRect** value are **CGPoint** and **CGSize** structures, respectively, so they can be copied into other variables or properties as any other values.

Listing 9-51: Accessing the structures inside a `CGRect` structure

```
var myrect = CGRect(x: 30, y: 20, width: 100, height: 200)

var mypoint = myrect.origin
var mysize = myrect.size
```

```
print("The origin is at \(mypoint.x) and \(mypoint.y)")
// "The origin is at 30.0 and 20.0"
print("The size is \(mysize.width) by \(mysize.height)")
// "The size is 100.0 by 200.0"
```

When we don't have initial values for the coordinates or the size, we can use the **zero** type property to create a structure with all the values initialized to 0.

Listing 9-52: Assigning empty structures to a `CGRect` variable

```
var myrect = CGRect.zero

print("The origin is at \(myrect.origin.x) and \(myrect.origin.y)")
// "The origin is at 0.0 and 0.0"
print("The size is \(myrect.size.width) by \(myrect.size.height)")
// "The size is 0.0 by 0.0"
```

The **CGRect** structure also includes properties to calculate values from the coordinates and size. For example, the **midX** and **midY** properties return the coordinates at the center of the rectangle.

Listing 9-53: Calculating the coordinate at the center of the rectangle

```
var rect = CGRect(x: 0, y: 0, width: 100, height: 100)

print("The horizontal center is \(rect.midX)")
// "The horizontal center is 50.0"
```

IMPORTANT

In this chapter, we have explored the part of **Core Graphics** used by modern frameworks to build user interfaces, but the framework is extensive and includes tools for the creation of custom graphics. For more information, visit our website and follow the links for this chapter.

Chapter 10

Regular Expressions

BASIC

10.1 - Standard Regular Expressions

Using the methods provided by the **Foundation** framework and the `String` data type, we can modify strings, insert or remove substrings, and determine whether a string contains another string. For simple tasks, these tools are more than sufficient. However, determining whether a string represents a phone number or an email address, or extracting values from more complex structures such as the contents of a spreadsheet, often requires iterating through characters one by one and comparing them with previous characters to identify valid or invalid patterns. This approach is cumbersome and error prone. To simplify this kind of processing, Swift provides support for regular expressions.

A regular expression is a sequence of characters that represent the pattern we want to identify in a string. It consists of common characters that match the characters in the string one by one, and also special characters that describe specific patterns or matches. For example, the expression `/message/` matches any string that contains the word "message". However, if we add the special characters `\s+` at the end (`/message\s+/`), the regular expression now matches a string containing the word "message" followed by one or more spaces. To differentiate special characters from common characters, they must be preceded by a backward slash, as in `\s` (the `s` represents a white space). There are dozens of special characters to represent anything we need. The following are the most frequently used.

`\s` and `\t` match a whitespace. The `\s` character matches any whitespace character, and the `\t` character matches only tab characters.
`\d` matches a digit (any number from 0 to 9).

To match a character from a group of characters, regular expressions include the following special characters.

`[]` matches any character in the square brackets (e.g., `[abc]` matches the character `a` or `b` or `c`). It can also match a character in a range of consecutive characters. The range is defined with a hyphen, as in `[a-z]` to match a lowercase letter from `a` to `z`, or `[a-zA-Z]` to match a lowercase or uppercase letter from `a` to `z`.
`[^]` matches any character different from those in the square brackets (e.g., `[^abc]` matches any character that is not `a` or `b` or `c`).
`.` (dot) matches any character except a new line (new lines are represented by the special character `\n`).

| (or) matches the character on the left or the right (e.g., **a|b** matches the character **a** or the character **b**).

These special characters match a single character. To specify quantity, regular expressions include the following special characters.

`*` specifies 0 or more occurrences of the previous character.
`+` specifies 1 or more occurrences of the previous character.
`?` specifies 0 or 1 occurrences of the previous character.
`{min, max}` specifies the minimum and maximum occurrences of the previous character (e.g., `{3, 5}` matches 3, 4, or 5 characters). If the maximum value is ignored, the expression matches the character at least the times specified by the minimum value (e.g., `{2,}` matches the character at least two times). And if only one value is declared, the expression matches the character exactly the times specified by the value (e.g., `{2}` matches the characters only two times).

There are also special characters to delineate the expression. The following are the most frequently used.

`^` matches the beginning of the string.
`$` matches the end of the string.
`()` define a subexpression (useful when we want to capture the value).

Regular expressions are defined by a combination of these special characters and also common characters, as we have seen before. For instance, if we have a string like "Name: John" and we want to know whether the string contains any name, we can match it against the regular expression `/Name:\s+[a-zA-Z]+/`. The slashes at the beginning and the end are the way to tell Swift that this is a regular expression. The string "Name:" matches exactly the same sequence of characters in the original string. The `\s+` characters tell the system that the string "Name:" must be followed by one or more spaces, and the `[a-zA-Z]+` characters indicate that after the space there should be one or more lowercase or uppercase letters. If the original string doesn't contain the string "Name:" followed by one or more spaces and one or more letters, we won't get a match.

To match a regular expression against a string, the Swift Standard Library includes the following methods.

firstMatch(of: Regex)

This method finds the first sequence of characters in the string that match the regular expression specified by the **of** argument.

wholeMatch(of: Regex)

This method matches the whole string against the regular expression.

prefixMatch(of: Regex)

This method matches the beginning of the string against the regular expression.

```
matches(of: Regex)
```

This method finds all the sequences of characters in the string that match the regular expression.

These methods take a value of type **Regex** (a structure defined to contain a regular expression) and return a value of type **Match** if a match is found or **nil** otherwise. The **Match** structure contains two properties: **output** with the strings that matched the regular expression, and **range** with a **Range** value that represents the range of the overall match.

For example, the following code processes the string and regular expression introduced before with the **firstMatch()** method to check if the string contains a name.

Listing 10-1: Using regular expressions

```
import Playgrounds

#Playground {
    let message = "Name: John"
    let regex = /Name:\s+[a-zA-Z]+/

    if let match = message.firstMatch(of: regex) {
       let found = match.output
       print("Found: \(found)")  // "Found: Name: John"
    }
}
```

This code defines a regular expression and assigns it to a constant called **regex**. The Swift compiler detects that the value is a regular expression and creates a **Regex** structure with it. Next, the **firstMatch()** method matches the string in **message** against the regular expression in **regex** and returns a value with the result. In this case, the string contains the string "Name:" followed by one or more spaces and one or more letters, so the match is successful. The part of the string that matches the regular expression is assigned to the **output** property of the **Match** structure returned by the method, so we assign it to a constant and print it on the console.

Do It Yourself

Update the **MyPlayground.swift** file in your project with the code in Listing 10-1. You should see the message "Found: Name: John" printed on the console. AI agents can create regular expressions for you. Ask your AI agent to modify the regular expression in Listing 10-1 to also include numbers. The agent will read the current expression and replace it with something like "/Name:\s+[a-zA-Z0-9]+/", so the name can now include numbers.

IMPORTANT

Declaring the regular expression between slashes, as we did in our example, allows Xcode to recognize it and provide feedback. If the expression is invalid, it is displayed in a single color, otherwise, the special characters are highlighted. This is the recommended notation in Swift, but the language provides others. For instance, we can create the **Regex** structure directly with the structure's initializer and the regular expression in quotes.

The values returned in the **Match** structure depend on the expression. In the previous example, the **output** property returns a single string with the sequence of characters that match the regular expression, but we can define subexpressions to capture specific values. For instance, if we want to only get back the name, we can define a subexpression using parentheses.

Listing 10-2: Capturing values with subexpressions

```
let message = "Name: John"
let regex = /Name:\s+([a-zA-Z]+)/

if let match = message.firstMatch(of: regex) {
   let found = match.output.1
   print("The name is: \(found)")  // "The name is: John"
}
```

In this example, the **output** property returns a tuple. The first element of the tuple is the string that matches the regular expression, as before, but the second value is the string that matches the expression between parentheses. (In this case, one or more letters after a space.)

The **firstMatch()** method finds the first sequence of characters that match the regular expression and returns that value. If we want to get all the matches in a string, we must implement the **matches()** method.

Listing 10-3: Capturing multiple values

```
let message = "Name: John, Name: George, Name: David"
let regex = /Name:\s+([a-zA-Z]+)/

let matches = message.matches(of: regex)
if !matches.isEmpty {
   let names = matches.map({ value in
      return value.output.1
   })
   let list = names.joined(separator: ", ")
   print("Names are: \(list)")
   // "Names are: John, George, David"
}
```

The **matches()** method returns an array of **Match** structures. Again, we use a subexpression to capture the names, so we loop through the array with the **map()** function, return the name from each match, and then join them with the **joined()** method to get the list of names separated by comma.

The Swift Standard Library includes a few more methods to take advantage of regular expressions. The following are the most frequently used.

split(separator: Regex)

This method divides a string by a separator and returns an array with the parts. The **separator** argument specifies the regular expression that matches the characters used to split the string.

replacing(Regex, **with:** String)

This method replaces the sequence of characters that match the regular expression specified by the first argument with the string specified by the **with** argument.

The **split()** method is useful when we have to process long texts or a text file line by line. In the following example, we use triple quotes to tell the Swift compiler to add the characters **\n** after each line of text to generate a new line (see Chapter 2, Listing 2-23). This is how usually text documents are structured. To read each line, we define a regular expression with the special character **\n** and then call the **split()** method to get each line of text in an array.

Listing 10-4: Processing multiple lines of text with a regular expression

```
let message = """
John
George
Martin
"""
let separator = /\n/
let lines = message.split(separator: separator)
print(lines)  // ["John", "George", "Martin"]
```

The **replacing()** method could be implemented in a similar way, but instead of using the regular expression as a separator, we can use it to replace the sequence of characters with another one. For example, we can replace each new-line character in our string (**\n**) with a comma to get all the lines of text in a single string.

Listing 10-5: Replacing the characters that match a regular expression

```
let message = """
John
George
Martin
"""
let separator = /\n/
let result = message.replacing(separator, with: ", ")
print(result)  // "John, George, Martin"
```

10.2 - Regex Builder

The regular expressions implemented so far match simple characters, like whitespaces or letters, but the complexity of regular expressions increases when we try to match patterns that can take many combinations of characters. For example, if we want to know whether a string represents an email address, we must determine if the string begins with a set of valid characters, such as letters and numbers, followed by the @ character, followed by the characters valid for a domain, including the right number of characters for the extension. The complexity of this type of regular expressions goes from something like `/[A-Z0-9._%+-]+@[A-Z0-9.-]+\.[A-Z]{2,}/`, which is capable of validating approximately 98% of email addresses, to regular expressions that extend for three or four lines of text to match all the possible email addresses. Constructing and understanding these regular expressions is not an easy task. For this reason, the Swift Standard Library introduces the **RegexBuilder** framework.

The **RegexBuilder** framework defines structures to represent every special character in a regular expression and others to represent special features. The following are the structures included to specify characters.

`CharacterClass``(Characters)`

This structure represents a group of characters and also special characters like whitespaces and new lines (similar to square brackets in literal notation). The initializer takes ranges of characters separated by comma, and also type properties to represent common characters, such as **`any`** (any character), **`digit`** (digits from 0 to 9), **`whitespace`**, and **`newlineSequence`**.

`Anchor`

This structure defines an anchor character, like the ^ and **$** characters used in literal notation to match the beginning and end of the string. The instances are created from the type properties **`startOfLine`**, **`endOfLine`**, **`startOfSubject`**, **`endOfSubject`**, **`endOfSubjectBeforeNewline`**, **`firstMatchingPositionInSubject`**, **`textSegmentBoundary`**, and **`wordBoundary`**.

`Lookahead``(Closure)`

This structure matches the characters returned by the argument without capturing them.

`ChoiceOf``(Closure)`

This structure matches different values, like the **|** (OR) in literal notation.

There are also structures to represent quantifiers.

`One``(Characters)`

This structure matches only one occurrence of the group of characters specified by the argument.

Optionally(RegexRepetitionBehavior, Closure)

This structure matches a character that may or may not be present. The first argument determines the type of matching. It is a structure with the type properties **eager** (default), **possessive**, and **reluctant**. And the second argument specifies the characters we want to match.

ZeroOrMore(RegexRepetitionBehavior, Closure)

This structure matches zero or more characters (similar to the * character in literal notation). The first argument determines the type of matching. It is a structure with the type properties **eager** (default), **possessive**, and **reluctant**. And the second argument specifies the characters we want to match.

OneOrMore(RegexRepetitionBehavior, Closure)

This structure matches one or more characters (similar to the + character in literal notation). The first argument determines the type of matching. It is a structure with the type properties **eager** (default), **possessive**, and **reluctant**. And the second argument specifies the characters we want to match.

Repeat(Characters, **count:** Int)

This structure matches the characters specified by the first argument the number of times specified by the **count** argument (similar to the {} characters in literal notation). The **count** argument can be replaced by a range of values to specify multiple quantities (2...4).

The framework also includes structures to capture values from the string.

Capture(Closure, **transform:** Closure)

This structure captures the sequence of characters that matches the expression provided by the first argument. The **transform** argument is a closure used to transform the captured value into any data type we want.

TryCapture(Closure, **transform:** Closure)

This structure captures the sequence of characters that matches the expression provided by the first argument, but unlike **Capture**, the structure returns a no-match if the value cannot be transformed.

The Regex Builder is built from a **Regex** structure. The structure includes an initializer that takes strings, structures, and regular expressions in literal notation to define the final expression. For instance, the following Regex Builder defines the same regular expression used before to determine if a string contains a name.

Listing 10-6: Defining a regular expression with a Regex Builder

```
import RegexBuilder
import Foundation
import Playgrounds
```

```
#Playground {
    let regex = Regex {
       "Name:"
       OneOrMore(.whitespace)
       OneOrMore {
          CharacterClass("a"..."z", "A"..."Z")
       }
    }
    let message = "Name: John"
    let result = message.matches(of: regex)
    if !result.isEmpty {
       print(result[0].output)
       // "Name: John"
    }
}
```

In this example, we first import the **RegexBuilder** framework to have access to the framework's definitions and then initialize the `Regex` structure to build our regular expression. In this case, we are looking for a sequence of characters that begins with the string "Name:", followed by one or more whitespaces, and one or more lowercase or uppercase letters. The patterns are declared one per line. We first declare the string "Name:", then use the `OneOrMore` structure with the `CharacterClass` structure returned by the `whitespace` property to match one or more whitespaces, and finally include another `OneOrMore` structure, this time with a `CharacterClass` defined with two ranges, one for lowercase letters and another for uppercase letter. The result is the same as before. The `matches()` method returns an array with a `Match` structure that contains the string that matches the entire expression ("Name: John").

If we want to capture the name, as we did in the example in Listing 10-2, we must include the `Capture` structure. In the following example, we use the `One` structure to ensure that the name is capitalized, and capture the name with the `Capture` structure.

Listing 10-7: Capturing a value with a Regex Builder

```
let regex = Regex {
   "Name:"
   OneOrMore(.whitespace)
   Capture {
      One(CharacterClass("A"..."Z"))
      OneOrMore {
         CharacterClass("a"..."z")
      }
   }
}
let message = "Name: John"
let result = message.matches(of: regex)
if let name = result.first?.output.1 {
   print("The name is: \(name)")  // "The name is: John"
}
```

This regular expression matches the string "Name:" followed by one or more spaces, as before, but now the name's first character is matched against an uppercase letter, so the string is captured only if the name is capitalized. The rest of the code is the same as before; we match the expression against the string and print the value captured by the **Capture** structure.

The **Match** structure returns substrings. These are instances of a **Substring** structure defined in the Swift Standard Library to store a slice of a string. But we can transform these values to any data types we want. For this purpose, the initializer of the **Capture** structure includes an argument called **transform**. The closure assigned to this argument is called with the value that matches the expression and from it we can convert it to a different data type and return it. For instance, in the following example we convert two values into integers.

Listing 10-8: Transforming values to the right data type

```
let message = "09 units, stock 190"
let regex = Regex {
   Capture {
      OneOrMore(.digit)
   } transform: { value in
      Int(value)
   }
   OneOrMore(.any, .reluctant)
   Capture {
      OneOrMore(.digit)
   } transform: { value in
      Int(value)
   }
}
let result = message.matches(of: regex)
if let units = result.first?.output.1, let stock = result.first?.output.2
{
   let total = units + stock
   print("Final Stock: \(total)")  // "Final Stock: 199"
}
```

The string we are processing in this example includes numbers at the beginning and the end. The first number represents the units to be added to the stock, and the last number represents the current stock. To get the first number as an integer, we capture one or more digits. (The **digit** property returns a **CharacterClass** structure that represents numbers between 0 and 9.) Capturing the last number is a bit tricky. Because we may have any characters in between, to match the text we use the **any** property, which returns a **CharacterClass** structure that represents any character. But this includes numbers, which means that the number at the end will also be matched by this pattern and the last **Capture** structure won't have anything else to match. By default, the behavior of the **OneOrMore** structure is determined by the **RegexRepetitionBehavior** structure returned by the **eager** property. This structure tells the system to match as many characters as it can. But we can change this behavior by assigning the **reluctant** property instead, as we did in our example. The structure returned by this property asks the system to match the current expression until any character matches the next expression, so when the number is found, the system moves to the next **OneOrMore** structure that matches digits and we are able to capture our second number.

Although we can transform any value we want, some like dates and complex numbers may require long patterns. To simplify our work, the **Foundation** framework includes properties and methods we can use to match these values. The following are the most frequently used.

localizedDecimal(locale: Locale)

This method returns a **FormatStyle** structure to match decimal numbers. The **locale** argument specifies the locale.

localizedCurrency(code: Currency, **locale:** Locale)

This method returns a **FormatStyle** structure to match currency values. The **code** argument can be specify as a string to represent the currency (e.g.: "USD"). The **locale** argument specifies the locale.

date(DateStyle, **locale:** Locale, **timeZone:** TimeZone, **calendar:** Calendar?)

This method returns a **ParseStrategy** structure to match a date. The first argument is a **DateStyle** structure that specifies the format of the date. The structure includes the type properties **abbreviated**, **complete**, **long**, **numeric**, and **omitted**. The **locale** argument specifies the locale, the **timeZone** argument the time zone, and the **calendar** argument the calendar we want to use to interpret the date.

dateTime(date: DateStyle, **time:** TimeStyle, **locale:** Locale, **timeZone:** TimeZone, **calendar:** Calendar?)

This method returns a **ParseStrategy** structure to match date and time. The **date** argument is a structure that specifies the format of the date. The structure includes the type properties **abbreviated**, **complete**, **long**, **numeric**, and **omitted**. The **time** argument is a structure that specifies the format for the time. The structure includes the type properties **complete**, **omitted**, **shortened**, and **standard**. The **locale** argument specifies the locale, the **timeZone** argument the time zone, and the **calendar** argument the calendar we want to use to interpret the date and time.

The following example shows how to match dates and currency. In this case, we process a string with multiple items and split the content in lines of text to process one line at a time, as we did in Listing 10-4.

Listing 10-9: Matching dates and currency

```
let usLocale = Locale(identifier: "en_US")

let separator = /\n/
let content = """
06/15/2025 Lamp $35.00
06/21/2025 Desk $250.50
06/29/2025 Chair $129.00
"""
let regex = Regex {
   Capture {
      One(.date(.numeric, locale: usLocale, timeZone: .current))
   }
```

```
    OneOrMore(.whitespace)
    Capture {
        OneOrMore(CharacterClass("a"..."z", "A"..."Z"))
    }
    OneOrMore(.whitespace)
    Capture {
        One(.localizedCurrency(code: "USD", locale: usLocale))
    }
}
let lines = content.split(separator: separator)
for line in lines {
    if let result = line.firstMatch(of: regex) {
        print("Date: \(result.output.1.formatted(date: .complete, time:
            .omitted))")
        print("Item: \(result.output.2)")
        print("Price: \(result.output.3)")
    }
}
```

When working with dates and currency, we must ensure that the locale we use matches the format of the input data. In this case, both the date and the currency in the text follow a format that is standard in the United States. For this reason, we create a **Locale** structure configured for that country and use it when defining the **Regex** structure.

The pattern in the regular expression matches a single date value, followed by a sequence of uppercase and lowercase letters, and finally a single currency value expressed in U.S. dollars. These three values are captured using **Capture** structures and printed to the console. Because the date is returned as a **Date** value, we can format it using the **formatted()** method introduced in Chapter 9. The result is shown below.

```
Date: Sunday, 15 June 2025
Item: Lamp
Price: 35
Date: Saturday, 21 June 2025
Item: Desk
Price: 250.5
Date: Sunday, 29 June 2025
Item: Chair
Price: 129
```

Figure 10-1: *Processing dates and currency*

IMPORTANT

This introduction to regular expressions only scratches the surface. Regular expressions support many patterns and techniques that allow us to extract and process text in powerful ways. Exploring them in depth is beyond the scope of this book. For additional resources and examples, visit our website and follow the links for this chapter.

Chapter 11
Swift Tools

BASIC

11.1 - Tools

Swift includes special keywords that can be added to our code to expand functionality, enforce requirements, or automatically generate additional code. These keywords usually appear prefixed with the `@` or `#` symbols and are interpreted by the Swift compiler at build time. They allow us to annotate declarations, modify how values are stored or accessed, and inject behavior that would otherwise require repetitive or complex code.

IMPORTANT

This chapter introduces several Swift tools, including property wrappers, attributes, and macros. These tools are widely used in modern frameworks such as SwiftUI and in advanced Swift features such as concurrency. In Chapter 12, we will learn how these tools are applied in the context of concurrency. For more information on SwiftUI, read our book *SwiftUI for Masterminds* (**www.formasterminds.com**).

BASIC

Property Wrappers

Property wrappers are a tool provided by Swift that allow us to encapsulate reusable behavior around a property. They are conceptually similar to the computed properties introduced in Chapter 4 (see Listing 4-15), but they can be applied consistently across multiple properties. For example, we can define a property wrapper that constrains a property's value to a specific range. Any property declared using that wrapper will then automatically accept only values within those limits.

A property wrapper is defined as a structure, but the definition must be preceded by the **`@propertyWrapper`** keyword and include a property called **`wrappedValue`** to process and store the value. The following example illustrates how to define a property wrapper that limits a property's value to a minimum of 0 and a maximum of 255.

Listing 11-1: Defining a property wrapper

```
import Foundation
import Playgrounds

#Playground {
    @propertyWrapper
    struct ClampedValue {
        var storedValue: Int = 0
        var min: Int = 0
        var max: Int = 255

        var wrappedValue: Int {
            get {
                return storedValue
            }
            set {
                if newValue < min {
                    storedValue = min
                } else if newValue > max {
                    storedValue = max
                } else {
                    storedValue = newValue
                }
            }
        }
        init(wrappedValue: Int) {
            self.wrappedValue = wrappedValue
        }
    }
}
```

This example defines a property wrapper called **ClampedValue**. The structure contains three properties to store and control the value. The **storedValue** property stores the current value of the property, and the **min** and **max** properties determine the minimum and maximum values allowed for the properties defined with this property wrapper. There is also the required **wrappedValue** property, defined as a computed property with a getter and a setter. The getter returns the current value of the **storedValue** property, and the setter checks whether the new value is within the minimum and maximum allowed before storing it. If the new value exceeds any of these limits, the values of the **min** or **max** properties are assigned to the **storedValue** property instead.

The code in Listing 11-1 defines the property wrapper, but it does not define any property of this kind. Implementing a property wrapper is easy. We simply declare properties as we normally do, but prefix them with the name of the property wrapper preceded by the `@` character.

Listing 11-2: Using a property wrapper

```
struct Price {
    @ClampedValue var firstPrice: Int
    @ClampedValue var secondPrice: Int
```

```
    func printMessage() {
        print("First Price: \(firstPrice)")
        // "First Price: 0"
        print("Second Price: \(secondPrice)")
        // "Second Price: 255"
    }
}
var purchase = Price(firstPrice: -42, secondPrice: 350)
purchase.printMessage()
```

The **Price** structure in Listing 11-2 includes two properties that use the **ClampedValue** property wrapper, **firstPrice** and **secondPrice**, as well as a method to print their values. Instances of the structure are initialized with the values **-42** and **350**. Both values exceed the limits established by the property wrapper, so the value stored in each property is the limit that was exceeded (**0** for **firstPrice** and **255** for **secondPrice**).

BASIC

Attributes

Attributes provide additional information about declarations, such as properties and methods, as well as data types like structures and classes. They are written by prefixing the attribute name with the **@** character and can include configuration values enclosed in parentheses. Swift includes a wide range of attributes, each designed to serve a specific purpose. The following are the most frequently used.

@available(Values)

This attribute is used to specify the minimum system version required to run the code. It accepts a list of arguments, separated by commas, that define the availability requirements for different platforms. The possible values are **macOS**, **iOS**, **watchOS**, **tvOS**, **visionOS**, and **anyAppleOS** (to include any Apple operating system), as well as special values like the * character to indicate all other platforms, or **unavailable** to indicate that the code cannot be used on that platform at all.

@escaping

This attribute is used to mark escaping closures, that is, closures that remain in memory after the function that received the closure finish executing.

@objc

This attribute exposes a declaration, such as a property, method, or data type, to the Objective-C runtime. It is commonly used when interoperating with Objective-C code, for example when passing values to legacy frameworks written in that language.

The **@available** attribute is commonly used in frameworks and APIs to tell developers what is available and what is not, but we can also use it in our own code to adapt functionality to older systems. In this case, all we need to do is specify the name and version of the system for which the code is available. For example, we can declare a method that is only available on iOS 27 or later, as shown below.

Listing 11-3: Specifying the availability of a function

```
@available(iOS 27.0, *)
func runFeature() {
    print("Running code for iOS 27 or newer.")
}
```

In this example, the **@available** attribute specifies that the **runFeature()** function is only available on iOS 27 or later. The * as the second parameter indicates that other platforms are not affected. This serves as a compile-time signal to anyone working on the project that the function must not be called on earlier versions. To enforce this restriction at runtime, we use the **#available** condition. This is an availability check that works with conditional statements such as **if else** to determine whether a specific system version is available. For example, we can use it to call the **runFeature()** function only when the application is running on iOS 27 or later, as shown below.

Listing 11-4: Calling a function only if available

```
@available(iOS 27.0, *)
func runFeature() {
    print("Running code for iOS 27 or newer.")
}
if #available(iOS 27.0, *) {
    runFeature()
} else {
    print("Running code for older OS")
}
```

Another common attribute we may need to use in our code is **@escaping**. This attribute allows us to keep a closure in memory even after the function that receives it has finished executing. This usually applies to asynchronous operations, as we will see in Chapter 12. To declare an escaping closure, all we need to do is add the **@escaping** attribute before the closure's type, as shown in the following example.

Listing 11-5: Declaring escaping closures

```
nonisolated(unsafe) var myclosure: () -> Void = {}

func passclosure(closure: @escaping () -> Void) {
   myclosure = closure
}
passclosure() { () -> Void in
   print("Closure Executed")
}
myclosure()
```

This example declares a variable called **myclosure** that stores a closure that doesn't receive or return any values (**() -> Void**), and then assigns an empty closure to it. After that, we define a function called **passclosure()** that receives an escaping closure and all it does is to assign that closure to the **myclosure** variable. Next, we call the **passclosure()** function with a closure that prints a value on the console, so now the **myclosure** variable contains that closure. Finally, we execute the closure in **myclosure** and the message is printed on the console.

> **IMPORTANT**
>
> When we define the data type of a closure, we must declare the data types of the values it receives and the data type of the values it returns. Therefore, if the closure doesn't return any value, we must declare the return type as **Void**, as we did in Listing 11-5.

In addition to these common attributes, there is another one we may need to apply when working with legacy frameworks. Many of these frameworks were written in Objective-C and therefore expect declarations that can be exposed to the Objective-C runtime. To make a Swift declaration available to Objective-C, we can use the **@objc** attribute. For example, the **Foundation** framework provides an older **scheduledTimer()** method, which creates a timer that executes a method referenced by a selector. Selectors are an Objective-C mechanism for referencing methods, so to use them in Swift, we must mark the method invoked by the selector with the **@objc** attribute, as shown below.

Listing 11-6: Declaring an Objective-C method

```
import Foundation
import Playgrounds

#Playground {
   class Clock: NSObject {
      var counter = 0

      func startTimer() {
         Timer.scheduledTimer(timeInterval: 1.0, target: self, selector:
            #selector(runCounter), userInfo: nil, repeats: true)
      }
      @objc func runCounter() {
         counter += 1
         print("Count: \(counter)")
      }
   }
   let clock = Clock()
   clock.startTimer()
}
```

In this example, we define a class called **Clock** that includes two methods: the **startTimer()** method to start a timer, and the **runCounter()** method to increment the value of a counter each time it is executed. The **startTimer()** method creates a timer that uses a selector to call the **runCounter()** method every second. Because this method is invoked through a selector, it must be marked with the `@objc` attribute so it can be accessed by the Objective-C runtime. As a result, the value of the `counter` property is incremented and then printed to the console once per second.

IMPORTANT

Note that classes intended to work with Objective-C APIs must inherit from the `NSObject` class. This class is defined in the **Foundation** framework and provides the basic behavior required by objects used in older Objective-C based runtimes.

BASIC

Macros

Macros are another tool provided by Swift to help simplify our code. A macro generates code automatically and injects it into our source code before the application is compiled. All we need to do is apply the macro, and the Swift compiler takes care of generating and inserting the required code for us.

There are two types of macros: freestanding macros and attached macros. Freestanding macros insert code into an expression, such as those assigned to variables, while attached macros modify a declaration, such as an enumeration, structure, or class. Freestanding macros are included in our code by prefixing the name with the # character, while attached macros use the @ character. We have introduced freestanding macros before. The `#Preview` and `#Playground` macros included in the template created by Xcode for new projects are freestanding macros that generate all the code necessary to run the app or execute additional code and display the results on the Canvas, but there are others. For example, below are some useful freestanding macros defined by the Swift Standard Library.

`#file`

This macro produces the name of the file.

`#filePath`

This macro produces the path of the file.

`#line`

This macro produces the line number in the code where the macro appears.

`#function`

This macro produces the name of the function in which the macro appears.

The following example shows how to use these macros in our code.

Listing 11-7: Implementing Freestanding macros

```
func showMacros() {
   print("File Name \(#file)")  // "File Name MyPlayground.playground"
   print("File Path \(#filePath)") // "File Name MyPlayground.playground"
   print("Line \(#line)")  // "Line 4"
   print("Function \(#function)")  // "Function showMacros()"
}
showMacros()
```

When the Swift compiler finds a macro, the macro is executed, the code generated by the macro is inserted into our code, and then the application is compiled. For instance, when the compiler finds the **#file** macro, the macro gets the name of the file and adds it to the string in the **print()** function. After all the macros are processed, the code is compiled and executed.

IMPORTANT

Macros are typically provided through Swift packages and can be shared among teams of developers or with the wider community. You do not need to create your own macros to build applications, but they are used extensively throughout Apple's frameworks. If you want to learn more about macros, visit our website and follow the links for this chapter.

Chapter 12
Swift Concurrency

BASIC

12.1 - Approachable Concurrency

Apple systems can take advantage of the many cores available in modern processors to execute multiple pieces of code at the same time, increasing the amount of work a program can perform at any given moment. This is useful not only for improving performance but also for keeping an application responsive. For example, in an app that allows users to download images from the web, we cannot force them to wait until a download finishes before doing anything else. The image should be downloaded in the background while the user is free to select another image or continue working with the app. To make this possible, the system divides work across separate CPU threads, each one capable of running its own sequence of instructions in parallel with the others.

BASIC

Threads

A thread is a path of execution that can run a sequence of instructions independently from others, allowing multiple operations to occur in parallel on the same processor. To perform multiple tasks at the same time, the system splits the work into processing threads and assigns them to the available CPU cores.

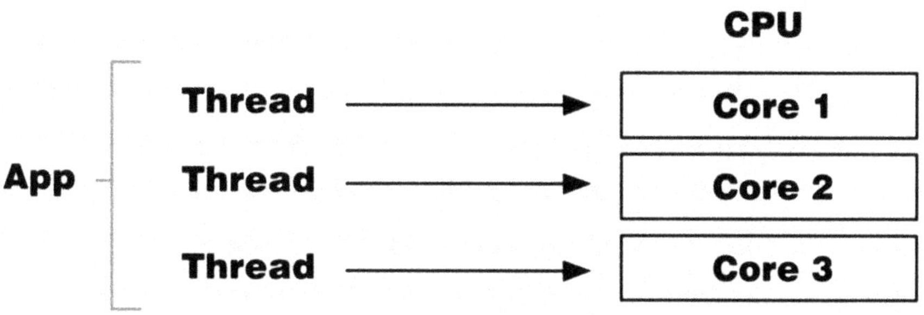

Figure 12-1: *Threads*

Of course, CPUs have a limited number of cores, and our app usually runs alongside many other applications and system processes. As a result, hundreds or even thousands of tasks may be active at any given time. The computer handles this workload by alternating between threads. The operating system schedules multiple threads on the same CPU core and rapidly switches between them, giving each thread a share of processing time until all the work is completed.

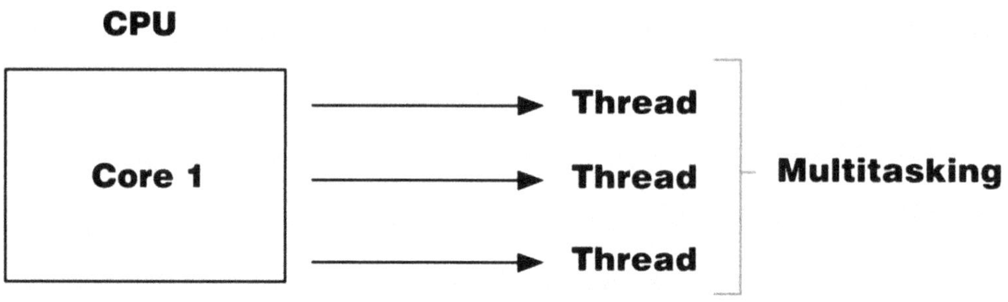

Figure 12-2: *Multitasking*

The system is responsible for assigning threads to specific cores and distributing processing time among them, but our app must indicate when additional threads are required. Every app is automatically assigned a single thread, known as the *main thread*, and it can create additional threads, commonly referred to as *background threads*. The main thread controls the user interface and responds to user interactions, while background threads are typically used for more demanding and time consuming tasks, such as downloading or processing images.

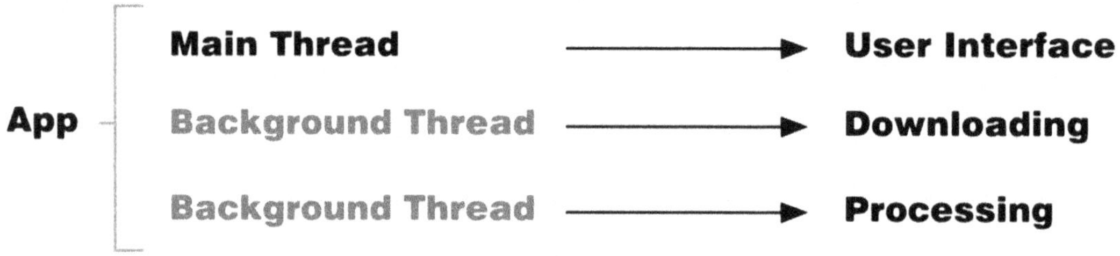

Figure 12-3: *Main thread and background threads*

When we create a new application, all code initially runs on the main thread, and it is up to us to decide when background threads are needed to process data more efficiently and keep the app responsive. Swift 6.4 defines three ways to execute our code: synchronously, asynchronously, and concurrently. The simplest approach is to run everything on the main thread. For example, if an application does not perform any demanding work, all tasks can be executed sequentially on the main thread, as shown below.

Figure 12-4: *Synchronous processing*

This is called synchronous processing because each task is executed in sequential order, one after another, and no task can begin until the previous one has finished. If an application performs time consuming operations, such as downloading an image from the web, those tasks can be performed asynchronously. An asynchronous task suspends its execution while waiting for an operation to complete, allowing the system to perform other work in the meantime. For example, if our app needs to download an image, we can perform the task asynchronously, so while this code is waiting for the image to come back from the server, the system can continue performing other tasks.

Figure 12-5: *Asynchronous processing*

Although asynchronous tasks are often sufficient to keep the user interface responsive, more processing intensive work can take too long to return control to the main thread, causing the interface to freeze or even the app to crash. In situations like this, we need to create additional threads to execute those tasks in the background. For example, if an app needs to download and process large images, those operations can be moved to background threads, allowing the main thread to continue responding to user interactions and updating the interface, as shown below.

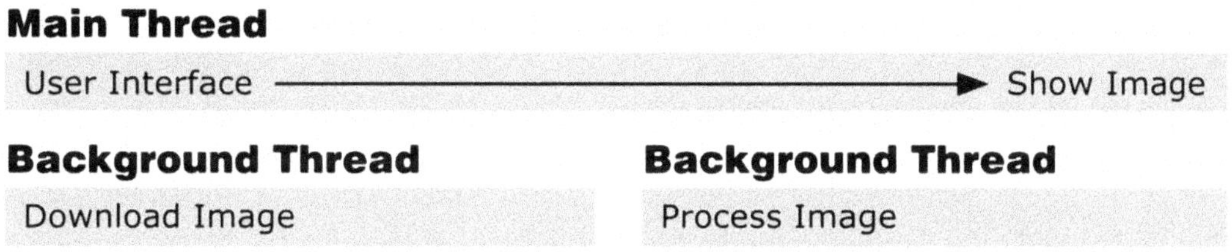

Figure 12-6: *Concurrent processing*

This is known as concurrent processing, in which multiple tasks run at the same time, and it is one of the most challenging aspects of app development. To implement this type of processing, we must decide which tasks should run on which threads, coordinate communication between them, pass data safely, and notify other threads when work is finished or results are available. To help manage this complexity, Swift 6.4 introduces a set of language improvements and compiler settings known as *Approachable Concurrency*. These features are designed to make it easier for developers to adopt concurrent code in their applications. With approachable concurrency, we can start by building our application to run synchronously on the main thread, and then add asynchronous tasks and concurrency only when needed.

BASIC

Configuration

When we create a new project, Xcode configures it with default settings. At the moment, new projects are configured to use Swift 5. If we are not yet sure whether our application will require concurrency, we can begin development using Swift 5 and switch to Swift 6 later when we are ready. This option is available in the project's settings. To access these settings, we need to select the project from the Navigator (Chapter 1, Figure 1-4, number 8), open the Build Settings panel, and then navigate to the Swift Compiler section, as shown below.

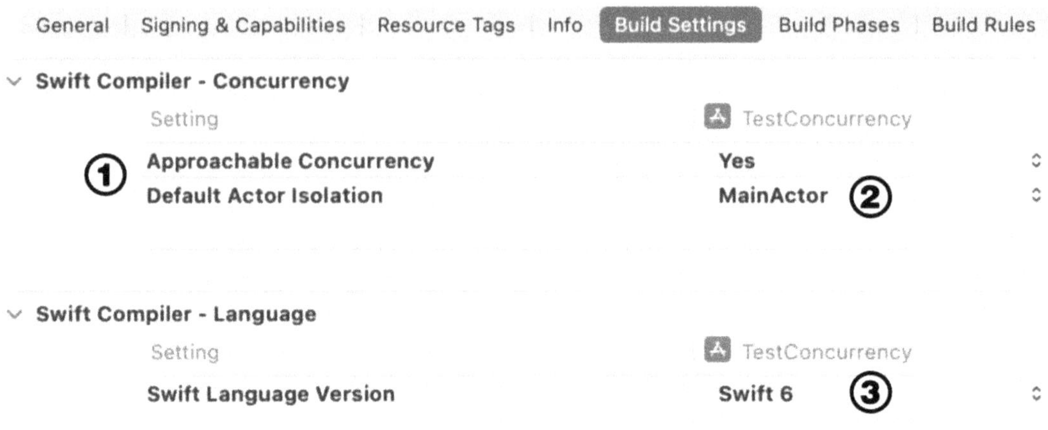

Figure 12-7: *Concurrency options*

At this point, there are three configuration options we need to set to enable Swift 6.4 concurrency in our app. Two of these settings control how Swift concurrency behaves (Figure 12-7, number 1). The first option is called **Approachable Concurrency**. When this option is set to **Yes**, the compiler enables a set of features that make it easier to adopt Swift concurrency in our application. The second option is called **Default Actor Isolation**. This option determines the execution context used by default (Figure 12-7, number 2). If we select **MainActor**, the compiler runs all code on the main thread (also known as the Main Actor), unless we specify otherwise. This simplifies development and allows us to introduce concurrency only when it is actually needed. The last option controls the version of the language we want to use (Figure 12-7, number 3). If we do not care about concurrency, we can develop the app using **Swift 5**, which is the default. However, if we want to implement approachable concurrency features, we need to set the language version to **Swift 6**.

Do It Yourself

Open your project, click the project's name at the top of the Navigator (Chapter 1, Figure 1-4, number 8), open the Build Settings panel, and navigate to the Swift Compiler section. Make sure the Approachable Concurrency option is set to **Yes**, the Default Actor Isolation option is set to **MainActor**, and the language version is set to **Swift 6**.

BASIC

Applying Concurrency

Swift's concurrency features are designed to help us create more responsive and capable applications for Apple devices. As a result, these capabilities cannot be fully tested in a **`#Playground`** macro. To learn how concurrency is applied and how it works, we need to create an application and work with views.

IMPORTANT

In this chapter, we implement concurrency using the **ContentView** view included in the template created by Xcode for a new project. These examples work with the project you have already used to test previous examples, so you only need to follow the instructions to see how they work. If you want to develop a deeper understanding of how these examples work and how to develop a full application with SwiftUI, read our book *SwiftUI for Masterminds* (**www.formasterminds.com**).

BASIC

12.2 - Asynchronous and Concurrent Tasks

As mentioned earlier, when we begin developing an app, all the code runs on the main thread, including our code and all the code that presents and manages the user interface. Although some applications can operate on the main thread without issues, we may soon find the need to implement asynchronous or concurrent code. For example, we may have a method in our app that is executed when the user presses a button. If this method takes too long to finish, the button will become unresponsive until the process is complete, as illustrated by the following code.

Listing 12-1: Running a synchronous task

```
struct ContentView: View {
    var body: some View {
        VStack {
            Text("Hello, world!")
                .padding()
            Button("Run Task") {
                let imageName = loadImage(name: "My Image")
                print(imageName)
            }
        }
        .font(.system(size: 30))
    }
    func loadImage(name: String) -> String {
        sleep(5)
        return "Name: \(name)"
    }
}
```

This example adds a text and a button to the initial view of our application. When pressed, the button executes a method called **loadImage()**. This method is responsible for downloading an image from the web. To simplify the example, we do not perform an actual download. Instead, we use the **sleep()** method provided by the Swift Standard Library to simulate the operation. This method takes a value that specifies how many seconds to wait and blocks the thread during that time, allowing us to observe the effects of running a demanding task on the main thread. In this case, we set the time to 5 seconds, so when we press the button, the method is executed, and the user interface becomes unresponsive for 5 seconds, as shown below.

Figure 12-8: *Running a synchronous task*

Do It Yourself

Select the **ContentView.swift** file in your project. Update the **`ContentView`** structure with the code in Listing 12-1. Select an iPhone simulator using the device button on the toolbar (Figure 1-4, number 4) and open the Canvas (Figure 1-4, number 6). You should see the interface shown in Figure 12-8, left. Click the Run Task button. After 5 seconds, you should see a message printed on the console. The button should be disabled until the process is complete, as shown in Figure 12-8, right.

IMPORTANT

The last example adds some code to the **`ContentView`** view defined by the Xcode's template to display a text and a button on the screen. These are structures defined in the **SwiftUI** framework. The **`VStack`** structure creates a vertical stack of views on the screen, the **`Text`** structure displays text and the **`Button`** structure shows a button that performs an action when clicked or tapped. This is all you need to know to test the examples in this chapter. For a deeper understanding of SwiftUI and how these structures work, read our book *SwiftUI for Masterminds*.

BASIC

Tasks

In the previous example, when we press the button, the **`loadImage()`** method performs a task and then returns a string. Because this method runs on the main thread, the interface is frozen until the process is complete. During this time, the button is disabled and the user cannot interact with it. Of course, this is not the desired behavior. Our app should always remain responsive, and time-consuming tasks should be executed as efficiently as possible. A simple solution is to perform this work asynchronously. Asynchronous tasks run independently and suspend their execution when they need to wait for an operation to complete, returning control to the main thread so the user can perform other tasks and the interface remains responsive.

To define asynchronous tasks, the Swift Standard Library includes the **Task** structure. The following is the structure's initializer.

Task(name: String, **priority:** TaskPriority, **operation:** Closure)

This initializer creates and runs a task. The **name** argument is a string to identify the task. The **priority** argument helps the system decide when to execute the task. It is a structure with the properties **background**, **high**, **low**, **medium**, **userInitiated**, and **utility**. The **operation** argument is a closure with the statements to be executed by the task.

The **Task** structure includes the following properties to cancel a task.

isCancelled

This property returns a Boolean value that indicates if the task was cancelled.

cancel()

This method cancels the task.

checkCancellation()

This method verifies whether the current task has been cancelled. If cancellation has occurred, it immediately throws a **CancellationError** error.

There are also a few type properties and methods available to get information from the current task or create tasks that perform specific processes. The following are the most frequently used.

currentPriority

This property returns the priority of the current task. It is a **TaskPriority** structure with the properties **background**, **high**, **low**, **medium**, **userInitiated**, and **utility**.

isCancelled

This property returns a Boolean value that indicates whether the current task was cancelled.

sleep(for: Duration)

This method suspends the current task the time specified by the **for** argument. The argument is a structure with the type methods **seconds(Double)**, **milliseconds(Double)** and **microseconds(Double)**.

The initializer of the **Task** structure receives a closure with the code we want the task to execute. Inside this closure, we can include any code we want, read properties and call methods, but if we want the methods to be executed asynchronously, we must indicate it explicitly. For this purpose, Swift defines the following keywords.

async

This keyword marks a method as asynchronous. It is declared in the method's definition after the parameter list and before the return type.

await

This keyword is used when calling an asynchronous method. It marks a suspension point where execution may pause and later resume.

To run an asynchronous task, we must create the task using the **Task** structure, define a method with the **async** keyword, and then call that method with the **await** keyword from within the task. The following are the changes we need to make to our previous example to run the **loadImage()** method asynchronously.

Listing 12-2: Running an asynchronous task

```
struct ContentView: View {
   var body: some View {
      VStack {
         Text("Hello, world!")
            .padding()
         Button("Run Task") {
            Task {
               let imageName = await loadImage(name: "My Image")
               print(imageName)
            }
         }
      }
      .font(.system(size: 30))
   }
   func loadImage(name: String) async -> String {
      try? await Task.sleep(for: .seconds(5))
      return "Name: \(name)"
   }
}
```

This example creates a task when the button is pressed. Inside the closure assigned to the task, we call the **loadImage()** method as before, but this time we prefix the call with the **await** keyword to indicate that the method executes asynchronously. To declare the method as asynchronous, we add the **async** keyword to its declaration. When the button is pressed, the task calls the **loadImage()** method, waits for it to finish processing, and then prints a message with the value returned by the method to the console.

The process performed by the method is the same as before: it waits for five seconds and then returns a string. However, instead of using the **sleep()** function from the Swift Standard Library, we now use the **sleep()** method provided by the **Task** structure to simulate the operation. This method suspends execution without blocking the thread, allowing the task to wait while the main thread continues processing user interactions. As a result, the operation runs asynchronously and the interface remains responsive.

Do It Yourself

Update the **ContentView** structure with the code in Listing 12-2. Open the Canvas and press the Run Task button. A message should be printed to the console after five seconds, as before, but this time the button remains active.

We can create as many tasks as needed, and each task can perform any operations we require. For example, we can use the same button to execute two different asynchronous methods, as shown below.

Listing 12-3: Running multiple asynchronous tasks

```
struct ContentView: View {
   var body: some View {
      VStack {
         Text("Hello, world!")
            .padding()
         Button("Run Task") {
            Task {
               let imageName = await loadImage(name: "My Image")
               print(imageName)
            }
            Task {
               let text = await loadText()
               print(text)
            }
            print("This runs outside the tasks")
         }
      }
      .font(.system(size: 30))
   }
   func loadImage(name: String) async -> String {
      try? await Task.sleep(for: .seconds(5))
      return "Name: \(name)"
   }
   func loadText() async -> String {
      try? await Task.sleep(for: .seconds(2))
      return "This is from loadText()"
   }
}
```

This example defines two asynchronous methods. The **loadImage()** method simulates an asynchronous operation that runs for five seconds and then returns a string, as in previous examples. The **loadText()** method behaves in the same way but waits for only two seconds before returning its result. When the button is pressed, the two tasks are created and executed in parallel. As a result, the message returned by the **loadText()** method is printed to the console after two seconds, while the message returned by **loadImage()** appears three seconds later.

Each task is executed independently of the rest of the code, so any code defined after the initialization of the **Task** structures continues executing sequentially and may complete before the tasks finish. In our example, we added a **print()** statement after the tasks are created, which causes the message "This runs outside the tasks" to appear on the console before either task has completed.

Do It Yourself

Update the **ContentView** structure with the code in Listing 12-3. Open the Canvas and press the Run Task button. You should see the message "This runs outside the tasks" printed to the console immediately, followed two seconds later by the message returned by the **loadText()** method, and three seconds later by the message returned by the **loadImage()** method.

In the last example, the tasks are independent of each other and therefore run in parallel. If we want to run an asynchronous task only after a previous task has finished, we must declare them within the same **Task** structure, as shown in the following example.

Listing 12-4: Running asynchronous tasks sequentially

```
struct ContentView: View {
   var body: some View {
      VStack {
         Text("Hello, world!")
            .padding()
         Button("Run Task") {
            Task {
               let imageName = await loadImage(name: "My Image")
               print(imageName)
               let text = await loadText()
               print(text)
            }
         }
      }
      .font(.system(size: 30))
   }
```

```
    func loadImage(name: String) async -> String {
        try? await Task.sleep(for: .seconds(5))
        return "Name: \(name)"
    }
    func loadText() async -> String {
        try? await Task.sleep(for: .seconds(2))
        return "This is from loadText()"
    }
}
```

In this example, we create a single task that calls two asynchronous methods. As before, both methods wait for a period of time and then return a string. However, because the methods are called sequentially, the task waits for the first method to finish before invoking the second one. As a result, the message produced by the **loadImage()** method is printed to the console first, followed by the message produced by the **loadText()** method.

IMPORTANT

A task can run any code you need, including both synchronous and asynchronous methods. When calling an asynchronous method, you must prefix the call with the **await** keyword, but synchronous methods are called as usual.

Although we can create **Task** structures anywhere in our code to initiate an asynchronous task, SwiftUI includes the following modifier to do it when the view appears. The task is perform as soon as the view appears and it is automatically canceled when the view disappears.

task(id: Value, **priority:** TaskPriority, Closure)

This modifier executes a task when the view appears. The **id** argument is a value used to identify the task (Every time this value changes, the task is restarted.) The **priority** argument is a structure that helps the system decide when to execute the task. The available values are **background**, **high**, **low**, **medium**, **userInitiated**, and **utility**. The last argument is a closure that contains the code the task will execute.

The **task()** modifier is useful when all we need is to run an asynchronous task after the views are loaded, as shown in the following example.

Listing 12-5: Running a task when the view is loaded

```
struct ContentView: View {
    var body: some View {
        VStack {
            Text("Hello, world!")
                .padding()
        }
```

```
        .task {
            let imageName = await loadImage(name: "My Image")
            print(imageName)
        }
    }
    func loadImage(name: String) async -> String {
        try? await Task.sleep(for: .seconds(5))
        return "Name: \(name)"
    }
}
```

The **loadImage()** method in this example performs the same operation as before, but because it is called from the **task()** modifier, it runs as soon as the view is loaded. Note that we do not include a button anymore, since it is no longer needed to start the task.

Do It Yourself

Update the **ContentView** structure with the code in Listing 12-5. Open the Canvas. After five seconds, you should see a message printed to the console with the value returned by the **loadImage()** method.

Asynchronous tasks can perform operations that last for a long time, and because they run independently of the main code, they do not automatically respond to user actions. However, we can interrupt them at any time by calling the **cancel()** method. This method marks the task as cancelled, so we must check this condition from within the task and decide how to respond. For example, we can inspect the value of the **isCancelled** property and stop the operation ourselves, as shown below.

Listing 12-6: Cancelling a task

```
struct ContentView: View {
    var body: some View {
        VStack {
            Text("Hello, world!")
                .padding()
            Button("Run Task") {
                let myTask = Task {
                    let imageName = await loadImage(name: "My Image")
                    print(imageName)
                }
                Timer.scheduledTimer(withTimeInterval: 2.0,
                    repeats: false) { timer in
                    myTask.cancel()
                }
            }
        }
        .font(.system(size: 30))
    }
```

```
    func loadImage(name: String) async -> String {
        try? await Task.sleep(for: .seconds(5))
        if Task.isCancelled {
            return "Task Cancelled"
        }
        return "Name: \(name)"
    }
}
```

The task in this example is defined as before, but it is assigned to a constant so it can be referenced later. The task calls an asynchronous method that runs for five seconds. However, immediately after the task is created, we set up a timer to cancel it. As a result, the task runs for only two seconds before it is cancelled.

Each time a task is cancelled by calling the **`cancel()`** method, we can check the value of the **`isCancelled`** property from within the task to confirm its state. This property returns a Boolean value that indicates whether the current task has been cancelled. In our example, we use this value only to return a message that reports the current state to the user, but we could perform any action we need, including stopping additional work or cancelling other tasks.

IMPORTANT

If we need to make sure that a task is performed even after it has been canceled, we can run the task from the **`withTaskCancellationShield (operation:)`** function. This is a function defined by the Swift Standard Library that ensures some cleanup work is still performed even when a task is canceled, such as when we need to close a file or a network connection. For more information on this function, visit our website and follow the links for this chapter.

BASIC

Concurrent Tasks

Asynchronous tasks execute code independently and return control whenever they need to wait for an operation to complete. For example, when a task downloads an image from the web, it sends a request to a server and then waits for a response. During this waiting period, control is returned to the system so the rest of the code can continue running and the application remains responsive. However, some operations are time-consuming and may freeze the main thread if they are not handled properly. In cases like this, we must perform the work concurrently.

To free the main thread and keep the application responsive, we must execute this work on a background thread. For this purpose, Swift 6.4 provides the following attribute.

@concurrent

This attribute tells the system to run the method on a background thread.

Implementing the **@concurrent** attribute is straightforward. All we need to do is identify the method that must run on a background thread and prefix it with it, as shown below.

Listing 12-7: Processing a high demanding task in a background thread

```
struct ContentView: View {
   var body: some View {
      VStack {
         Text("Hello, world!")
            .padding()
         Button("Run Task") {
            Task {
               let imageName = await loadImage(name: "My Image")
               print(imageName)
            }
         }
      }
      .font(.system(size: 30))
   }
   @concurrent
   func loadImage(name: String) async -> String {
      sleep(5)
      return "Name: \(name)"
   }
}
```

This example implements the **sleep()** method used in previous examples to simulate a long-running operation (see Listing 12-1), but now the **loadImage()** method is marked with the **@concurrent** attribute, so it runs on a background thread and the user interface remains responsive.

With the **@concurrent** attribute, we can not only define a concurrent method but also perform concurrent tasks. If we have a simple task that needs to run in the background, we can include the **@concurrent** attribute in the definition of the **Task** structure, as shown below.

Listing 12-8: Defining a concurrent task

```
struct ContentView: View {
   var body: some View {
      VStack {
         Text("Hello, world!")
            .padding()
         Button("Run Task") {
```

```
                Task { @concurrent in
                    sleep(5)
                    print("From concurrent task")
                }
            }
        }
        .font(.system(size: 30))
    }
}
```

In this example, we define a task that simulates a time-demanding operation for five seconds and then prints a message to the console. Because we specify the **@concurrent** attribute in the closure, the entire process runs on a background thread, allowing the interface to remain responsive.

PRO

Isolation Domains

As with asynchronous tasks, we can create as many concurrent tasks as needed, allowing multiple operations to run at the same time. This flexibility can introduce a problem known as a data race. A data race occurs when two or more concurrent tasks attempt to access or modify the same data simultaneously. To help prevent data races, Swift introduces the concept of isolation domains. An isolation domain is an independent execution context that protects its data from being accessed concurrently by other threads. Each time code runs in a different execution context, its values are isolated from the rest of the program. Swift includes many tools for creating and controlling these isolation domains. The most important of these are actors.

Actors are data types that isolate parallel tasks from each other. They are reference types, similar to classes, but they strictly control how their data is accessed. By requiring asynchronous access to their stored properties and methods, actors ensure that only one task can interact with their mutable state at a time, providing a built-in and reliable defense against data races.

Actors are like classes, but instead of the **class** keyword, they are declared with the **actor** keyword, as shown below.

Listing 12-9: Protecting data with an actor

```
actor ItemData {
    var counter: Int = 0

    func incrementCount() -> String {
        counter += 1
        return "Value: \(counter)"
    }
}
```

```
struct ContentView: View {
    var item: ItemData = ItemData()

    var body: some View {
        Button("Run Task") {
            Task {
                await loadImage(name: "My Image")
            }
        }
        .font(.system(size: 30))
    }
    @concurrent
    func loadImage(name: String) async {
        sleep(5)
        let total = await item.incrementCount()
        print("Total: \(total)")
    }
}
```

In this example, we define an actor called **ItemData** with a property and a method. The view includes a button to call an asynchronous method, as before, but now the method executes a method in the **ItemData** structure. The result is the same as calling a normal method in a class, but the difference is that the data in the actor is now protected, so no data race can occur. Note that because access to a method defined in an actor is asynchronous, we use the **await** keyword to call the method. The actor makes our task wait until no other task is using the method anymore before giving us access to it.

Do It Yourself

Update the **ContentView.swift** file with the code in Listing 12-9. Open the Canvas and press the Run Task button. After five seconds, you should see a message in the console with the current value of the **counter** property. You will not notice anything different from calling a method on a class, but now the **counter** property is protected by the actor, so there is no risk of a data race occurring if later we try to modify the same value from another method.

As we already mentioned, the actor isolates the properties and methods from the rest of the code and other threads, but in some circumstances this isolation is not required. Swift offers the following keyword to break isolation from an actor.

nonisolated

This keyword detaches a declaration, including structures, classes, properties, and methods, from the actor.

Nonisolated properties and methods may be necessary to conform to protocols and can also simplify our code when all we need is access to immutable values in an actor. For instance, in the following example, we add a constant to the **ItemData** actor called **maximum** and a method that prints its value. Because the value of the constant never changes, we can declare the method **nonisolated** and call it without waiting for the actor to grant access.

Listing 12-10: Defining a non-isolated method

```
actor ItemData {
   var counter: Int = 0
   let maximum: Int = 50

   func incrementCount() -> String {
      counter += 1
      return "Value: \(counter)"
   }
   nonisolated func maximumValue() -> String {
      return "Maximum Value: \(maximum)"
   }
}
struct ContentView: View {
   var item: ItemData = ItemData()

   var body: some View {
      Button("Start Process") {
         let value = item.maximumValue()
         print(value)
      }
      .font(.system(size: 30))
   }
}
```

BASIC

Main Actor

When an app is launched, the system assigns it a thread. This thread, known as the main thread or main queue, is responsible for managing the application life cycle, processing user input, responding to events, and updating the user interface. To protect the data on this thread, the system also creates an actor called *Main Actor*.

The Main Actor controls access to all data related to the user interface and user interaction. As a result, attempting to modify the user interface from a background thread causes Xcode to report an error. Swift offers several ways to work within this isolation boundary. One simple approach is to move the operation into a method that runs on the Main Actor, as shown in the following example.

Listing 12-11: Modifying the user interface from a background thread

```
struct ContentView: View {
   @State private var message = "Hello, world!"

   var body: some View {
      VStack {
         Text(message)
            .padding()
         Button("Run Task") {
            Task {
               await loadImage(name: "My Image")
            }
         }
      }
      .font(.system(size: 30))
   }
   @concurrent
   func loadImage(name: String) async {
      sleep(5)
      await changeMessage(name: name)
   }
   func changeMessage(name: String) {
      message = "\(name)"
   }
}
```

In this example, we define the same **loadImage()** method from previous examples and an additional method called **changeMessage()** to perform the task. Because this method is defined within the **ContentView** structure, and this structure is assigned to the Main Actor by default, the method also belongs to the Main Actor and therefore has access to the actor's values. As a result, when the user presses the Run Task button, the **loadImage()** method is executed, this method executes the **changeMessage()** method on the Main Actor, and this method updates the value of the **message** property to display a new text on the screen. Note that because the **changeMessage()** method is defined in the Main Actor and we are calling it from a background thread, we must prefix the call with the **await** keyword to wait for the Main Actor to give us access to it.

Figure 12-9: *Modifying the interface from a background thread*

Do It Yourself

Update the **ContentView.swift** file with the code in Listing 12-11. Open the Canvas and press the Run Task button. After five seconds, you should see the text "My Image" appear on the screen, as shown in Figure 12-9, right.

Because the Default Actor Isolation option is set to **MainActor** (Figure 12-7, number 2), every declaration is assigned to this actor by default. However, Swift also provides the following attribute to assign a declaration to the Main Actor explicitly.

@MainActor

This attribute assigns a declaration, including structures, classes, properties, and methods, to the Main Actor.

Because everything runs on the Main Actor by default, we rarely need to apply this attribute to a method or data type. However, it becomes useful when we need to access or update the user interface from a background thread. In the following example, we show how to create a task on a background thread that executes on the Main Actor.

Listing 12-12: Modifying the user interface from a background thread

```
struct ContentView: View {
   @State private var message = "Hello, world!"

   var body: some View {
      VStack {
         Text(message)
            .padding()
         Button("Run Task") {
            Task {
               await loadImage(name: "My Image")
            }
         }
      }
      .font(.system(size: 30))
   }
   @concurrent
   func loadImage(name: String) async {
      sleep(5)
      Task { @MainActor in
         message = "\(name)"
      }
   }
}
```

This example works as before, but because the task is not marked to run in the Main Actor by default, we had to declare the **@MainActor** attribute to tell the system to run the code in the main thread.

Most of the time, only part of our code deals with the interface, but the rest can be executed in the current thread. For cases like this, the **MainActor** class includes the following method.

run(body: Closure)

This type method executes the closure specified by the **body** argument on the Main Actor.

The following example shows how to implement this method to perform the same task as before.

Listing 12-13: Running code in the Main Actor

```
struct ContentView: View {
   @State private var message = "Hello, world!"

   var body: some View {
      VStack {
         Text(message)
            .padding()
         Button("Run Task") {
            Task {
               await loadImage(name: "My Image")
            }
         }
      }
      .font(.system(size: 30))
   }
   @concurrent
   func loadImage(name: String) async {
      sleep(5)
      Task {
         await MainActor.run {
            message = "\(name)"
         }
      }
   }
}
```

PRO

Parallel Tasks

As always, we can include any code we need inside a concurrent method, including calls to additional methods. If these additional methods perform demanding operations and those operations are independent of one another, we can ask the system to create additional background threads to run them. These are usually called parallel tasks and are defined using the **async let** statement.

The **async let** statement is all we need to run several methods at the same time within a concurrent task. However, because these methods run on the Main Actor by default, running them on a background thread requires detaching them from the Main Actor using the **nonisolated** keyword (see Listing 12-10). The following example shows how to split a task into multiple concurrent methods using the **async let** statement and how to detach them from the Main Actor with the **nonisolated** keyword, so they can run in parallel and in background threads.

Listing 12-14: Runing multiple concurrent tasks

```
struct ContentView: View {
   var body: some View {
      VStack {
         Text("Hello, world!")
            .padding()
         Button("Run Task") {
            Task {
               let imageName = await loadImage(name: "My Image")
               print(imageName)
            }
         }
      }
      .font(.system(size: 30))
   }
   @concurrent
   func loadImage(name: String) async -> String {
      async let t1 = taskNumber1()
      async let t2 = taskNumber2()
      return "Values returned: \(await t1) / \(await t2)"
   }
   nonisolated func taskNumber1() -> String {
      sleep(5)
      return "Task 1"
   }
   nonisolated func taskNumber2() -> String {
      sleep(5)
      return "Task 2"
   }
}
```

In this example, the **loadImage()** method calls two additional methods: **taskNumber1()** and **taskNumber2()**. Because these methods perform demanding operations, we use the **async let** statement to run them on separate background threads. Note that because these methods run concurrently, we must wait for their results using the **await** keyword (**await t1** and **await t2**). When the user presses the Run Task button in the interface, the task calls the **loadImage()** method, which in turn calls **taskNumber1()** and **taskNumber2()**. Since all this work runs on background threads, the operations are performed efficiently without interrupting the user interface.

Do It Yourself

Update the **ContentView.swift** file with the code in Listing 12-14. Open the Canvas and press the Run Task button. The interface should remain responsive, and you should see a message printed to the console when all methods finish executing. Each method takes five seconds to finish processing, but because we are running everything in parallel, you will see the final message in the console after only five seconds.

The **nonisolated** keyword can be applied directly to methods, as we did in previous examples, or to entire data types. For example, if we move our app's functionality into a structure and want all the methods in that structure to be detached from the Main Actor, we can declare the entire structure as **nonisolated**, as shown below.

Listing 12-15: Declaring a structure `nonisolated`

```
nonisolated struct ApplicationData {
   @concurrent
   func loadImage(name: String) async -> String {
      async let t1 = taskNumber1()
      async let t2 = taskNumber2()
      return "Values returned: \(await t1) / \(await t2)"
   }
   func taskNumber1() -> String {
      sleep(5)
      return "Task 1"
   }
   func taskNumber2() -> String {
      sleep(5)
      return "Task 2"
   }
}
struct ContentView: View {
   let appData = ApplicationData()

   var body: some View {
      VStack {
         Text("Hello, world!")
```

```
            .padding()
        Button("Run Task") {
            Task {
                let imageName = await appData.loadImage(name:
                    "My Image")
                print(imageName)
            }
        }
    }
    .font(.system(size: 30))
  }
}
```

This example works exactly the same as the previous one, but all the functionality is now defined in an additional structure called **ApplicationData**. The advantage of declaring the entire data type as **nonisolated** is that every property and method becomes non isolated, so we can run them on any thread we want.

> **IMPORTANT**
>
> Being non isolated, means that the data type doesn't belong to any thread in particular. If the data type is initialized on the main thread, it now belongs to the main thread; if it is initialized on a background thread, then it belongs to that background thread. By declaring them **nonisolated**, we are telling the compiler that they can be called from any thread.

PRO

Data Races

When working with multiple concurrent threads, we may encounter situations where data needs to be passed between them. Value types, including custom structures and data types such as **Int** and **String**, are safe to send across threads because they are copied. When a method running on one thread is called form another thread with one of these values, the system creates a copy and passes that copy to the method, leaving the original value unchanged. Objects, however, are reference types. When an object is passed to an actor, only a reference is sent, which means that the same object can still be modified elsewhere in the code. This can easily lead to a data race. To ensure that values send from one thread to another are safe to use, the Swift Standard Library defines the following protocol.

Sendable

This protocol tells the system that the values created from the data type can be safely shared between asynchronous threads.

Value types, such as **Int** and **String**, collections that include value types and sendable values, such as arrays and dictionaries, and data types defined in the Main Actor are considered sendable. This means that, in most cases, we do not need to explicitly adopt this protocol, although it may be required in certain situations. For example, even though structures are inherently safe, we can make them conform to this protocol to ensure that no unsafe properties are added later. Classes can also be considered safe if they contain only immutable values. However, subclasses may introduce unsafe behavior, so the class must be marked with the **final** keyword to prevent subclassing, as shown below.

Listing 12-16: Defining a sendable class

```
nonisolated final class Product: Sendable {
   let name: String

   init(name: String) {
      self.name = name
   }
}
actor ItemData {
   var stock: Int = 100

   func sellProduct(product: Product, quantity: Int) {
      stock = stock - quantity
      print("Stock: \(stock) \(product.name)")
   }
}
struct ContentView: View {
   var item: ItemData = ItemData()

   var body: some View {
      Button("Run Task") {
         Task {
            let product = Product(name: "Lamp")
            await showStock(product: product)
         }
      }
      .font(.system(size: 30))
   }
   @concurrent
   func showStock(product: Product) async {
      await item.sellProduct(product: product, quantity: 5)
   }
}
```

This example illustrates a situation in which a data type may need to conform to the **Sendable** protocol. The code defines a class called **Product** that is marked as **final**, so no subclasses can be created from it, and includes an immutable property of type **String**. This means that the class is thread-safe, but we still need to make it conform to the **Sendable** protocol to let Xcode know that it is safe to pass these values between threads.

To verify that no issues occur, we define an actor called **ItemData** with a method that receives **Product** values, and then create a concurrent task that calls this method. The **Product** instance is created on the Main Actor, passed to a concurrent task, and then used to call the method on the **ItemData** actor, but because the **Product** class conforms to **Sendable**, the entire operation is valid and Xcode does not report any errors.

Do It Yourself

Update the **ContentView.swift** file with the code in Listing 12-16. Open the Canvas and press the Run Task button. You should see a message on the console. Remove the conformance to the **Sendable** protocol. Xcode should then display an error indicating that sending the **Product** object to the actor may cause a data race.

If we really need to include unsafe values and we know for sure that they are not going to be modified from different threads, we can explicitly declare it unsafe with the **nonisolated** keyword and the parameter **unsafe**. For example, global variables are not safe. Many tasks can access a global variable simultaneously. One way to solve this issue is to turn it into a constant, but if we still need to modify its value, we can use the **nonisolated(unsafe)** keyword to tell the system that we are going to take care of safety ourselves.

Listing 12-17: Declaring a global variable unsafe

```
nonisolated(unsafe) var myvalue = "Hello!"

struct ContentView: View {
    var body: some View {
        Button("Run Task") {
            Task { @concurrent in
                myvalue = "Goodbye!"
                print(myvalue)
            }
        }
        .font(.system(size: 30))
    }
}
```

In this example, we have a global variable called **myvalue**. If we declare it as a normal variable, Xcode will return an error, but because we know that only one task is accessing the value at a time, we can declare it unsafe to avoid the warnings.

Swift also offers the following attribute to suppress warnings and data race errors produced by old frameworks.

@preconcurrency

This attribute tells the Swift compiler that the code was designed before concurrency was available.

This attribute is useful when working with old frameworks that have not yet implemented Swift concurrency. We can declare it when the framework is imported (e.g. **`@preconcurrency import OldFramework`**) or before the name of an old protocol (e.g. **`class MyClass: @preconcurrency OldProtocol`**). This tells Xcode to ignore the warnings and allows us to work with those frameworks in Swift 6.4.

> **IMPORTANT**
>
> How you protect data in Swift depends on the characteristics of your application, the organization of your code, and the frameworks you use. In this section, we explored most of the tools provided by Swift 6.4 to implement concurrency, but additional tools are available depending on the language version and the platform. AI agents are trained to understand concurrency and generate safe code. Ask your agent for help resolving data race errors or developing safe code when you are not sure how to approach it.

BASIC

12.3 - Asynchronous Access

Sometimes, information is returned as a sequence of values, but those values may not be available all at once. In these situations, we can access the values asynchronously. Swift provides several ways to process this kind of data, including asynchronous sequences and SwiftUI tools for loading images.

PRO

Asynchronous Sequences

Asynchronous sequences are processed like arrays, but their values are produced asynchronously, so we must wait for each value to become available. Swift provides the **`for await`** statement for this purpose. Using this statement, we can build a **`for in`** loop that waits for each value and executes the associated code as soon as it is received.

Although most of the time we will just consume asynchronous sequences produced by Apple's frameworks, we can also create our own. To create these sequences, the Swift Standard Library provides the **`AsyncStream`** structure. The following is the structure's initializer.

`AsyncStream(Type, bufferingPolicy: BufferingPolicy, Closure)`

This initializer creates an asynchronous sequence. The first argument is the data type the sequence produces. The **bufferingPolicy** argument is an enumeration that determines how the sequence manages its capacity. The possible values are **`unbounded`**, **`bufferingOldest(Int)`**, and **`bufferingNewest(Int)`**. And the last argument is a closure that produces the values.

The closure assigned to the **AsyncStream** structure receives a **Continuation** structure that provides access to the sequence. To produce values and finish the sequence, this structure includes the following methods.

yield(Value)

This method produces the next value in the sequence. The argument specifies the value that the sequence emits.

finish()

This method produces the value **nil**, indicating the end of the sequence.

The following example demonstrates how to create an asynchronous sequence. It takes three values from an array and returns them one by one at three-second intervals.

Listing 12-18: Defining an asynchronous sequence

```
struct ContentView: View {
   let list = ["image1", "image2", "image3"]

   var body: some View {
      VStack {
         Text("Hello World!")
            .padding()
         Button("Run Task") {
            Task {
               let stream = AsyncStream { continuation in
                  Task {
                     for image in list {
                        continuation.yield(image)
                        try? await Task.sleep(for: .seconds(3))
                     }
                     continuation.finish()
                  }
               }
               for await item in stream {
                  print(item)
               }
            }
         }
      }
      .font(.system(size: 30))
   }
}
```

This example simulates the asynchronous download of images from the web. We begin by creating an **AsyncStream** structure and using a **for in** loop to iterate over the values in an array of strings. During each iteration, we call the **sleep()** method to introduce a delay before producing the next value. This delay is used only to simulate the time required to download an image. We then call the **`yield()`** method on the **`Continuation`** structure to add the current value to the sequence. After the loop reaches its final index, we call the **`finish()`** method to signal the end of the sequence.

The **`for await`** loop at the end of the task listens to every value produced by the **`AsyncStream`** structure and prints it on the console. The loop runs until the value produced by the sequence is equal to **`nil`**.

Do It Yourself

Update the **ContentView.swift** file with the code in Listing 12-18. Open the Canvas and press the Run Task button. You should see the values in the **list** array printed on the console every three seconds.

PRO

Task Group

A task group is a container that manages a dynamically generated set of tasks. After the group is created, tasks can be added as needed by the application, and the values they produce can be consumed asynchronously as they complete. The Swift Standard Library provides the following global methods to create a task group.

`withTaskGroup(of:` `Type,` **`returning:`** `Type,` **`body:`** `Closure)`

This method creates a task group. The **of** argument defines the data type returned by the tasks, the **returning** argument defines the data type returned by the group, and the **body** argument is the closure where the tasks are defined. If no values are returned, the arguments may be ignored.

`withThrowingTaskGroup(of:` `Type,` **`returning:`** `Type,` **`body:`** `Closure)`

This method creates a task group that can throw errors. The **of** argument defines the data type returned by the tasks, the **returning** argument defines the data type returned by the group, and the **body** argument is the closure where the tasks are defined. If no values are returned, the arguments may be ignored.

The group is defined by an instance of the **TaskGroup** structure, which includes properties and methods to manage the tasks in the group. The following are the most frequently used.

`isCancelled`

This property returns a Boolean value that indicates whether the group was cancelled.

`isEmpty`

This property returns a Boolean value that indicates whether the group has any remaining tasks.

addTask(priority: TaskPriority?, **operation:** Closure)

This method adds a task to the group. The **priority** argument is a structure that helps the system decide when to execute the task. The structure includes type properties to defined standard priorities. The currently available are **background**, **high**, **low**, **medium**, **userInitiated**, and **utility**. And the **operation** argument is a closure with the code to be executed by the task.

cancelAll()

This method cancels all the tasks in the group.

A task group produces a generic asynchronous sequence, which means both the tasks and the group itself can return values of any type. For this reason, the methods used to create a task group require two parameters. One parameter specifies the type of values produced by the individual tasks, and the other specifies the type of values produced by the group as a whole. The two methods available to create a task group are the same. The one we implement depends on whether we want to throw errors or not. These methods create a **TaskGroup** structure that works with the data types specified by the arguments and send the instance to the closure. Using this value inside the closure, we can add to the group all the tasks we want, as shown below.

Listing 12-19: Defining a task group

```
struct ContentView: View {
   var body: some View {
      VStack {
         Text("Hello World!")
            .padding()
         Button("Run Task") {
            Task {
               await withTaskGroup(of: String.self) { group in
                  group.addTask(priority: .background) {
                     let imageName = await self.loadImage(name:
                        "My Image 1")
                     return imageName
                  }
                  group.addTask(priority: .background) {
                     let imageName = await self.loadImage(name:
                        "My Image 2")
                     return imageName
                  }
                  group.addTask(priority: .background) {
                     let imageName = await self.loadImage(name:
                        "My Image 3")
                     return imageName
                  }
                  for await result in group {
                     print(result)
                  }
```

```
                }
            }
        }
    }
    .font(.system(size: 30))
  }
  func loadImage(name: String) async -> String {
     try? await Task.sleep(for: .seconds(3))
     return "Name: \(name)"
  }
}
```

In this example, we create a task group that doesn't throw errors. The group doesn't return a value either, but the tasks return a string, so we declare the **of** argument of the **withTaskGroup()** method as a **String** data type (**String.self**). The tasks are added to the group one after another. Each task performs the same process; they call the **loadImage()** method asynchronously and get a string in return.

Because a task group produces an asynchronous sequence, we can iterate though the values with a **for in** loop, as we did before. Every time a task is completed, the group returns the value produced by the task until no tasks remain, in which case the value **nil** is returned to indicate the end of the sequence.

> **IMPORTANT**
>
> Task Groups store the tasks in sequence. You can remove, filter, or even check whether a group contains a specific task. The topic is beyond the scope of this book. For more information, visit our website and follow the links for this chapter.

BASIC

Asynchronous Images

Although the tools introduced in this chapter allow us to perform any type of asynchronous or concurrent task we need, SwiftUI offers the **AsyncImage** structure to simplify our work when loading images. The view created by this structure takes care of downloading an image from a server and displaying the image on the screen when it is ready. The following are the most frequently used initializers.

AsyncImage(url: URL, **scale:** CGFloat, **content:** Closure, **placeholder:** Closure)

This view downloads an image from a server and displays it on the screen. The **url** argument is a **URL** structure with the image's url, the **scale** argument is the scale we want to assign to the image (1 by default), the **content** argument is a closure to process the image, and the **placeholder** argument is a closure that returns a view to show in place of the image while we wait for the image to download.

AsyncImage(request: URLRequest, **scale:** CGFloat, **content:** Closure, **placeholder:** Closure)

This view downloads an image from a server and displays it on the screen. The **request** argument is a **URLRequest** structure that defines the URL and configuration options for the network request, the **scale** argument is the scale we want to assign to the image (1 by default), the **content** argument is a closure to process the image, and the **placeholder** argument is a closure that returns a view to show in place of the image while we wait for the image to download.

The location of the image is determined by the **URL** structure defined in the **Foundation** framework. This structure is used to store the addresses of local and remote documents, files, and resources. The following are the initializers we need to create URLs to access documents and resources on the web.

URL(string: String)

This initializer creates a **URL** structure with the URL specified by the **string** argument.

URL(string: String, **relativeTo:** URL?)

This initializer creates a **URL** structure with the URL specified by the arguments. The URL is created by adding the value of the **string** argument to the value of the **relativeTo** argument.

URL(dataRepresentation: Data, **relativeTo:** URL?, **isAbsolute:** Bool)

This initializer creates a **URL** structure with the URL specified by the arguments. The URL is created by adding the value of the **dataRepresentation** argument to the value of the **relativeTo** argument. The **isAbsolute** argument is a Boolean value that determines if the URL is absolute or not (it includes all the information required to access the resource).

IMPORTANT

There are two types of URLs: secure and non-secure. Non-secure URLs use the **http** protocol (Hypertext Transfer Protocol), while secure URLs use the **https** protocol (Hypertext Transfer Protocol Secure). Because non-secure URLs expose data to potential security risks, Apple requires the use of secure URLs for all apps submitted to the App Store.

Loading an image with an **AsyncImage** view is straightforward. All we need to do is provide the image URL and implement the view using that value, as shown below.

Listing 12-20: Loading an image asynchronously

```
struct ContentView: View {
   let website = URL(string: "https://www.formasterminds.com/
      images/coverseriesapplefull.png")
```

```
    var body: some View {
        VStack {
            AsyncImage(url: website)
        }.padding()
    }
}
```

In this example, we store a URL in a constant and then implement the view to load the image. Although the image is effectively loaded and displayed, the **AsyncImage** view doesn't allow any configuration, so the image is shown in its original size.

Figure 12-10: *Image loaded asynchronously*

If we want to configure the image, we must provide a closure for the **content** argument. This closure receives an **Image** view that we can configure with view modifiers.

Listing 12-21: Configuring the image after it is downloaded

```
struct ContentView: View {
    let website = URL(string: "https://www.formasterminds.com/
        images/coverseriesapplefull.png")

    var body: some View {
        VStack {
            AsyncImage(url: website, content: { image in
                image
                    .resizable()
                    .scaledToFit()
            }, placeholder: {
                Text("No Image")
                .font(.system(size: 30))
            })
        }.padding()
    }
}
```

When we provide the **content** argument, the **AsyncImage** view delegates the job of displaying the image to the **Image** view received by the closure, so we can configure this view as before. In this example, we resize the image with the **resizable()** modifier and scale it to fit within the view with the **scaledToFit()** modifier. Note that we have also defined the **placeholder** argument to show a temporary image while the final image is downloading.

Figure 12-11: *Image configuration*

Do It Yourself

Update the **ContentView.swift** file with the code in Listing 12-21. Open the Canvas. After a few seconds, you should see the cover of our book Apple Intelligence for Masterminds replacing the placeholder text, as shown in Figure 12-11.

IMPORTANT

The **Image** view is a SwiftUI view that loads and displays images on the screen. To learn more about the **Image** view and SwiftUI, read our book *SwiftUI for Masterminds*.

The previous example loads the image directly from a URL. If we need more control, we can use a **URLRequest** structure. This is a structure defined in the **Foundation** framework that allows us to configure additional properties for the request, such as the HTTP method, headers, timeout interval, and cache policy. The following is the structure's initializer.

```
URLRequest(url: URL, cachePolicy: CachePolicy, timeoutInterval: TimeInterval)
```

This initializer creates a **URLRequest** structure for the URL specified by the **url** argument. The **cachePolicy** argument is an enumeration that determines how the request interacts with the cache. The possible values are:

useProtocolCachePolicy (default), **reloadIgnoringLocalCacheData**, **reloadIgnoringLocalAndRemoteCacheData**, **reloadIgnoringCacheData**, **returnCacheDataElseLoad**, **returnCacheDataDontLoad**, and **reloadRevalidatingCacheData**. The **timeoutInterval** argument is the maximum time allowed for the system to process the request (60.0 seconds by default).

Depending on what we need, we can create the request with just a URL or specify a cache policy. For example, if we want the image to be downloaded from a cache instead of always loading it from the server, we can specify the **returnCacheDataElseLoad** policy, as shown below.

Listing 12-22: Loading an image from the cache when available

```
struct ContentView: View {
    let imageURL = URL(string: "https://www.formasterminds.com/
      images/coverseriesapplefull.png")!

    var request: URLRequest {
        var request = URLRequest(url: imageURL, cachePolicy:
            .returnCacheDataElseLoad)
        return request
    }
    var body: some View {
        VStack {
            AsyncImage(request: request, content: { image in
                image
                    .resizable()
                    .scaledToFit()
            }, placeholder: {
                Text("No Image")
                    .font(.system(size: 30))
            })
        }.padding()
    }
}
```

The code in this example is very similar to the one before, and we get the same results, but now we use a **URLRequest** configured to check the cache first, so if the image was downloaded before, the app uses that image instead of downloading it again from the server.

Where To Go From Here

The Swift programming language is open source and has therefore been adopted by many companies and organizations to build tools and run production systems. However, it is still used primarily to develop applications for Apple devices and platforms. If you want to learn how to build applications for these devices, we recommend the other books in our series. **SwiftUI for Masterminds** will teach you how to build apps for iPhones, iPads, and Macs, and **Apple Intelligence for Masterminds** will teach you how artificial intelligence works and how to incorporate it into your applications. For more information about Swift 6.4, see the official documentation at **https://docs.swift.org/swift-book/documentation/the-swift-programming-language**.

SwiftUI for Masterminds

How to take advantage of SwiftUI and AI Agents to develop insanely great apps for iPhones, iPads, and Macs

How to use the SwiftUI framework to create amazing applications for iPhones, iPads, and Macs. After reading this book, you will know how to define interactive views, create custom layouts, build graphics and animations, store information permanently on device, and gain all the skills you need to design and develop modern applications.

Apple Intelligence for Masterminds

How to create intelligent applications for iPhones, iPads and Macs

How to take advantage of Apple Intelligence to create intelligent applications for iPhones, iPads, and Macs. After reading this book, you will know how to integrate artificial intelligence into your applications, how to use Apple Intelligence and Siri effectively, and how to train your own models to build innovative and revolutionary applications.

www.formasterminds.com

Index

R

S

T

U